Praise for *HOT SEAT*

"Jeff has delivered the most insightful perspective on GE over a remarkable period of change and growth with the same intellectual energy, self-reflection, and bold leadership that he used in running the company for more than sixteen years. This book is the definitive account of how it all unfolded."

—Geoff Beattie, chairman and CEO, Generation Capital

"*Hot Seat* is bravely honest in a way few CEO books have ever been. Jeff shows deep humility, taking you inside the boardroom during an extraordinary time in GE, and American, history. It is fascinating insight from a career filled with incredible highs and lows, and Jeff does not shy away from any of it. This is a must-read book for every CEO, aspiring business leader, or anyone who has to manage teams, big and small."

—Jeff Zucker, president, CNN

"*Hot Seat* provides a detailed inside view of the intense challenges in leading the most successful diversified industrial company of the twentieth century into a turbulent twenty-first century. The book reveals the enormous energy, passion, and commitment needed to navigate a highly complex and global business. Jeff's energetic and charismatic leadership style, based on his unwavering commitment to innovation, customers, and employees, is seen through incredible events and business portfolio challenges. *Hot Seat* also provides many insightful business and leadership lessons."

—Joseph M. Hogan, president and CEO, Align Technology

"*Hot Seat* is an interesting and captivating read. It chronicles Jeff Immelt's career at GE, how he spent his time, especially as CEO, how he himself grew over time and helped develop others. The book provides useful background and perspective on the many critical decisions he made—selecting leaders, buying and selling businesses, where to invest and where not to. Like any big company, people may or may not agree with his decisions, but Jeff's rationale is explained clearly. The lessons learned about business leadership are extremely valuable and thought-provoking. We can all learn something from *Hot Seat*. I recommend it highly."

—Omar Ishrak, executive chairman, former CEO, Medtronic

"The metric that matters in a business leadership book is how many pages you underline things on because you know you want to remember and refer back to them. *Hot Seat* scored one hundred and ninety-two for me. If you're looking for a 'How great was I?' memoir, move to the next book. If you want the real lessons of leading one of the world's most complex companies through sixteen of the world's most challenging and least predictable years, take a seat and turn to page one."

—Andrew Robertson, president and CEO, BBDO Worldwide

"Read this book. You'll be a better leader for it."

—David Rogier, founder and CEO, MasterClass

"In this artfully told biography, Jeff Immelt offers a master class to today's CEOs who are building global businesses as they encounter unprecedented pace of change and tail risks. The reader is afforded a rare window to see how lonely leadership can be at critical times and teaches key leadership lessons that are both timely and timeless. We learn so much on how to run our businesses more effectively and be better human beings, making this not only a must-read book but a go-to reference."

—K. R. Sridhar, founder and CEO, Bloom Energy

HOT SEAT

Hard-won Lessons
in Challenging Times

JEFF IMMELT

FORMER CEO OF GENERAL ELECTRIC

WITH AMY WALLACE

HODDER &
STOUGHTON

First published in Great Britain in 2021 by Hodder & Stoughton
An Hachette UK company

3

Copyright © Jeffrey Immelt 2021

Interior design by Erika R. Genova

A CIP catalogue record for this title is available from the British Library

Hardback ISBN 9781529358698
Trade Paperback ISBN 9781529358735
eBook ISBN 9781529358704

Printed and bound in India by Manipal Technologies Limited, Manipal

Hodder & Stoughton policy is to use papers that are natural, renewable
and recyclable products and made from wood grown in sustainable
forests. The logging and manufacturing processes are expected to
conform to the environmental regulations of the country of origin.

Hodder & Stoughton Ltd
Carmelite House
50 Victoria Embankment
London EC4Y 0DZ

www.hodder.co.uk

Dedicated to my family

CONTENTS

Prologue *1*

Chapter 1: Leaders Show Up. **7**
    Threading the Needle 9
    Stoking GE's Growth Engine 12
    Waking to a Nightmare 14
    Facing Disaster .17
    Absorbing Fear .19
    Putting Customers First 22

Chapter 2: Leaders Learn Every Day. **27**
    "Don't Complain—Fix It!" 30
    Be Willing to Stand Apart 32
    Choose Purpose Over Money 34
    See Through Your Customer's Eyes 36
    Learn to Take the Heat 41
    Get a Thicker Skin 44
    Valuing Growth .46
    Launching the LightSpeed 48
    Who's Next in Line? 50
    Your Peers Promote You 54

Chapter 3: Leaders Invest in Growth. **57**
    A Time for Change 61
    Technology First .63
    Protect the Builders 67
    Fulfilling the Dreamliner Dream 71
    Don't Fall in Love with an Idea 76
    Pivot to Grow 77
    Seize Opportunity 81
    Don't Be Afraid to Act 87

Chapter 4: Leaders Are Systems Thinkers 93
    Communicating with the World 96
    Green Is Green. 99
    The Digital Future 107
    Competing for Talent. 112
    Bringing the Team Along 113
    Not Finishing the Job 116

Chapter 5: Leaders Persevere in a Crisis. 119
    Bundle at Your Peril 121
    Beware a Cold Snap 123
    Darkness Visible 126
    Rolling Paper 132
    "Let's Get the Money" 133
    Fishing for an Anchor 136
    The Killer Chart 138
    Stepping into Liquid 141
    Cutting the Dividend. 143

Chapter 6: Leaders Make Big Companies Small 149
    Facing Reality 151
    Retaining the Best 153
    It Starts with You 154
    The Soul of GE. 160
    Reimagining Crotonville 161
    Leadership Explorations 163
    Valuing Everyone 166

Chapter 7: Leaders Compete Around the World 173
    Becoming the Jobs Czar 179
    There's Always a Crisis Somewhere 182
    Investing in Local Capability. 185
    Persisting Through Volatility 187
    Cementing Relationships. 190
    Hiring Local Teams. 194
    China Matters Most 196
    A Little Bit of We. 204

Chapter 8: Leaders Manage Complexity 207
    Creating Incremental Value 209
    Pattern Recognition 211
    An Aspiration to Lead 213
    Private Equity: A Modern Conglomerate? 216
    Developing Trustworthy Leaders 220

A Bias for Innovation 222

Constantly Simplifying 224

Operational Transparency 229

Peer Learning & Peer Pressure 230

Chapter 9: Leaders Solve Problems **233**

Managing Risk 234

Welcome to the Hotel California 238

Shooting for the Moon 239

Keeping the Lid on Tight 243

Secretive No More 250

Leveling with Our People 251

Activists Abound 254

Sell, Sell, Sell! 256

Mission Accomplished 258

Chapter 10: Leaders Are Transparent **261**

A Simple Deal (in a Market We Knew) 263

A Position of Strength 265

A Leader Stops Leading 268

Integrating Alstom 269

Overt Transparency 271

Close the Deal, Lose the Leader? 276

The Business Suffered 278

Chapter 11: Leaders Are Accountable **285**

Grooming the Candidates 287

The Home Stretch 291

Valuing the Company 292

Every Job Looks Easy (Until You're the One Doing It) 300

Activist Investors Weren't the Answer for GE 301

A Short Tenure 303

Chapter 12: Leaders Are Optimists. **309**

Owning Some Mistakes 312

The Case for Listening (Most of the Time) 315

Life After GE 316

Change for the Better 318

Acknowledgments 321

Index 325

PROLOGUE

In October 2017, as I stepped down after thirty-five years at General Electric, I wasn't sure I could write this book. My sixteen years as CEO had given me a front-row seat to history, and I'd learned some tough lessons I believed others could benefit from. But my tenure had ended badly. Many business books begin with a tacit promise: "Let me tell you how to be like me: an unmitigated success!" Clearly, I couldn't say that.

My legacy was, at best, controversial. GE won in the marketplace but not in the stock market. I made thousands of decisions impacting millions of people, often in the midst of blinding uncertainty and second-guessed by countless critics. I was proud of my team and what we'd accomplished, but as CEO, I'd been about as brilliant as I was lucky, by which I mean: too often I was neither. Maybe it would be better not to write a book at all.

Then, in June 2018, something happened that changed my mind.

I'd agreed to teach a class at the Stanford Graduate School of Business. Its title was a mouthful—Systems Leadership for the Digital Industrial Transformation—but at the class's core, it was about perseverance through change. I'd never been a professor before, but my co-instructor, a venture capitalist and longtime Stanford lecturer named Rob Siegel, was there to help me. Together we recruited leaders from the world's biggest companies to give our sixty-seven students firsthand accounts of the challenges they faced, and so far, the guests had all been terrific. The CEO of Align Technology had told our students about using 3D printers to create custom-made trays to straighten customers' teeth; the CEO of John Deere had explained why trust is key to selling tractors; and the former CEO of Legendary Entertainment (the maker of films like *Jurassic World*) had explained his plan to use artificial intelligence to "wake up" sleepy businesses not known for innovation.

Then, mid-semester, *Fortune* magazine published a lengthy article under the headline "What the Hell Happened at GE?" The story, by Geoff Colvin, had what I perceived to be many errors of both fact and implication. The story suggested that there had been no succession planning to find my replacement (there had), and it laid the problems caused by GE's financial arm, GE Capital, solely at my feet (many were inherited). But most striking was its histrionic tone. GE, it said, was an "unholy mess," while I was "inept." I suspected more than one of Colvin's sources were people I'd fired— not exactly impartial. But readers had no way of knowing that.

No one is immune to criticism; certainly not me. There'd been a lot of negative media coverage since I'd left GE, and I'd often winced while reading it. But this time I saw an opportunity. I'd been struck by how little patience our students seemed to have for rehearsed speeches or simplistic lists of how-tos. Their favorite question seemed to be "How did you figure it out?" They were hungry to learn how to survive in an uncertain world, and now I realized I was preeminently qualified to weigh in.

So I asked my co-instructor to send out an email inviting all the business school's students to a previously unscheduled forum. The title: "Jeff Immelt—Unplugged." The assignment: ask me anything.

At 5 p.m. the following Friday, the school's biggest classroom was packed. One of our students had volunteered to bring wine and cup-cakes, so the mood was oddly festive. "A lot has been written about me lately, and about GE," I said, kicking things off. "I thought you might have questions."

For the next hour or so, they asked, and I answered. The queries started off polite, like, "What's the hardest thing you dealt with as a leader?" I talked about some of GE's struggles—after 9/11, through the financial crisis of 2008 and 2009, and the meltdown of Fukushima's nuclear reactors (which had been designed by GE). Another student asked about one of my favorite topics, globaliza-tion. I described how my team had made GE more nimble by build-ing capable teams on the ground throughout the world and moving decision-making power to them in their markets.

But other students were more pointed. "What went wrong in GE Power?" asked one. Another bore down on the *Wall Street Journal's* assertion that I'd created a culture of "success theater" within GE, encouraging people to paint a positive picture, no matter what.

I remember the sun was starting to set on the trees outside the classroom windows when a student raised his hand. I could see a printout of the *Fortune* story on his desk. "How could you let this hap-pen?" he asked. All I could tell him was the truth: I'd worked hard not to let it. "I feel terrible about the company's troubles," I said. "I know some feel that I have let them down, and that will weigh on me for the rest of my life. But merely blaming the past isn't helping GE win, nor is letting lies go unchallenged and be treated as truth. GE is losing customers and talent. They aren't fixing the right problem."

I wanted the students that day to see that I could own not being perfect, and I could also defend myself when merited, without sounding thin-skinned. That is what leaders do.

Only later did I realize that the forum had had an unintended consequence. It had made me see, for the first time, not only that I could write this book but that I should.

I approached the project as an interrogation—of myself and of my tenure. Everybody, including me, remembers a "truth" that includes their best self. It's a human defense mechanism. The reason to do a book like this, I felt, was to go deeper and not rely merely on my own recollection of events. With the help of my cowriter, I sought out and interviewed more than seventy people, inside and outside GE, who had insights and memories that made this book better. Some of them told stories I hadn't remembered until I heard them again. Others corrected errors. Most vital, many of these people pushed me to confront some of the questions my critics have asked. Questions such as: Why, when GE got out of the insurance business, did we not sell our long-term-care assets? Why did I so strongly support GE's acquisition of the French power company Alstom when the world seemed to be moving toward cleaner energy? Why did my immediate successor have such a short tenure (and what did that say about my succession process)? And yes, with a nod to my Stanford students, what the hell happened at GE Power?

In 2001, I'd become CEO of a company where perception didn't equal reality. The company I had inherited from Jack Welch had a strong culture and great people. But we had run out of ideas. A year before, while I was running GE Healthcare, I had tried to buy an ultrasound company called Acuson, but Jack said no because it was located in Mountain View, California, and "people are crazy out there." I disagreed; its location would have given us a foothold (as it did for our rival Siemens, which later bought it) in Silicon Valley, a place famous for innovation. While some within GE believed that the company would always be guaranteed great results, I worried that we'd become too entrenched and not curious enough.

For at least a decade, we'd used our financial-services colossus, GE Capital, to fuel our growth and support our industrial businesses. But when I took over, few observers grasped how little we'd been investing in those industrial businesses. We were a sprawling conglomerate that encompassed everything from jet engines to TV networks to insurance policies for cats and dogs. Yet we were valued like a tech company, trading substantially above the value of the businesses we had.

So as CEO, I threw myself into improving the company, reinvesting in the industrial portfolio, improving our technology, and expanding our global footprint. And I did it without speaking a single negative word about Jack Welch.

This was a risky choice. It's difficult to drive change while your team feels everything is already perfect. But at the time, that approach felt right. My predecessor was viewed as the best CEO in history. My hope was to preserve his legacy by fixing what I saw to be broken before it caught up with us. But too often during my tenure, our desire to protect GE by growing it would take a back seat when crises threatened the company's success—and sometimes even its survival.

The GE story could not be more personal for me. I'm the son of a man who worked as a GE purchasing agent for thirty-eight years. Before becoming CEO, I'd worked my way up within the company, learning inside three GE divisions. I was the ultimate grinder—a true believer, with a tattoo of the GE "meatball," as insiders call the company logo, on my left hip to prove it. (More on that later.) I was the guy who worked every weekend, who never spent a penny to decorate his office, who brought his own stamps to work to stick on personal mail. If I'd had a mantra, it would have been: it isn't about me, it's about GE.

During the five decades I'd experienced GE up close, first through the lens of my father's experience and then through my own, its culture had always been about teamwork and confronting problems, not about pointing fingers. I had the privilege of leading this iconic American company during a pivotal time. I knew world leaders—Obama, Putin, Merkel, Xi, and yes, Trump—because GE's preeminence in so many industries made it worth their while to know me. I can't tell you how many times as CEO that I wanted to say, "Okay, what the heck are we going to do now?" But just like in that classroom at Stanford, I always showed up. I never once went to work with a frown on my face or blamed others for a problem that I could help fix.

Leadership is an intense journey into yourself. If you can go to bed feeling beaten up and rise the next morning ready to keep listening and learning, then I believe you can lead. I like to quote Mike Tyson: "Everybody has a plan until they get punched in the mouth." The trick is to stay open to new ideas, even when your ears are ringing. You're not going to get everything right. I sure didn't. If all you want to do is cover your ass, you shouldn't sign up to be CEO.

When trouble erupts on a global scale and disruption is constant, leaders often lack control. In situations like this, all you have is your willingness to make decisions and to persevere. The goal is survival, by which I mean progress, not perfection. Here's the bottom line: leaders' biggest decisions are always scrutinized, and mine were no exception. I only wish you could stand in my shoes and see what I saw in the crucial moments—there were probably ten thousand of them—when my team had to act. I'd be curious to see what you'd do.

When I give speeches these days, I ask my audiences two questions. "How many of you are geniuses?" I say, and no one moves. "How many of you think you're lucky?" I continue, and a few people raise their hands. "Okay," I say, "if you're not a genius and you're not lucky, my story is for you."

I know that some will read this book with an eye toward how I treat Jack Welch. I'll confess that following him had its challenges. But my decisions were my own. The times in which we led were so different that comparing them was never a priority to me. I leave that to others. But readers will see how much I learned from Jack, and how much I admired him, even though I knew he had flaws.

This book is my account of what I learned in my time atop one of America's biggest and most-heralded corporations—of what it meant to be in the hot seat, having full responsibility for one of the most rewarding, most challenging, most scrutinized jobs in the world. I've tried to capture how I think the business world has changed over the past two decades. I've called out some ideas we championed that succeeded at GE, and some that didn't. I've explained how we survived both. No one hands a CEO a manual on his or her first day that spells out how to make difficult decisions. My hope is that by talking about the lonely job of leadership, I can encourage readers to keep pushing forward. I've been frank about the obstacles I faced as I sought the path forward, even when I was in my own way. My story is raw but always honest. And it begins on my first Monday as CEO: September 10, 2001.

CHAPTER 1

Leaders Show Up

In the summer of 2001, just weeks before I stepped into the CEO's job at GE, I went on a golf trip with some of my college buddies. I'm not a great golfer, but my friends had invited me to the Skokie Country Club outside of Chicago, and I was looking forward to a little R & R. Ducking into the locker room to change my shoes, I encountered a club member who introduced himself and asked what I did. "I work for GE," I said, omitting my new job title on purpose.

The man didn't skip a beat. "Ah, GE! Jack Welch!" he replied. "I feel sorry for the poor son of a bitch who's taking his place." I don't remember how I played that day, but I do recall that my friends and I laughed for four hours about that guy. Everybody seemed to know I was taking over for the most famous CEO in history.

Every CEO's relationship with his or her predecessor is complicated. It's a little like my relationship with my late mother-in-law: we both loved my wife, but in different ways. Jack and I both loved GE, but not in the same way. We were of different generations; when I'd

ɔme to GE and for years after, he was my hero. I loved having
s my boss. I paid attention to how easily he could talk to anyone—foremen on the factory floor, customers, other CEOs. He was
accessible and informal, and that was seductive. Everyone at GE
felt they worked for Jack, and they knew what to expect from him. I
marveled at his ability to connect.

Jack could be bombastic—he upped the theater quotient in
many meetings—but people enjoyed his directness. Meanwhile,
metrics mattered. Yes, we sometimes got buried in them. But mostly
they kept us accountable. Jack knew how to set priorities and stick
to them. That, I wanted to emulate.

But there were other Welchisms I didn't plan to copy. Over the
years Jack had collected a group of idol worshippers and sycophants
around and outside the company who fostered an unrealistic view
of GE and of Jack himself. They loved to tell Jack Welch stories,
reliving the past over and over. Jack's 1980s mantra "Only be in businesses in which you rank number one or number two" was fine in
principle, but it had become outdated. GE needed to grow, and to do
that, we had to enter businesses in which we were behind. I tried to
be respectful of what had come before but not kneel to it. And I had
little tolerance for those who objected to change by saying, "But this
isn't the way we used to do it."

Jack had announced I would be his successor just after Thanksgiving 2000. Over the next ten months, as CEO-in-waiting, I spent a
lot of time with him. He and I attended a business dinner in London,
for instance, just a few months before he stepped down. At one point
during the meal, Sir George Simpson, a legendary British executive
known for turning around struggling companies, leaned across the
table and teased, "Jack, how do you do it? How do you get a 50 PE
with that bag of shit you've got?"

I laughed, but I was shocked to hear Simpson joke about something
that no one within GE would have ever dared say. A company's PE, or
price-to-earnings ratio, reflects how much confidence the market has
in the company's future growth. The more investors are willing to pay

per share relative to the company's current earnings, the higher that company's perceived potential. In 2001, if you'd divided the price of GE stock by its earnings per share (EPS), you would, indeed, have gotten a ratio of fifty. But that obscured the fact that several of GE's businesses were pretty average; the luster of GE inflated their value. In Jack's twenty years at GE's helm, the company's value had risen a staggering 4,000 percent. But Jack led GE during a time of consistent economic expansion, and that streak was about to end.

GE was founded by one of the greatest inventors the world has ever seen, Thomas Edison, and for most of the twentieth century, even until 1986, GE had more patents than any other corporation. But the company had deemphasized technology, and GE was not even in the top-twenty ranking of companies holding patents. Instead of innovation, Jack had been focused more on management techniques such as Six Sigma that were used to eliminate mistakes.

Six Sigma is a data-driven methodology invented by a Motorola engineer named Bill Smith in 1980. It trains managers to be experts (called Black Belts) in improving business processes to reduce product defects. Given that GE made machines that could not fail (aircraft engines and MRI scanners, for instance), it's easy to understand why in 1995, Jack made Six Sigma's five systems (Define, Measure, Analyze, Improve, and Control) central to his business strategy. Six Sigma helped to reinforce a culture of efficiency, but it wouldn't help us grow.

Other than Six Sigma, Jack's primary focus was financial services, which gave GE most of its profit growth. By the time he stepped down, among GE top officers there were five times more finance leaders than engineers. I feared that during times of slowing growth, relying on money lending over innovation would be a recipe for failure.

THREADING THE NEEDLE

My first Monday as CEO was September 10, 2001, and that meant introducing myself, via simulcast, to GE's three hundred thousand employees. I'd spent months getting ready for this moment, weighing how much to say and how to say it. When you replace somebody famous, especially somebody you respect and admire, you have to thread a very particular kind of needle. My plan was to express optimism and pride in our company, while also signaling coming change.

I knew that GE's people wanted to follow their leader. If a new leader was merely critical and denounced his or her predecessor's legacy, a couple of things would happen. First, a culture of blame would infect people at all levels of the company. Second, accountability would evaporate. Those associated with the predecessor's "mistakes" would come to work feeling unmotivated. GE's people wanted to be led forward with confidence, not to look backward in shame.

I was proud of GE's preeminence in aircraft engines, gas turbines, railroad locomotives, and medical imaging equipment. Nonetheless, as I walked onstage at the John F. Welch Leadership Development Center (a place GE people call Crotonville), I was worried about what I saw as looming headwinds.

I knew that our biggest industrial business—GE Power—was in the midst of a bubble. In a normal year, we shipped twenty to thirty gas turbines in the United States. But this was the era of deregulation and blackouts in California. From 1999 to 2002, we would ship a thousand heavy-duty turbines domestically, pulling forward a huge amount of demand. There was about to be a major lull in that market that would last an entire generation.

I also had concerns about how we ran our insurance business and about our pension earnings. Because the stock market had been so strong in the late 1990s, the investment returns from our pension plan far exceeded the amount we needed to fund it. That excess accounted for 10 percent of our earnings per share, but I worried that wasn't going to last.

Crotonville is GE's corporate university—some within the company simply call it GE's soul. The campus is located on a tree-filled fifty-nine acres up the Hudson River, an hour north of New York City, in Ossining, NY. It is a place I visited many times over my nineteen years as a manager in GE's Plastics, Appliances, and Health-care businesses. Now, as I entered the sunken auditorium, a place known as "the Pit," I settled into a director's chair next to the event's moderator, CNBC anchor Sue Herera, who introduced me as GE's new CEO.

It was humbling to look out into the faces of the hundreds of GE employees who filled the room and to know that hundreds of thousands more around the world were watching. I could see some of them, too, displayed on huge TV monitors. The folks from Power Systems, based in Atlanta, Georgia, waved hello, as did members of the Plastics team in Bergen op Zoom, the Netherlands. The GE Capital group piped in from Stamford, Connecticut; the Aircraft Engines team from Cincinnati, Ohio; and the Medical Systems people from outside of Milwaukee, Wisconsin. Associates in Scotland and Wales, as well as other teams around the United States, were also watching.

I started my remarks with some personal history. My older brother and I were raised in Cincinnati by my father, Joe, and my mother, Donna, a third-grade teacher. Both my parents grew up during the Depression, and I never forgot how lucky my father felt to have a job as a middle manager at GE's Aircraft Engines division. For many of those years, he went to work in GE Aviation Building 800, a World War II–era structure that was built underground to protect it from enemy artillery. (He might as well have been a coal miner, he often joked, for all the sunshine he saw.) Every day, he took his lunch—two boiled eggs—and ate it in the break room.

I remembered many Saturdays sitting next to him on the front seat of the family Buick, which he would park just outside the gates of our municipal airfield, Lunken Airport. Built in 1930, the airport is a beaut, with an art deco terminal. The Beatles landed there during their first US tour in 1964. But for my dad and me, Lunken was all about aircraft. Peering together through the chain-link fence, we'd watch planes land as he narrated the action: "That's a 707—the same plane the president of the United States has," he'd say. Or: "That's a 727. It's got three engines, but they aren't ours—they're Pratt &

Whitney." (Pratt & Whitney was GE Aviation's big rival in those days.) I also remembered that whenever my dad had a great boss, he was motivated, and when he had a lousy boss, he was neither challenged nor happy. The worst kind of boss, he always used to say, was one who criticized all day long but never offered solutions.

I wanted to be a great boss. So I told my colleagues that I believed the CEO should be the most competitive person at the company—to establish, from the top, the will to win. As I'd risen at GE, I'd often wondered why it had become a company that didn't respect engineers. We had adapted a "fast-follower" strategy—we left innovation to other companies, and then we hurried to catch up—so we had let our research center erode. We had refused to do any tech acquisitions for fear that they would dilute our quarterly earnings, lowering the stock price. Now I told GE's people that I wanted technology to be our core competitive advantage. I wanted GE, once again, to be a place where innovation could thrive.

After my remarks, I fielded questions from employees around the world for about half an hour. Then I jumped in the car and headed to GE's then headquarters in Fairfield, Connecticut. Stepping into what had been Jack's third-floor office there, I experienced a sort of déjà vu. I'd been in the windowed room so many times over the years to meet with Jack. Now the massive oak desk was mine to scribble on and the sweeping views were mine to survey. The place was beautiful, but I didn't plan to spend much time there. I did my best work out of the office.

STOKING GE'S GROWTH ENGINE

For the remainder of that first Monday as CEO, the phone wouldn't stop ringing. One key call was from Denis Nayden, the head of GE Capital. Nayden was intense. He'd spent his whole career at GE, starting in air-rail financing after graduating from the University of Connecticut. At GE Capital, Nayden had come up under CEO Gary Wendt and developed a reputation as Wendt's pit bull, before succeeding him in 1998. "Gary's more strategic," Nayden explained to one interviewer. "I'm good at execution." Now Nayden had something he wanted to execute on: he told me he'd reached a final agreement with Xerox to buy its credit company.

GE had created GE Capital to provide in-house financing for some of GE's most expensive products, such as railroad locomotives and airplane engines. But in the years before I took over, GE Capital had grown into a humongous enterprise that provided credit services to every industry imaginable, from automotive to consumer electronics, flooring, healthcare, home furnishings, insurance, jewelry, landscaping and irrigation, mobile homes, outdoor power equipment, pool and spa, power sports, recreational vehicles, sewing, sporting goods, travel, vacuum, and water treatment. If you had a credit card from Walmart or the Home Depot or Lowe's or even Harrods, it was really from GE Capital. We made car loans in Europe and invested in commercial real estate in Florida. We were the world's biggest lessor, with hundreds of thousands of cars, trucks, railcars, airplanes, and satellites.

In 1980 GE Capital accounted for 20 percent of GE's earnings; twenty years later, it contributed more than twice that. And for many years, it had a strong business model. We had low financing costs, supported by GE's industrial cash. We were a very good, hands-on commercial lender, feeding off the weaknesses of banks. We'd help niche businesses with operations, floor plans—anything to give them an edge. For ten years running, GE Capital's earnings grew about 20 percent a year. Best of all: because our financial arm was linked to our industrial businesses, its earnings were accorded the premium multiple of an industrial company, not the typical discount of a finance business. Had GE Capital been a stand-alone bank, its PE would have been 12 to 15. Under the umbrella of Big GE, which borrowed money inexpensively, GE Capital's earnings were accorded a 30 or 40 PE. That translated into about $250 billion more value for our investors.

When I took over, however, GE Capital was seen as something

of a mystery by analysts, by investors, and even by executives within the company. Jack Welch himself had long used a phrase that prescribed how we should assess GE Capital: "The Blob Theory." That meant: don't look at the elements that make up the Blob, just look at the results. It may sound crazy now, but that was how people in and outside the company valued GE Capital.

Even good ideas can be taken to bad extremes. Our investments in insurance, particularly, were indicators of how far we'd gotten off track. In the late nineties, GE Capital had loaded up on primary-care insurance, reinsurance (property and casualty) assets, and long-term care insurance. Insurance had become our largest business within GE Capital. It seemed to me that we had overpaid for acquisitions, leveraged them too aggressively, and sold investments to make our quarterly earnings. And due to the long-tail nature of the assets, a complete exit would be impossible.

And yet . . . especially after you added in real estate loans and credit card debt, business was booming at GE Capital, which generated nearly 50 percent of GE's earnings in 2001. Nayden's phone call about Xerox at the end of my first Monday as CEO only confirmed that he wanted to drive that number higher.

I left the office and boarded a GE jet bound for Seattle, where I was due to speak at an aeronautical conference the next day. Upon arrival, I checked into a hotel and fell into bed exhausted but pleased that Day One had gone well. I was asleep before midnight.

WAKING TO A NIGHTMARE

Tuesday morning, September 11, I awakened just after 5 a.m. so I could hit the gym before paying a visit to one of GE's best customers, Boeing. When I turned on the TV above my stair-climber machine, however, every channel was broadcasting images of a fire burning on the 110-story north tower of the World Trade Center. The first reports I heard speculated that a small private aircraft had mistakenly veered off course. But as I kept stepping—right, left, right, left—a second plane hit the south tower, and this one was anything but small. Thanks in part to my dad's tutelage at Lunken Airport, I knew how to recognize a Boeing 767. Something was horribly wrong.

I left the gym and hurried to my room. I knew my wife, Andy, and my fourteen-year-old daughter, Sarah, were in New Canaan, Connecticut, where we'd just moved from Milwaukee. Assured my family was safe, I flipped on the TV and made my first call, to GE's chief financial officer, Keith Sherin. He was watching the news, too, and at first we didn't say much as the unfathomable images sunk in. Would anyone above the damaged floors escape, Sherin and I wondered, and if so, how? Meanwhile, both of us knew that GE held all the reinsurance on 7 World Trade Center, a forty-one-story building right next to the twin towers. We had insured the insurance company that held that policy.

At 6:59 a.m. Seattle time, the south tower collapsed. I couldn't believe what I was seeing. Twenty-nine minutes later, the north tower fell, and 7 World Trade Center would soon crumble as well, leveled by the incredible force with which the twin towers had crashed down. Soot and an eerie white ash engulfed all of Lower Manhattan.

I called Andy Lack, the number-two executive at NBC, which GE owned. Because his boss, Bob Wright, was traveling, I designated Lack to be our point person in New York City. He was getting feedback from the news division that the two planes that had hit the twin towers, along with another that struck the Pentagon and a fourth that had crashed in a field in Pennsylvania, were coordinated hijackings—acts of terrorism. This was gut-wrenching for the nation. It also had immediate implications for GE's Aviation division. For the first time ever, a plane had been used as a weapon, and we owned twelve hundred of them. The jet engine business was core to GE's future.

As our newscasters began to report estimates of the number of lives lost, I tracked down Wright, the CEO of NBC, in Los Angeles. Together we decided that the network would broadcast ad-free until further notice. It could cost millions of dollars, but it was an easy call. Nearly three thousand people were dead, more than six thousand were injured, and our country was on the brink of war. It just didn't feel right to have advertisements punctuating what at this point was near-constant coverage of the attacks.

We'd soon learn that GE was connected to nearly every part of the tragedy. Planes powered by GE engines had just destroyed real estate that was insured by GE-held policies. The TV network I was watching—NBC—was owned by GE. Two GE employees—an NBC technician who worked at the top of one of the twin towers and a woman from our Aviation division who was on one of the downed flights—had lost their lives.

The towers fell on a Tuesday. On Wednesday, Andy Lack and I got the idea that GE should donate $10 million to the families of the firefighters and other first responders. I had Mayor Rudy Giuliani's cell phone number, so I dialed. I thought I'd get his assistant, but Giuliani answered on the second ring. I told him our idea and that we wanted to do it quietly. Giuliani wasn't having it. "Bullshit, Jeff!" he said. "I'm going to use your donation to shame other companies into giving!" In an hour or two, he had created a fund and announced our gift. He would use GE's seed money to raise hundreds of millions of dollars.

While that felt good, it didn't erase the terror I was feeling. By the end of my first week as CEO, GE's shares had dropped 20 percent, decreasing the company's market capitalization by $80 billion.

Sometime during this period I called up G. G. Michelson, the pioneering R. H. Macy executive who was then on GE's board of directors, for a reality check. Michelson was a rock. She'd broken through many a glass ceiling, attending Columbia Law School when few women did, negotiating with Teamsters and other union leaders on behalf of the Macy's department store chain, often serving as the only woman on the corporate boards that clamored for her time. She'd had a rough upbringing—she spent some time in orphanages while her mother, who would die when she was eleven, battled tuberculosis. I sensed that, as somebody who'd weathered the worst storms, she'd give solid advice. When I told her how I was analyzing GE's priorities, she was encouraging. "You're doing great," she said. "Trust your instincts." I was so grateful that I admitted something I hadn't planned to reveal: "Look," I told her. "I feel like I want to vomit *all* the time."

FACING DISASTER

The first days after 9/11 were a blur. The nation's airspace had been deemed unsafe for commercial flight, and that left my executive team stuck in different cities. I was in Seattle; Keith Sherin—GE's CFO—was in Boston; Dennis Dammerman, GE's vice chairman and former CFO, was in Palm Beach; Bob Wright was in LA. So my team and I began having conference calls every six hours.

Keeping on top of all the issues we faced was mind-boggling. We had a customer named Atta who'd used one of our flight simulators. We needed to find out if he was the hijacker Mohamed Atta, who'd piloted the American Airlines flight that crashed into the north tower. (It took us a while, but the answer was, thankfully, no.) Next we needed to determine what our exposure was for the reinsurance on 7 World Trade Center. (We'd soon take a $1 billion write-down.) I reached out to the families of the GE employees who had died and composed an email of reassurance to be sent to GE's people—the first time in history that an all-employee email was sent within GE. I was worried about my country, my company, and my family, all at the same time. The length of my to-do list was both terrifying and motivating.

I was determined to protect GE's most vulnerable customers: the nation's airlines, which bought our aircraft engines and leased our planes. My approach was the inverse of the spiel we've all heard before takeoff, when flight attendants advise you, in case of emergency, to put on your own oxygen mask before helping others. I knew the best way to protect GE was to put the airlines' welfare first, though that would prove to be difficult.

I couldn't get home to Connecticut until Thursday night, more than forty-eight hours after the attack. I was glad to be reunited with my wife and our daughter, who was starting her freshman year in a new high school. Our move from Milwaukee, where I'd been running GE Healthcare, had already uprooted her, and I knew that was tough for a teenager. But being the new kid in a place shaken by tragedy would prove even harder.

Six days after the attacks, on a Monday, the stock market opened for the first time since 9/11. By the end of that week, the Dow Jones Industrial Average had fallen 14.3 percent, then the largest one-week point drop in history. That meant $1.2 trillion in value, gone. I tried to stay calm, but GE was getting crushed. I heard from several share-holders, including our biggest one: "We didn't realize GE was so big in insurance!" I wanted to say, "We've never hidden it. Didn't you examine our holdings when you bought our stock?" Instead I kept quiet.

Every day I woke up and got on the stair-step machine, trying to assert normalcy one footfall at a time. That was also my motivation for approving a full-page ad that GE placed in the *New York Times*, the *Wall Street Journal*, and nearly every major newspaper in the country. It featured a drawing of a solemn-faced Statue of Liberty, rolling up one sleeve and appearing to step off her pedestal. "We will roll up our sleeves," the ad said. "We will move forward together. We will overcome. We will never forget."

Even when flights began to return to normal schedules, few customers wanted to fly. The airlines were hurting, and that wasn't good for GE. As I finish this book, in 2020, the coronavirus has had a similar impact on the industry—and maybe even worse. Then as now, I believed it was important to solve our own problems, while also helping our customers. In the toughest times, you always remember who extended a helping hand.

Most evenings during this period, my executive team would get on the phone to discuss our exposure. Every night brought a new challenge—and when I say "new," I'm not kidding. At times I felt like I was learning to speak a second language. Someone would say, "Okay, we've got to buy a billion dollars of American Airlines EETCs tomorrow or else they're going to go bankrupt." EETCs, enhanced equipment trust certificates, are a type of bond. "Hey," I asked Dammerman the first time he used the acronym in my presence, "what the fuck is an EETC?" My learning curve could not have been steeper.

Dennis Dean Dammerman, who we all called by his nickname "Triple D," was as tough-minded a finance guy as they come. In 1984, he'd been just thirty-eight when Jack Welch made him the youngest CFO in GE history, and by 2001, he'd seen it all. Maybe that's why he was so calm in the face of chaos. He'd been a mentor to me; he was the first person at GE to interview me when I was still in business school, and I'd always been grateful for his support. Now, though, I was even more grateful for his unflappability.

ABSORBING FEAR

The best leaders absorb fear. I'm not talking about soothing people by blowing smoke or giving false assurances. I'm talking about giving people the truth but also giving them a way forward. In the wake of 9/11, GE's people needed to hear, and to believe, that we had a plan and that, working together, they could help us execute it. They didn't need to hear that I was so agitated that I struggled to keep food down.

True leaders are frank, but they don't traffic in panic. The best leaders acknowledge mistakes, but they don't tear their colleagues down just to ease their own discomfort. Transparency is an admirable goal. But the real goal is to solve problems. When leaders merely unload their burdens without offering a plan of action, that's selfishness masquerading as candor—the arrogance of false piety.

GE couldn't afford for the airlines to fail, so between September 11 and December 1, GE lent them tens of billions of dollars. Even as we bailed them out, however, we also had to play the heavy. At this point, airlines could fly internationally only into and out of countries that had passed a special terrorism exception to insurance. In those early days, only a few countries had done so. We needed to be sure that if a leased GE airplane was used in a future terrorist attack, we wouldn't be liable. So at the end of each workday, we'd have to place calls to airlines in countries that hadn't passed the test.

Night after night, we'd dial up either the airline CEOs or the presidents of the countries themselves and deliver the bad news: "You can't fly GE airplanes tomorrow, because you haven't passed the terrorism exception." Dammerman would call up the leader of Poland or Japan or Australia and say, "Hey, tomorrow you can't fly those eight GE planes you lease from us." The leader would say that was unacceptable, and Triple D would counter that he wasn't asking; he was telling. Sometimes these calls got heated. "That's bullshit," the guy on the other end of the phone would yell, to which Triple D would bark, "Hey, don't fly the goddamned planes or you're going to get sued!" I'll never forget watching Triple D slam down the phone one night after one of these contentious back-and-forths. I waited a beat before I turned to him with a smile. "Can you make my next call?" I asked. "Because you do it so well!"

I was also dealing with stuff that had been underway before the tragedy. The Xerox deal that Denis Nayden had pitched me on September 10 had not been completed, and soon, I heard from Ann Mulcahy, the company's new CEO. She knew we had the right to walk away, and given what had just happened, we had every reason to. But I knew that would put Xerox in a difficult spot. I invited Mulcahy to lunch, and with her assurances, I decided we'd proceed. Did GE need to absorb another credit company in this business climate? No. But America's corporations—like the nation itself—were under siege. We had to stick together. (In the end, we made a little money on the deal, and Xerox stayed in business.)

Another issue that had been simmering was GE Capital's role in financing the bankruptcy restructuring of the steel industry, which had been overleveraged when 9/11 triggered a steep decline in steel prices. We were among a consortium of investors involved in rescuing Bethlehem Steel, led by the private-equity firm of Wilbur

Ross (much later, he'd become the nation's secretary of commerce, appointed by President Donald Trump). Decisions had to be made by late September, and the deal's urgency necessitated that I get personally involved. During one difficult meeting in New York City, we were all getting hung up on tiny details when Ross looked up from across the huge conference table and declared, "Let's do the easy things first. We can tackle the tough ones later, once we get momentum." It was such helpful, commonsense advice.

Friday, September 21, was my first meeting with analysts as CEO. I came prepared with five or six charts that illustrated how we would survive if the airlines went bankrupt. I'd played offensive tackle in college, and I tend toward football metaphors. So as I walked analysts through our thinking, I said, "I'll play a little offense here. We didn't dust off the playbook and start practicing on September eleventh." I stressed that GE had been trimming costs for more than a year and that the power market—though showing signs of a coming crater— was still in a good cycle. Our diversified portfolio would enable us to offset losses in insurance and aircraft engines. That was the beauty of a conglomerate, I said—when one sector was down, chances were another was up. Everyone gave me high fives that morning. Even Jim Cramer, the voluble, wild-eyed former hedge fund manager and prognosticator on CNBC's *Mad Money*, praised my performance.

After the analysts meeting, I did an interview on CNBC, and then started to make my way down to Ground Zero. I'd been offered an up-close tour of the devastation. On the way, I stopped at St. Vincent's Hospital, where GE had sent some of our portable CT scanners on the morning of the attacks. The hospital administrators I met explained that, while they were grateful, they hadn't had much use for the scanners. After about 11 a.m. on September 11, ambulances stopped delivering injured people. You either lived or you died that morning, they said.

I continued south, to Wall Street. Beth Comstock, GE's head of corporate communications, was with me. Placing our full-page Lady Liberty ad in the nation's newspapers had been Comstock's idea, so we were both truly moved when we walked onto the floor of the New York Stock Exchange and were greeted with a cheer. The ad was taped to the walls of many traders' kiosks.

Minutes later, we arrived at Ground Zero, where we were given hard hats, work boots, and face masks to protect our lungs. I met Thomas Von Essen, the fire chief who was coordinating the cleanup. He led us into the twisted wreckage, and I was stunned to see that ten days after the attack, fires were still blazing. The smell of incinerated plastic and wire was so sharp it hurt to breathe. Von Essen had been among the first responders. Listening to this bone-weary public servant, still so professional even amid his grief, I was overwhelmed.

Mathematicians use proofs called "existence theorems" to conclude there is only one solution to a particular problem with a particular set of conditions. I was a math major in college, so this is a familiar concept to me. But during this period I remember thinking that there was no existence theorem for this particular set of conditions because it was so abnormal. As my team rallied in the short term to support part of our customer base (the airlines), we were also trying to think about how our industrial company needed to change for the long term. All we could do was make decisions, one by one. Standing amid the smoldering wreckage, I told Von Essen that GE's leadership training program would help the New York Fire Department try to replace the many leaders it had lost. It was the least we could do.

PUTTING CUSTOMERS FIRST

On September 22, President George W. Bush signed into law the Air Transportation Safety and System Stabilization Act, which aimed to maintain a "safe, efficient and viable" commercial aviation system in the United States. In addition to providing immediate cash infusions to the airlines and liability protection for the carriers whose jets had been hijacked on 9/11, the act created a board to evaluate and approve loan guarantees to airlines that needed it—essentially providing credit that was not otherwise available. That bailout board was made up of Alan Greenspan, the chairman of the Federal Reserve, Secretary of the Treasury Paul O'Neill, and Secretary of Transportation Norman Mineta. Greenspan was in full bloom at that time, at the height of his power. O'Neill had run Alcoa, the aluminum company, and Mineta was the former secretary of commerce. I think he thought his second cabinet position would be an easy, cushy gig. How hard could it be to oversee the nation's highways and flyways? Suddenly he had one of the most difficult jobs on earth.

I would soon be making regular trips to DC to plead the airlines' case to Greenspan, O'Neill, and Mineta. You may wonder why the CEOs of the airlines didn't do this themselves, but given their financial challenges, which included having too much debt, they hadn't been hugely respected even before 9/11. Most of the airlines had been on their backs before the attacks, so afterward, no one believed their lobbying efforts would be effective.

GE, meanwhile, was overexposed to aviation. In the boom times of the late nineties, we'd turbocharged our aircraft purchases and ended up with a fleet of twelve hundred aircraft—significantly more than any other company. So I had an incentive to become the airlines' de facto spokesman.

What GE did for a struggling Phoenix-based airline called America West is a terrific example of how we tried to impact the aviation industry during this time. Doug Parker was America West's CEO in 2001, and before the attacks, he'd managed to line up some much-needed financing with the help of GE and the European aeronautics company Airbus. When 9/11 made that financing disappear—no one wanted to lend to an overleveraged airline whose business has dropped 80 percent—America West seemed headed for liquidation. That's when I encouraged Henry Hubschman, the head of the GE Capital Aviation Services division, to get involved. Ever unruffled and logical, Hubschman put the head of our Washington division on the case, and GE's lobbyists helped Parker convince Greenspan, O'Neill, and Mineta that this smaller carrier did, indeed, deserve loan guarantees. The result: America West survived. That may not mean much to those who've never heard of the airline, but it had many positive ripple effects. First, America West's thirteen thousand employees kept their jobs. Four years later, when US Airways was about to go under, America West pulled together a plan—again with GE's help—to bring them out of bankruptcy, saving another thirty thousand jobs. Arguably, America West ushered in a period of industry consolidation that would benefit not just individual carriers but also consumers. Parker is now CEO of American Airlines.

Another story: Right after 9/11, a thirty-seven-year-old Malaysian entrepreneur named Tony Fernandes approached GE Capital seeking to lease two Boeing 737s. Fernandes believed the time was right to enter the no-frills travel market. He'd mortgaged his home to buy AirAsia, a heavily indebted subsidiary of the Malaysian government, and he needed to lease some planes. Because he had no collateral, GE Capital told him no. But he wouldn't be denied, which I found out when, somehow, he showed up in my office.

"Look, I know you've got a million things going on right now," he said. "But I can do this if you just get me some planes!" I must have been late for a meeting on bankruptcy or some other dreaded fiasco, because his optimism swayed me. "I'm so swamped, let's just do it," I said.

Man, did my people excoriate me for that later—and rightly so. They'd already shown him the door! But Fernandes made good on his promise. AirAsia was out of debt in just one year, he became a multibillionaire, and from that point on, GE got all of AirAsia's business.

I couldn't have known it then, but 9/11 would mark the end of an era—and an abrupt one. No American executives my age had ever before encountered tail risk—which is basically something that is unlikely to happen, but then *does* happen. Once you encounter tail risk, though, you never forget it. The tranquil nineties—when the world was at peace, China was still a sleeping giant, and the US economy was growing 4.5 percent a year like clockwork—had been the "trust me" decade. But after the terrorist attacks, and the faltering economy and shoddy business behavior that soon followed, trust evaporated.

As I finish this book in 2020, I see the next generation of leaders grappling with the COVID-19 crisis. They are learning that especially in a crisis, people want to be led. They don't expect perfection, but they want to know where you stand. They want to hear you articulate what drives your thinking. They want simple words based on trust, honesty, and consequences. That's how I tried to communicate in 2001.

About two weeks after the attacks, I remember looking out my office window and feeling, for the first time, like the worst might be over. "We're going to make it through this," I said out loud. I swear it was only minutes later that the phone rang. It was Bob Wright calling from NBC and his voice was grave. Our *Nightly News* anchor Tom Brokaw had just received an envelope containing a threatening handwritten note: "09-11-01," read the letter, which also included what looked like anthrax spores. "This is next. Take Penacilin [sic] now. Death to America. Death to Israel. Allah is great." I put Wright on hold for a moment while I let out a scream. The hits, they just kept coming.

Three days later, on September 28, Brokaw's personal assistant Erin O'Conner came down with flu-like symptoms and broke out with reddish-black sores. It had, indeed, been anthrax in that envelope. That would have been terrible news about any employee, but O'Conner was a new mom, so it felt even worse. While she ultimately would recover, those events only heightened the fear and uncertainty within GE. As we revamped our corporate security company-wide, I continued to think about how 9/11 would alter my plans to move GE into the future.

CHAPTER 2

Leaders Learn Every Day

I n the months following 9/11 it was hard not to feel untethered, as if anything could happen. An October 2001 editorial in the *New York Daily News* sticks out in my mind. "To the city and the nation, the events of Sept. 11 were apocalyptic," the piece began. "To General Electric, they apparently were a convenient diversion." The paper then went on to accuse GE of using this national catastrophe as an opportunity to negotiate with the Environmental Protection Agency "under cover of a distracted public." Our alleged goal: to "weasel out" of our obligation to clean up the polluted Hudson River.

Maybe I was just tired, but the piece made me angry, and I wrote to the newspaper's owner, real estate investor Mort Zuckerman, to tell him so. It was crass, I said, to imply that GE, which for eighty-plus years had worked closely with the US military to build jet engines to keep America safe, would use the murder of 2,996 Americans as a negotiating tactic. It wouldn't be the last time I'd shake my head in disbelief.

On October 11, 2001, one month after the terrorist attacks, GE reported its third-quarter earnings. Thankfully, they had risen 3 percent over the same period the previous year. There was more good news: while stocks in general were up about 11 percent since hitting rock bottom three weeks earlier, GE's share price had risen about 29 percent.

But just when I thought I could catch my breath, the world learned that Enron's earnings were a sham. In the year 2000, the Texas energy corporation had been the world leader in electricity, natural gas, and other related products and services, with reported revenues of $111 billion. Now, just a year later, its complex, obfuscating financial statements and its unethical misrepresentations of its earnings would cause it to collapse, rocking much of the corporate landscape, and especially GE Capital.

You're a "trust me" company until you're not. When Enron executive Jeffrey Skilling testified in front of Congress and compared Enron to GE, I knew we were in trouble. While GE wasn't guilty of the kind of financial scamming that Enron was accused of, the scandal shined new light on the complexity of some of our holdings. Watchdogs were calling for increased corporate transparency. I needed to move fast to get GE in line with changing norms.

In January 2002, I was watching TV in CNN's green room, waiting to do an interview about GE's just-announced fourth-quarter earnings. I watched as CNN's anchors grilled the on-air guest who preceded me: Joseph Berardino, the CEO of Arthur Andersen, one of the Big Five accounting firms. My whole life, I'd heard Arthur Andersen referred to with nothing but respect. But now, since the firm had been discovered to have shredded documents relating to its audits of Enron, it was an embarrassment. Within months, Arthur Andersen would surrender its licenses to practice as CPAs. It was unprecedented.

A month later, in February 2002, the GE board met in Salt Lake City during the Winter Olympics. The Enron scandal had made it essential that we dig deep, together, into the GE Capital balance sheet. At this meeting, I grasped for the first time how much more work our board and senior executives needed to do in order to fully understand the nitty-gritty workings of GE Capital.

We also dissected many of the esoteric financial materials we owned, including special purpose vehicles, or SPVs, the incorrect use of which was at the center of Enron's misdeeds. We had a lot of them, and while we had been using them correctly, we realized we needed to have fewer of them. I remember during this twelve-hour marathon of a meeting, I looked over at Shelly Lazarus, a great advertising leader who had just joined the GE board. I could tell she was thinking to herself, "What have I gotten myself into?" I could relate, to some degree.

More than 9/11 or the dot-com bubble bursting, Enron's failure transformed GE's business forever. Before Enron, neither analysts nor investors ever asked us how GE Capital worked. And then it changed in an instant—and we responded.

In the first half of 2002, we added Bob Swieringa, a former member of the Financial Accounting Standards Board, to the GE board. We asked longtime GE director Douglas "Sandy" Warner, the former chairman of the board of J.P. Morgan & Co., to chair our audit committee (and the corporate audit staff began reporting directly to the board). For the first time, we began requiring board members to visit several GE businesses each year without me or any other corporate executive present. The goal: to ensure transparency between the board members and our division heads. Finally, we instituted a fifteen-person "disclosure committee" that approved all public investor statements. By the time the Sarbanes-Oxley Act became law in the summer of 2002, reforming the rules that determined what public companies had to share with investors, these practices were underway at GE, and we never wavered.

If the back-to-back challenges of 9/11 and the Enron debacle had taught me anything, it was that in crisis, you can bring to bear only the tools you have in your toolbox. In my twenty years at General Electric, I'd worked in three divisions: Plastics, Appliances, and Healthcare. Each had taught me important lessons about leadership and about myself. I'd also participated in a grueling, three-way runoff to determine who would be Jack's successor. That process in itself was an education you won't get in any business school. I'd always believed an important determinant of success could be found in how one answered three questions: How fast can you learn? How much can you take? And what will you give to those around you? I knew a lot of my strengths and weaknesses, but did I have all the tools I needed? It was time to take stock—to examine the lessons I'd learned and the areas in which I still needed to grow.

"DON'T COMPLAIN—FIX IT!"

My parents' own upbringings had left no room for laziness. My maternal grandmother was a full-time secretary in the 1940s, having been widowed when my mom was twelve. My dad, the youngest of ten children, began working before he finished high school, making Helldiver bombers for Curtiss-Wright, the aircraft manufacturer. At eighteen in 1946 he joined the navy and spent time on a destroyer in the Pacific.

My parents taught my older brother, Stephen, and me that it was up to each individual to make his or her way in the world. They never took a steady job for granted or, say, the ability to buy a house. They'd never been bailed out by anyone, and they made clear that we shouldn't expect to be either. They were not didactic people, but they wanted us to never see ourselves as victims. If my brother or I came home with a complaint, they would say, "Don't complain—fix it!"

They also instilled in us the importance of being yourself. "Phony" was the worst thing they could say about somebody. There weren't a lot of phonies in Finneytown, the suburb of Cincinnati where, in 1961, my parents paid twenty-three thousand dollars for a yellow three-bedroom brick split-level on a cul-de-sac. I was five years old then, Steve was nine, and our tidy but chockablock housing development was nearly brand-new. Our address was 9060 Cotillion Drive, and several of the surrounding street names shared a similar cheerful grandeur: Cherry Blossom Lane, Fontainebleau Terrace. But Finneytown wasn't grand. It was solidly middle-class.

The moms of the kids I hung out with mostly stayed home to raise them (my mom had quit teaching when Steve was born). The dads included an insurance salesman, a schoolteacher, a pharmaceutical salesman, and a GE machinist—what people back then called "respectable" jobs. My dad's job was no different. As a frontline manager in the sourcing department at GE Aircraft Engines, he was a white-collar professional.

I've often joked that while we lived on Cotillion Drive, not one of my neighbors would ever attend a cotillion. Hell, we didn't even have air-conditioning. When I was a freshman in high school, I used to come home after football practice during the hottest Ohio months and head straight to the basement to lie on the cool concrete floor. It was the only way I knew to stop sweating. I remember when I was sixteen, my dad finally sprang for central AC. The day it was installed will always be one of the most vibrant, happy moments of my life, right up there with marrying my wife and welcoming the birth of my daughter.

I loved football, but it was baseball that instilled in me the connection between teamwork and mutual respect. It was my senior year in high school, circa 1973, and I was on the pitcher's mound. I was a six-foot-four-inch, curly-haired seventeen-year-old, decked out in my white uniform with a big red Finneytown *F* over my heart.

I looked into the stands, where my parents were sitting, as always. Whether I was here or on the football field or the basketball court, I was used to looking up and catching my dad's eye after a good play. Steve was in college by this point, so the Immelt pride was focused laser-like on me. It felt good.

I was in the zone that day. I just kept striking batters out. I was on track for a great game. Still, at one point, when our shortstop made an error, I couldn't hide my frustration. Tugging off my glove, I threw it into the dirt. For me the moment was fleeting; I retrieved my catcher's mitt and moved on. Next time I glanced toward the fan section, however, I noticed my dad was missing. That was odd. As we won the game, I wondered what was wrong.

After our coach sent us home, I set off across the athletic field on foot. Dad used to say our house was just a driver and a nine iron from the high school (he had no golf club membership; he liked to whack balls off our front porch). So it took me all of five minutes to walk to Cotillion Drive. I found him in our kitchen. "Dad, where did you go?" I asked, a little steamed. "That was the best game I've had all year." He didn't hesitate, and he didn't hold back. "You know," he said, "if you're going to make an ass of yourself and embarrass one of your teammates, I don't have to sit there and watch it." My dad is not a massive guy—I had three inches on him by then. But I felt puny when he told me, "That is not the way I expect you to behave. You should never show up anyone on your team. Not ever."

I don't remember the score of that game. What I do remember is how hot my face felt. The sting of shame. My dad had called me out for behaving like someone I didn't want to be. He always urged us to treat people with respect, no matter where they came from or how much money they had.

Dad likes to joke that his sons were raised out of the Book of Proverbs, by which he meant a set of truisms he repeated (and lived by). Deal with a problem when it's small—that was one of his favorites. Another one was: you either make it for yourself or you don't; no one will do it for you. And then, of course, my father's favorite saying: fair is fair. These fundamentals would later color my management style.

BE WILLING TO STAND APART

I was a good athlete but not a gifted one. All my successes came from working hard. All summer long I'd be running and weight training, and all that conditioning paid off: my senior year of high school, I had the most varsity letters of anyone at Finneytown High, and several terrific colleges recruited me to play football. When I visited Dartmouth, however, I felt like I'd found a new home. In the end, it came down to Dartmouth and Vanderbilt, which offered me a better financial-aid package. But I was smitten. I told my dad if he'd let me join the Dartmouth Big Green, I'd borrow as much money as I could and work during the summers to make up the difference.

I kept that promise. On summer breaks during college, I worked construction, helped out at a scrap yard, and made and warehoused parts for Ford Motor Company. I'd come home right after finals, throw down my dirty laundry, and the next day report to work on an assembly line in a Ford parts depot. I made eight dollars an hour—big money for me. I think I pocketed three thousand dollars that summer.

During the school year back in New Hampshire, meanwhile, I worked closely with mathematician and computer scientist John G. Kemeny, the Hungarian émigré who was best known for codeveloping the BASIC programming language. He was a genius teacher and also the president of Dartmouth in the years I was there. But my time on the football team taught me as many enduring lessons as my professors did. During my sophomore year, for example, our team had been favored to win the Ivy League, but we'd been playing poorly. We'd lost two games in a row when the team gathered for our regular Monday meeting.

Mike Briggs was the first to speak. Mike was a senior—a second-string quarterback who worked his ass off in practice but always rode the bench. "I've got something I need to say," he said, "and Reggie"—he looked at a teammate named Reggie Williams—"it's about you."

We all held our breath. Reggie, ripped like a Greek god, was a superathlete who always started. But he didn't expend much effort except during games. "You've got God-given talent," Mike told Reggie. "I mean, you're easily the best player on the team. But you just don't give a shit about any of us." Reggie didn't know what to do. He'd been raised, I think, not to show any weakness. But that reluctance to be vulnerable—to admit the team mattered to him—was costing him in ways he hadn't understood. I found out later that another teammate of ours, a guy named Harry Wilson, took Reggie out after practice and told him he needed to face it: Mike's criticism was spot-on.

That moment changed Reggie. He became a great team member and leader, and he would go on to play in the NFL for fourteen years. (Harry Wilson, meanwhile, would have a son, Russell, who is a quarterback for the Seattle Seahawks.) I absorbed the lesson: if you have something to say, speak up, even when it's difficult.

CHOOSE PURPOSE OVER MONEY

After I graduated college in 1978, I applied to Harvard Business School. I still had some growing up to do—I'd enjoyed my frat partying days—and I thought grad school would help me buckle down. Thanks in large part to one of my football coaches, Jake Crouthamel, who wrote me a strong recommendation, Harvard let me in. But I needed to save some money, so I deferred for two years and headed home to Cincinnati for a job at Procter & Gamble.

I worked in brand management for P&G's Duncan Hines division, and one of my bullpen mates was Steve Ballmer, who would later become employee number two at Microsoft. Had you seen us then, flinging paper clips at each other over the walls of our cubicles, you'd never have guessed that we'd both become CEOs before we turned fifty. Instead of poster boys for upward mobility, Ballmer and I were more like something you'd see in a *Dilbert* cartoon.

Still, we worked long hours at those shiny Formica desks. Our big three products were boxed mixes for blueberry muffins, brownies, and Moist & Easy Snack Cake. The goal: for Duncan Hines to take market share away from Betty Crocker. There were many strategic discussions about how best to do that. To match Betty Crocker's brownies signature—a little can of Hershey's chocolate in every box—Duncan Hines had added a "liquid flavor packet" to its mix. It was our job to sell it. We debated whether we should focus our promotional efforts on areas of the country where Duncan Hines was already strong or try to force our way into Betty Crocker territory. We also learned to think analytically about pricing. If you could sell two boxes of muffin mix by offering thirty cents off, that was better than selling one at full price.

Ballmer and I were both headed to grad school. He left first for Stanford. I'd stick around a little longer before going east. Stepping onto that redbrick campus in Cambridge I was wowed: at Harvard there was actual ivy. But belying my soon-to-be fancy pedigree was this reality: I was broke. I had a credit card with a two-hundred-dollar limit, and Visa seemed always to be asking me to cut it in half and mail it back to them. To keep costs down, I volunteered to be the fourth guy in a three-bedroom apartment in a place called Peabody Terrace. My room was, literally, a closet.

I enjoyed HBS. The case-study approach was invigorating. So were my fellow students. Classrooms had tiered, amphitheater-like seating, and my friends and I snagged seats in the back row, an area HBS folks call "the Skydeck." We Skydeckers could size up every-one below us and whisper a little more without getting scolded. I sat next to Judy Kent (who I introduced to Jamie Dimon, another classmate in our second year; he later married her—and became chairman and CEO of JPMorgan Chase, the largest of the big four American banks). On the other side of me was Sue Zadek, who my roommate Steve Mandel would eventually wed. (Steve would become a hedge fund manager and philanthropist; he founded Lone Pine Capital after serving as managing director at Tiger Management.) Other classmates of mine would go on to similar heights: Steve Burke would become CEO of NBCUniversal; Scott Malkin would found Value Retail; and my best friend Pete Maglathlin and his wife, Laurie, would lead the mail-order giant MBI.

I didn't have a grand plan for my career. If you'd asked me then what I read regularly, I would have answered: *Sports Illustrated*. When I graduated in 1982, it seemed everybody was going into investment banking. But not me. I'd worked one summer at Boston

Consulting Group, and while I liked my colleagues there, I found the job unsatisfying. Ultimately BCG offered me a job that paid fifty thousand dollars a year. Morgan Stanley made a similar offer. That was good money in 1982, and I had student loans from both Dartmouth and HBS to pay down. But the abstract nature of that kind of work held no appeal to me. I wanted to work at a place that made things that made customers' lives better.

When GE offered me a job that paid thirty thousand dollars a year, my reaction was "Okay! Let's go!" I loved GE, having grown up in its embrace.

Around that time I met a famous banker at Morgan Stanley, a guy named Joe Fogg. When I told him I was going to work for GE, he scoffed. "If you worked for Morgan Stanley, you would be presenting to Jack Welch in your first year," he said. "If you go to work for GE, you're not going to meet him for twenty years."

I never forgot that, even as I proved Fogg wrong: about a year after I began at GE, I would meet Jack face-to-face when he summoned six young managers to his office. He told us our supervisors had recommended us, and for about an hour, he talked with us about GE's goals and how to get there. I was exhilarated, at twenty-seven years old, to have that time with him. Afterward, he sent me a handwritten note that said, "Hey, great job. Really impressive." I sent a copy of it to my parents, but I kept the original. I still have it.

SEE THROUGH YOUR CUSTOMER'S EYES

When I arrived at GE in 1982, my first big assignment was in the Plastics division. I moved to Dallas to become sales manager of the Southwestern district. I managed an office that sold a product called Noryl—little pellets of plastic—to businesses that molded them into instrument panels or car bumpers or hundreds of other products. Our main customers were independent automotive and computer companies across seven states.

I managed eight salespeople. If you've seen the TV series *The*

Office, you can imagine the cast of characters. There was one tall Texan sales rep who wore cowboy boots and didn't have a college degree. There was another guy whose male-model good looks seemed always to open doors before he even asked. There was one woman who was so intense she seemed always on the brink of suing someone, but her fearsomeness worked for her. And then there was Andy, the woman I would eventually marry. She likes to tell the story of how she and the other salespeople greeted me my first day. The short version is: with suspicion. Part of the problem was sartorial. My wardrobe consisted of five Brooks Brothers suits. They pegged me as a stuck-up Harvard guy.

I listened when the boot-wearing sales rep confided, "You've gotta lose the suits. You look like a dork." He took me shopping for blazers and khakis and, yes, my own pair of cowboy boots. I'd often say to my people: "I'll come out on sales calls with you, if that will help. But you're going to get me the business." After that, they realized I would pitch in, not just give orders.

Andy and I became friendly colleagues in Texas that year. Born in Panama, as a small child she'd moved around South America— Venezuela, Brazil—because her dad worked for Ford Motor Company exports. When she was ten, the family moved to Birmingham, Michigan, outside of Detroit. Living around the world, Andy had learned how to talk to anyone. I always tell people: "There's nobody who doesn't like my wife." She is genuine. No BS. And she was a hell of a saleswoman.

The culture of the Plastics division was wild and crazy and proud of it. Some guys would drink four martinis at lunch. Not for nothing did we call ourselves "Mad Dog Plastics." As a chemical engineer, Jack Welch himself had started in the Plastics division, and he'd helped create the work-hard-play-hard culture in part because that approach gave us a competitive advantage. Our chief rivals were German chemical companies—Bayer, BASF—whose salespeople tended to be buttoned-up rule followers. By contrast, GE Plastics led with its lack of bureaucracy. We'd do almost anything to get a sale.

I think Jack gave Plastics a loose rein because he saw its business as unique. In most sectors, you compete with your competitors to enlarge your slice of an existing pie. But in the 1980s in Plastics, it wasn't about fighting over market share; it was about creating market share. We wanted to bake a bigger pie—to expand the number of products that could be made of plastic—and we were always inventing new polymers and resins. If you made something out of metal, we would find a way to make it better out of plastic.

I've never been a huge drinker. I'm the guy at the table who orders a glass of merlot to fit in, takes a sip, and then flags down the waitress to request a Diet Coke. My bigger vice in those years was Dunkin' Donuts. But I understood the power of camaraderie. I'd show up at the parties, stay for a while, then head home.

During these years, I learned how to sell by doing it. My mentor was my boss, Patrick Dane Baise, or "P.D." He was one of the best belly-to-belly salesmen I've ever seen—street smart, strategic, and blunt. "Get your shoes shined," he'd bark. "You won't book orders with dirty shoes." He had incredible instincts. How do you seal a deal? When do you walk away? P.D. had answers. He taught me how to choreograph our team's pitches to potential buyers and what to say when we got an initial "No!" He taught me not to waste time on irrelevant stuff.

Here's a classic P.D. story. One day, one of GE's strategic planners called him up with a question. "P.D.," he said, "what's GE's share of polycarbonate in the Western region?" P.D. didn't hesitate. "Hang on," he said, putting his hand over the phone for a second. "Forty-seven percent!" The guy thanked him, and P.D. slammed down the phone. "I don't really know the exact answer," he admitted, "but if that guy knew it, he wouldn't call me. And why should we spend a couple of weeks figuring out if it's forty-six or forty-eight? What's the difference?"

This, too, is pure P.D.: he used to mock boast about his alma mater, Marshall University, which he called "the Harvard of West Virginia." P.D.'s confidence and lack of pretention was disarming. And man, what a teacher he was.

P.D. taught me that real leaders make timely decisions, and then stand behind them, even when criticized. Being a good manager wasn't a popularity contest. It demanded bravery and the willingness to be accountable. P.D. tutored me in the art of figuring out and catering to customers' needs, while also making a profit. And he showed me how important it is to take a chance on your people, by taking a chance on me.

These were the early days of maquiladoras. There was a tax-free zone in Mexico and people were building factories there. I told P.D. that our customers were sometimes frustrated by the time it took us to deliver our products. I wanted to store inventory nearby, in Mexico. "If you give me forty-five thousand bucks to buy a warehouse down there, and let me stock it, I will lose fewer orders," I told him. P.D. said yes, we bought the warehouse, and I never lost an order again.

Soon, I'd be transferred to Chicago, where I was responsible for selling those same plastic pellets to the whole western half of the United States. Andy and I started dating then, and given what good friends we were already, our relationship moved pretty fast. We got married in February 1986, and a lot of our Plastics buddies were there to cheer us on. Our daughter, Sarah, was born a year later.

In December 1987, I got a bill from Harvard for twenty-five thousand dollars. I'd signed a five-year balloon extension when I graduated, and suddenly, my student loans were due. Andy started crying. "What are we going to do?" she asked. "We're not going to have a Christmas!" Meanwhile, I was muttering to myself: "Fuck, I knew I'd forgotten about something!" I wasn't getting rich at GE, and we had bills to pay. We had no savings, and we were living paycheck to paycheck. But I was learning what I needed to know to succeed.

While I was way down in the ranks, I felt as though I worked for Jack Welch, and that was all right with me. I loved the guy and was inspired by him. Early in his reign as GE chairman, after he eliminated more than a hundred thousand jobs to fulfill his dictum that GE should be in businesses only where it was a market leader, he'd been tagged with the moniker "Neutron Jack." But the nick-name captured only one facet of him. I've never seen anyone better at evaluating the pros and cons of an idea. I'd heard about Jack's temper, and I had colleagues who compared him to General Patton, but I was never afraid of him. To me, his frankness was part of his appeal.

There has been so much written about Jack Welch. But if I were asked to name the most important lesson he taught me it would be: how to lead an enterprise at scale. Jack created a culture in which everybody counted and each individual voice mattered. He expected GE managers to be out of their offices and known to all. (Bureau-crats who holed up behind closed doors left the company, not always voluntarily.)

Jack paid little attention to protocol or organizational charts. He'd call anyone himself. He built horizontal cohorts of managers. He believed that even when they were in different GE businesses, these managers could execute and drive change across the company. He paid special attention to the top five hundred GE leaders. At this level, Jack controlled compensation and promotions, and everyone knew he trusted his own instincts about people. "You work for me," he'd often say. "The businesses just rent you."

Jack dominated the communication channels and controlled the messaging within GE. From him, I learned that good leaders speak in one voice to the entire company (thousands) and in subtly dif-ferent voices in an auditorium (hundreds), a conference room (ten people and up), or one-on-one. Jack understood the context of what he said and the impact he had on each group. He would change the tone and vocabulary.

Once when I was running the Healthcare business, Jack came to town to give me my job review. We were at odds over personnel—Jack wanted me to hire a chief financial officer whom I didn't think was the right fit. So I pushed back, which could sometimes be dan-gerous with Jack. He tore into me, questioning my judgment, my loyalty. He could be blistering when he wanted to win. A moment later, though, when he went next door to meet with some union leaders, he was charming and engaging—a different person.

One union leader had been married four times and was now remarried to his first wife. Jack spent fifteen minutes asking the guy how, exactly, was that working out? He was playful and familiar, without crossing any lines. Then he shifted gears, laying out the parameters of what would be possible in the next contract negotiation. It was masterful.

LEARN TO TAKE THE HEAT

It may sound weird to say it, but I am certain that I would never have become GE's CEO if I hadn't first learned to fix refrigerators. In 1989, however, when GE moved me, Andy, and our daughter to Louisville, Kentucky, so I could become head of customer service for GE Appliances, I wasn't so sure it was a promotion.

GE's refrigerators had begun failing at an alarming rate. The problem, we soon figured out, was faulty compressors. Compressors, which push refrigerant vapor into a unit's outer coils, have to work harder when the weather gets hot. So the hotter it got, the more our compressors failed. First, we heard from customers in Puerto Rico. Then Florida. After a little investigation, we determined that every single compressor inside 3.3 *million* refrigerators was going to fail, one by one, in a wave that would roll across the country from the warmest spots to the coolest. We figured refrigerators in Maine would be the last to give out, but their time would come. Each repair would cost us $210—more than half what customers had paid in the first place. It was a disaster.

We had to brief Jack, so the president of the Appliances division, the CFO, and I headed to GE's Connecticut headquarters. In the boardroom, about twenty guys sat around a huge table, with Jack at the head. My boss gave a few remarks, as did the CFO. Then they turned to me to make a detailed presentation about how quickly the compressors would die. I'd brought charts and graphs and a knowledgeable assistant—a GE statistician who I'd asked to help me explain how the failure was going to unfold. The stats guy was in his early sixties, near the end of his career, and he was scared to death.

I started off by describing how the repairs worked. I knew the details firsthand, since all the managers, including me, had been donning coveralls and going out on repair calls. (I will never forget what it feels like to reach under a failed unit, only to have melting ice cream run down my arm.) I talked about how we were trying to be as efficient as possible, but given that there were millions of affected fridges, the company would have to take a $500 million charge— then the biggest write-off in the history of GE. I'll never forget Jack's reaction. Flinging his head back in his chair so violently that he was looking at the ceiling, he screamed, "AAAAAAAAHHHHH!"

The meeting got worse from there. Several people tried to appease Jack. "You know, maybe if we sprayed zinc oxide on all the compressors, they wouldn't fail," offered Walt Robb, who ran GE's Research Lab. Jack's reply? "Walter, shut the fuck up!" When Robb kept talking, Jack wouldn't have it. "Shut the fuck up," he repeated, "or I'm going to throw you out the window!" Then the statistician I'd brought with us stood up to speak, but he was so mortified, no sound would come out of his mouth. He was like the Tin Man in *The Wizard of Oz*: total lockjaw. So I got up again and tried my best to explain the guy's failure-curve charts and the logarithms he'd brought that predicted where the next wave of outages would hit. I was out of my depth, and Jack knew it. "You don't know what you're talking about!" he yelled.

To be fair, if there were ever a time to lose it, this may have been it. Imagine: there was a global shortage of compressors, so for a while we replaced broken compressors with other faulty compressors that we knew would soon break. How's that for demoralizing? Every unit we fixed, we knew we would soon have to fix again. Not only did that anger our customers, it also put even more stress on our overworked service techs. We hired extra guys to handle the work, but when we got ahead on the repairs, we had to lay people off. Each time we solved a problem, another one cropped up.

There were environmental concerns as well. To replace a bad compressor, our guys would tear open a refrigerator and put a rag over one of the hoses to keep it from releasing too many chlorofluorocarbons, or CFCs (commonly known as Freon). When a customer in Washington State asked the tech what he was doing, the tech explained, "I don't want you to have to listen to the CFCs escaping." Well, this customer happened to be an environmentalist with connections. She called US senator Al Gore. Next thing I know, I'm in Gore's office getting my ass handed to me.

Remember that in 1988, the damage that our repairmen could cause by letting CO_2 loose into the atmosphere was not commonly understood. But Gore knew more than the rest of us, and when I arrived for our meeting in Washington, DC, he made that clear. I started off polite: "Senator Gore, I'm here to listen. I really want to understand what your problem is."

Gore was blunt. "My problem," he said, "is you're going to kill us all."

I must've mumbled something defensive—"Well, I don't think so, really"—because his voice rose. For fifteen minutes, he schooled me, at top volume, on something I'd not yet heard of: climate change. Instead of hating him for it, I came away admiring him. For years afterward, whenever someone mentioned Gore, I'd say: "He is worthy of our respect because he can deliver the groceries when he has to."

In all, I oversaw seven thousand employees in multiple disciplines. To do that well, I couldn't just rely on my sales skills. My office was in what was called Building 6—a cavernous, empty factory in Appliance Park where we'd made air conditioners until Jack moved that division to Asia. I used this shelled-out space to host town hall meetings, where I leveled with people about the direness of the situation. But I learned to stay focused on the parts of the problem that my workers could control, such as reducing the time it took to make a repair. The standard was 106 minutes. We launched sessions where we shared best practices, so people could learn from one another. Then we had contests, with prizes for those who fixed units faster. This way people could win, even as we were fixing a mess.

It was the largest product recall in the history of GE, and I was right in the middle of it. But I will always be grateful I did that job, because it was so unrelentingly impossible. Once you've pushed through a problem that at first seemed unfixable, the obstacles that come afterward don't hit you quite as hard.

In big companies, hundreds of people can be involved in decisions. When the decision works, thousands take credit. When decisions fail or face challenges, most grumble, "I told them not to do that." This idea is as true in the boardroom as it is on the assembly line. What was impressive—and instructive—about the compressor crisis was that Jack owned his decisions. He was solid in the face of second-guessers, and he was willing to sacrifice short-term profits to protect consumers. I learned an important lesson that I would later try to model for my people.

GET A THICKER SKIN

After Appliances, in 1992, I went back to Plastics. I had profit-and-loss responsibility for two-thirds of the business, or all of the Americas. This assignment took me to Pittsfield, Massachusetts.

In 1994, inflation drove up oil prices, and the components we used to make our polymers and resins now cost more. As a result, GE Plastics missed its earnings for the year by $50 million. Given that, when GE's top managers gathered in Boca Raton, Florida, in January 1995 for our annual three-day, invite-only retreat, I suspected Jack Welch would buttonhole me. Indeed, on the meeting's final evening, I was walking to the elevator with a group of guys when Jack grabbed me by the arm. "You just had the worst year in the entire company," he yelled. "You were the worst *person* in the entire company. You!"

My colleagues scattered, disappearing down hallways and around corners like church mice. I was suddenly alone. "I know you can do better," Jack barked. "I'm going to give you a chance to turn it around, but I'm going to take you out if you can't get it fixed." I knew he wasn't kidding. "Look," I said, "if the results aren't where they should be, you won't have to fire me, because I'm going to leave on my own." Luckily, I'd already figured out what it would take to improve: I needed to raise our prices. But it wasn't going to be easy.

The automotive industry was the biggest, most important end user of GE's plastic pellets, which they made into bumpers and dashboards and the like. Their buyers were known by the GE salespeople to be especially fearsome. Whenever a GE sales team went to Detroit, we'd gather at a Shoney's restaurant across the street from the General Motors purchasing department to prepare for what was always a hard sell. Imagine a group of grown men chewing their fingernails, queasy with nervousness. That was us. The reason we were so nervous? A formidable executive named Harold Kutner, who was GM's vice president of worldwide purchasing.

Kutner was a legend. He'd been at GM for nearly twenty years at that point, having started his career there at twenty-three. But rumor had it the Buffalo native had gotten his first job at the age of eight and never taken a day off since. He liked to describe himself as "tough but fair," but to us, he was pure alpha male, and he expected us to obey. So in 1994, when I told him prices on GE pellets were going up, I wasn't surprised when he refused to pay. In response, I stopped shipping him pellets, which was a declaration of war. Without pellets, GM would have to shut down production lines.

When I showed up in Detroit to meet with Kutner about the impasse, Jack called my automotive sales leader and me to talk tactics. We were sitting in the GM parking lot, in a rented car, when Jack told me that this negotiation was important and that he expected me to prevail. This was classic Jack. He didn't care that there were several management layers between him and me.

Minutes later, I entered a GM conference room, and Kutner started screaming. "You motherfucker," he yelled, "I'm going to put you on the front page of the *Wall Street Journal*. I'm going to send your company down in flames. Jack Welch is going to be everyone's enemy. And it's all because of you!" I sat there and took it. My strategy was to keep him talking—or screaming—until he calmed down enough to strike a deal. It took hours, but I held my ground. GM agreed to pay ten cents more per pound of Lexan, GE's polycarbonate resin thermoplastic, which we liked to say was flexible enough to make something as delicate as a DVD, but strong enough to stop a bullet. GE Plastics would not miss its numbers again as long as I was there.

VALUING GROWTH

In 1996, Jack Welch picked me to be the CEO of GE Healthcare, which was then called GE Medical Systems—or GEMS. I was honored. To my mind, no division of the company better represented what I loved best about GE: that it made complex, reliable products that helped people live better lives. I couldn't wait to move my family to Milwaukee.

It was a complicated time to be managing GEMS. First Lady Hillary Clinton had spearheaded an initiative to reform healthcare soon after her husband was elected, but her goal of achieving universal coverage had failed to garner sufficient support from the Democratically controlled Congress in 1994. Still, with even the possibility of a single-payer system on the horizon, the healthcare industry contracted. It would be even more difficult to transform GEMS from an afterthought inside GE to a major revenue creator.

My arrival in Wisconsin coincided with the best year in GE's history, but GEMS was on a slow-growth trajectory; for the three years before my arrival, the division's results had been flat. The reasons were clear: we had all our eggs in the diagnostic imaging basket, and the imaging products we sold already had majority market share. But given that GEMS was a $3.5 billion business in a $4 *trillion* industry, I felt that needed to change. To speed up growth, I had three options: expand the market for our existing products globally, offer new and different products in the imaging space, or acquire adjacent businesses that would help us push into new areas. I decided to do all three.

Our first acquisition on my watch was of a company called Diasonics Vingmed Ultrasound. We knew about Diasonics because before my arrival, my predecessor had recruited its product development manager, Omar Ishrak, to lead GE's global ultrasound business. At that point, GEMS had less than 10 percent of the ultrasound market, but Ishrak had a plan to grow our market share. He wanted to launch a demonstrably better machine every year, while at the same time lowering the cost 10 percent each year. His big goal— which was audacious at the time—was to build a low-cost ultrasound machine on the back of a personal computer. Diasonics, a Norwegian firm, had started to work on that problem, and Ishrak believed that once a PC-based unit became possible, the resulting products could transform GE from the seventh-largest ultrasound provider into the first.

Many people, both in GE corporate and at Diasonics, were skeptical of the deal. But I believed in Ishrak. Born in Bangladesh, with a PhD from King's College London, he was one of the best leaders I had ever seen. In your career, you meet only a handful of leaders who have the trifecta of being able to innovate, execute, and develop talent. Ishrak was entrepreneurial, he knew how to use leverage, he was great with people, and—most strikingly—he was willing to be different. I encouraged the entire Healthcare team to emulate him.

All of that colored how I looked at the Diasonics deal. I knew Ishrak could do what he said with the company, so I overrode the naysayers. Now my GEMS CFO, Keith Sherin, and I traveled to Horten, Norway, where we encountered Diasonics' humble headquarters building. I remember it struck me as little more than a shed. But we did the deal, paying $228 million.

That deal doubled the size of our ultrasound division while granting us a foothold in cardiac ultrasound, an area in which we'd lagged. The Diasonics deal also helped us accomplish something else: make our business truly global. For years GE had formed joint ventures with little ultrasound companies in South Korea, India, China, and Japan in order to gain access to their sales channels. GE would help fund their ultrasound research but didn't monitor it closely; the real goal of the JV relationships was to sell our more expensive MRI machines and CT scanners. Ishrak changed that, creating a global engineering group in ultrasound to find out what our capabilities were around the world, and then put them to use. Under Ishrak, this team worked together to invent that PC-based machine he'd dreamed of—a series of products that we called Vivid. And he wisely sought a dedicated sales team for ultrasound, so that those lower-priced products would get the attention they needed in the market.

The Diasonics acquisition was the perfect example of how marrying a big company to a small one could pay off. Diasonics brought us technical expertise, knowledge of the industry, and a close relationship with customers. GE gave Diasonics the access to capital it needed to grow and improve. More important, GE had the ability to open doors that a small company didn't. The right merging of big and small, I saw, could be a formula for more than one future success.

Within just a few years, Ishrak's hard work would pay off handsomely. By the time I left GEMS in 2000, GE was the global leader in ultrasound.

LAUNCHING THE LIGHTSPEED

For years we'd been working to invent a top-flight multi-slice CT, or computer tomography, scanner. These machines, which use X-ray beams to enhance imagery and gather diagnostic information more quickly than single-slice scanners, were already being developed when I became CEO, but I was an early and enthusiastic booster. I wanted GE to be a technical leader because I thought that was the only way we'd be number one.

It took years of development and testing to pull it off. But when we introduced our LightSpeed QX/i in 1998, we were thrilled with the results: a body scan with our product took about twenty seconds, or about the time the average sick person could hold his or her breath. Previously, a lesser-quality scan had taken nine times that.

We decided to launch the LightSpeed QX/i at a celebration in New York City. We invited our customers to NBC's Studio 8H at Rockefeller Center, where *Saturday Night Live* was shot each week, and then back to the Waldorf Astoria hotel to see our machines up close and talk to the engineers who'd invented them. GEMS had never rolled out a product with so much fanfare or in such a glamorous location, but we worked to make the product—not the surroundings—the focus. I invited Jack, who schmoozed with attendees and lauded the scanner for enabling everyone to "see and touch the results of Six Sigma." As Carl Ravin, then the chairman of radiology at Duke University, said at the launch: "I now understand what Six Sigma means: you just plug it in, and it works."

Soon, the LightSpeed QX/i would become GE's fastest selling CT scanner ever. It met the needs of three types of customers: those with the most difficult patients to diagnose; those with the highest patient volumes; and those in very competitive environments, where it paid to offer the superior experience that this machine did. It didn't hurt that almost all clinical users considered themselves to be in one or more of these categories.

There was just one problem: once we'd taken hundreds of orders, we discovered that we were having trouble making a key feature of the machine—the detector, which "catches" data once a photon has passed through a patient's body. So much for just plugging it in and having it work! Most companies (GE included) would rush products to market, which meant they had reliability problems and often lacked a full range of features (it was standard to fix those glitches later, on-site). But with the LightSpeed QX/i, we'd thought we'd worked out the kinks beforehand. Now I had to call Jack and say, "We've got good news and bad news. The good news is we've gained ten points in market share, and this has been the most amazing product launch ever. The bad news is we don't know how to make our detectors."

I reached out to a brilliant GE engineer—a Belarusian named Mike Idelchik—who'd worked on many GE products from aircraft engines to X-ray tubes, and begged him to find a solution. Thanks to Idelchik, I would soon be able to call Jack back: the problem was fixed.

I'd set out to grow GEMS, and my team had delivered. Within three years, division sales had increased by 75 percent. In 2000, we were a $6 billion-plus business (up from $3.5 billion when I arrived); services alone had reached $3 billion in annual sales. We'd also broadened the culture to include people from outside GE who had diverse backgrounds and work experiences that made us better.

WHO'S NEXT IN LINE?

Around the same time as the LightSpeed launch, Jack Welch and the GE board of directors were getting serious about picking Jack's successor. In 1998, in secret, they chose three finalists: Jim McNerney, who led GE Aviation; Bob Nardelli, who led GE Power and was so close to Jack that some called him "Little Jack"; and me.

In the years since, no one has handled the run-up to succession the way Jack did. Though he wouldn't officially announce the finalists' names until mid-2000, the rumor mill insured that for years before that, the three of us found ourselves in a very public runoff. It felt like a month didn't go by without another magazine article about who might take the reins from Jack, who *Fortune* had just dubbed "Manager of the Century." The process was contentious, distracting, and at times just weird.

McNerney, Nardelli, and I were told we would stay in our jobs until Jack's successor was named and that the two candidates who didn't get picked would have to leave GE. Jack believed that if the two who'd been passed over stayed at GE, some employees would remain more loyal to them than to the new CEO. He didn't want the

new leader to be hindered by cliques and divisiveness. He was entitled to that view, of course, but the result was that he set up an all-
or-nothing cage match between three of his most trusted lieutenants.

When Jack announced his retirement date—April 2001—the
mood began to intensify. To reassure Wall Street, he named seconds
in command at Aviation, Power, and GEMS: Dave Calhoun, John
Rice, and Joe Hogan. These three would take over when McNerney,
Nardelli, and I were either promoted or forced out. I liked Hogan,
who I'd known since we overlapped at Plastics, and I knew he'd
make a great GEMS CEO. But I thought forcing two top-performing
people out of the company was wrong. There was no reason the
runners-up for Jack's job needed to exit GE; all of us were competent, experienced leaders who put up good numbers for the company.
It seemed like Jack was creating drama, milking his own departure
for all it was worth.

Some of the process, I'll admit, was invigorating. Instead of
merely calling the candidates back to headquarters to meet with
board members, Jack encouraged GE's directors to come see us in
action in our various divisions. Those visits forced me to think about
the big picture at GEMS—always a valuable exercise, but one that
can be overlooked when you're in the weeds of day-to-day management. Explaining to the board why we'd made decisions and where
we hoped to improve was clarifying.

I understand why Jack wanted us candidates to schmooze with
board members in relatively relaxed settings, like playing golf and
gathering for regular dinner dances, but it increasingly felt to me like
the succession race was overshadowing the ongoing business of GE.
I'll never forget the time I missed a meeting of the GE Capital board,
which Jack had appointed me to as part of my continuing leadership
education. I had a good reason for my absence: I was in Malaysia visiting GEMS customers. But Jack came down on me hard. I needed
face time with the board, he said; it was important to be seen.

I pushed back. If board members didn't like me putting customers first, so be it, I told him. I wanted to be judged for my work, not

my ability to schmooze. While I would do anything for GE, I refused to make campaigning a full-time job. I was just forty-four. I wanted to succeed, but I knew if Jack chose either of my rivals, I would find another job. It just felt wrong to shirk my immediate responsibilities in the hopes of someday taking on Jack's.

Then Jack changed the timetable. In October 2000, he announced GE would be buying Honeywell, the American multinational conglomerate—GE's biggest acquisition ever. His rationale was that the acquisition would reset the company at 70 percent industrial, 30 percent financial—a worthy goal. But to oversee the integration of the two behemoth industrials, Jack said he would remain as CEO through the end of 2001—eight months longer than he'd planned. The news concerned me. I was sick of being in limbo. The constant under-the-spotlight attention was embarrassing. So I did two things to get my mind right. First, I asked Joe Hogan, my GEMS second in command, to come with me to China. We were starting to manufacture CTs there, and we had the beginning of an ultrasound position, so there was plenty of business for us to do. But I also just wanted to get out from under the succession spotlight. I knew China would clear my head.

The second action I took was to call an executive headhunter I knew named Gerry Roche. When I returned from China, Roche—a legendary recruiter at Heidrick & Struggles—flew to Milwaukee, and we had dinner. I told him I'd hit the wall. I've never run marathons, but I imagined this felt like being at mile twenty-six and learning the course had been changed to add ten extra miles. The hoopla had worn me out. I just wanted to work—to do my job, whatever job it was, in peace. I told Roche I wanted to discuss other options. He was a pro, so he ticked off a few jobs that he thought might be interesting. But then he leveled with me: "Jeff," he said, "don't do this. I know you're under a lot of stress, but don't spend time on anything but GE. You've got plenty of time to find a job if this doesn't go your way." I remember feeling such respect for Roche. Had he taken me on, like I wanted him to, he would have made money. But instead he told me to sit tight. And it turned out, he was right.

On the day after Thanksgiving 2000, at about five thirty in the afternoon, the phone rang at Andy's and my vacation house in South Carolina. It was Jack. He said he'd made up his mind: he wanted me to succeed him. I was flattered, of course, and a few minutes later, I felt enormous pride when I called my mom and dad to tell them the news (my dad ended the call with a half-joking directive: "Do something about the pension!"). But in the moment, hearing Jack's voice on the phone, I was just glad that the race was over.

"Pack a bag," Jack said. A plane was on its way to pick up Andy and me and to deliver us to his home in Palm Beach, where GE's leadership team was gathering. Before we hung up, Jack added one final cloak-and-dagger-ish flourish: I would not be traveling under my own name, and we wouldn't be flying on a GE jet. If he directed a GE plane to pick me up, he said, the whole company would know his decision within hours. Instead, to ensure that my appointment wouldn't leak before Jack announced it two days later, we boarded a rented jet and I posed as James Cathcart, the son of GE's longest-serving director, Silas Cathcart, the retired CEO of Illinois Tool Works Inc.

Once Andy and I touched down in Florida, the weekend was jam-packed. Jack and I spent Saturday together, talking about the company. Notably, he didn't say why he had picked me. He was all about the future, not the past. Saturday night we all had a celebratory dinner, but to preserve secrecy, it was a catered supper at Jack's home, not at a restaurant. On Sunday, Jack flew to Cincinnati to tell McNerney the bad news, then on to Albany, New York, to have the same conversation with Nardelli. Andy and I flew to New York City to prepare for a Monday news conference, again at Studio 8H, at which Jack's decision—nearly six and a half years in the making—would finally be revealed.

The announcement was pretty straightforward—just Jack and me and a podium, surrounded by media. When it was over, I headed to the airport to fly to Chicago. The annual meeting of the Radiological Society of North America—a huge event for GEMS—was already underway, and I had no intention of missing it. We had CT scanners to sell.

Jack never told me or, I think, anyone else why he chose me over McNerney and Nardelli. "I had to go with my gut" was all he would say. While McNerney took it in stride, Nardelli hammered Jack about why he wasn't chosen. "I told Jack," Nardelli said in an interview with *Fortune*, "'I need an autopsy here . . . Tell me what I could have done better . . . Give me a reason.'" But Jack wouldn't explain.

McNerney went on to run 3M and, later, Boeing, and he and I maintained a great relationship. Nardelli? Not so much. He became CEO of the Home Depot, and by the end of his first year there, he'd ended GE's lighting contract with the home improvement giant and had given the Home Depot's credit card—which had long been handled by GE Capital—to a bank. In other words, of the three products GE sold at the Home Depot—appliances, light bulbs, and credit cards—Nardelli kicked us out of the two that made GE money.

YOUR PEERS PROMOTE YOU

I remember a few months after I was named CEO-in-waiting, I was to speak, as usual, at our annual Boca Raton managers meeting. I'd thought a lot about how to begin, and when I took the podium, an idea came to me. "When I look out into this audience," I said, casting my gaze over GE's six hundred top executives, "what do I see?" I let the question hang there for a moment. "I see friends," I said.

Of course, these people were much more than that. They were smart, experienced leaders, great collaborative colleagues. But with those opening words, I hoped to send a message: We were all in this together. We were peers.

The proposed Honeywell acquisition, meanwhile, had hit a road-block. We'd thought that because Honeywell and GE did not make the same things and did not compete head-to-head, regulators wouldn't hesitate to approve it. And indeed, the US Justice Department had given the go-ahead in May 2001. But then the European Commission coined a new term—the "range effect"—that interpreted and applied antitrust law very differently. In essence, it asserted that the merger would reduce competition inside the European Union.

In mid-2001, the European Commission rejected GE's acquisition of Honeywell International. We could still do the deal, but we'd have to dispose of several divisions of Honeywell. Jack and I both felt that doing so would remove some of the strategic logic of the deal, so we decided to walk away. We had positioned the merger as a way to make GE less dependent on financial services—a goal I was still committed to achieving. But we'd have to find another way. The deal's demise also taught me about the pitfalls of corporate globalism. Despite GE's size and success, many in the EU viewed it with suspicion and that kept the deal from getting done. (The "range effect" argument, meanwhile, has never been used again.) I would strive for years to correct this problem.

I still wonder if we should have pushed harder to complete the Honeywell deal. For one, Jack's main argument for pursuing it—diluting GE Capital's dominance by making our industrial arm bigger—had not been a worry for our investors. Now it was top of mind, and would remain so.

Moreover, while we'd balked at concessions the European Commission had asked for (to preserve competition, they wanted us to divest GE of some aviation assets), I'm not sure we sufficiently thought it through. If we'd succeeded in making the deal work, it would have reset GE as an industrial powerhouse with relatively minimal reliance on financial earnings.

With Honeywell off the table, Jack announced he was stepping down, and GE spent the next two months celebrating his incredible tenure. When you own a TV network, you never lack for well-produced events. The parties for Jack—as for most retiring executives in this period—were extravagant, with tightly edited videotaped testimonial reels and endless buffet tables.

In all, I spent nine months as Jack's wingman—officially, my title was GE's president and chairman-elect. Jack was spending most of his time writing his first book, *Jack: Straight from the Gut*, but he was generous with me. Still, to walk into a room with Jack was to feel like a flea on the back of an elephant. He was one of the most powerful people in the world, and I knew it would be difficult to start building my own credibility within GE until he left. Now he gave me a final bit of advice. "Remember," he said, "when you go home at night, it's because you're tired or because you want to see your family. It's not because your work is done. Your briefcase is never empty."

Days before I took the reins from Jack, *Fortune* published a piece entitled "It's All Yours, Jeff. Now What?" In it, they noted that just to maintain GE's current level of growth, the company would have to expand by roughly $17 billion in that year—"the equivalent of one 3M . . . Next year it will have to grow by a Federal Express, and in 2003 by a Coca-Cola. . . . Immelt thus finds himself about where Sandra Bullock was in the movie *Speed*: driving an enormous vehicle that, should it slow down for any reason, will blow up."

GE was 109 years old, and I was about to become its ninth chairman and CEO. I was as ready as I would ever be.

CHAPTER 3

Leaders Invest in Growth

Anyone who's worked with me knows I'm fastidious about being on time. I usually arrive early. Among the many lessons my parents taught me about respecting others, this one stuck: unless you're early, you're going to be late. So on September 28, 2001, when I kept Kathy Cassidy, an executive in GE Capital's real estate division, waiting outside my office for more than two hours, she suspected something was up. That morning Tom Brokaw's assistant had opened a letter that was laced with anthrax, and I'd spent the day strategizing with the NBC team.

"I'm so sorry, Kathy," I said when I finally rushed in. She'd been patient long enough, so I got straight to the point: I had a pressing problem I needed help solving. "Will you please become treasurer of GE?" I asked. Thank goodness she said yes.

When I became CEO, GE's Treasury department was suffering from years of neglect. To most people within GE, Treasury was a mysterious back office, staffed by two hundred people who did something that most people didn't understand. At first, I didn't understand it either. I needed Cassidy to educate me. Her first day as treasurer was December 1. Three days later, Enron failed, prompting a bond crisis of extreme magnitude. WorldCom, the telecommunications company, went bankrupt in January 2002, fueling even more panic. Throughout, Cassidy kept a level head. She said she needed me to do something Jack Welch had never done: sit down with the credit ratings agencies—Moody's Investors Service and Standard & Poor's—upon which we depended for our AAA status.

At that point GE was one of only six corporations in the nation with a triple-A credit rating. This rating allowed us to borrow money inexpensively, and that made us money. We'd loan out that cheaply borrowed money at a higher rate, a process known as rolling commercial paper. But to maintain the AAA rating we had to keep a significant amount of cash on hand. We hadn't done that.

How big a problem was this? Enormous, as Cassidy discovered when she began setting up meetings for me to visit the ratings agencies. "I hope you know we're about to downgrade GE," an executive at Moody's told her. Shocked, she asked him what he was talking about. He was happy to fill her in: Moody's was concerned about our lack of cash, especially in the context of our huge insurance business, which we were levering eight to one (meaning we had eight dollars of debt for every one dollar of equity). To put that in context, everyone else in the insurance space was levering it two to one. And months earlier, Moody's had sent Cassidy's predecessor a letter warning that if we didn't improve our liquidity, we'd lose our AAA rating. Our Treasury department never responded.

Cassidy did some digging and discovered that her predecessor had, indeed, received the letter, but he'd ignored it, thinking it was an idle threat. But that had been a mistake, and now I had to try to repair the relationship.

At a meeting with Moody's in March 2002, my team and I were making the case for not downgrading us when one of Moody's top executives lit into me, saying how arrogant and rude GE Capital people were. He showed me a series of emails from a few members of our GE Capital team. "Arrogant" was an understatement. We needed an attitude adjust-ment. We also needed to shrink GE Capital's $250 billion debt.

That was made only more clear when, days later, Bill Gross of PIMCO (the world's largest fixed-income investment company) publicly questioned GE's credit and credibility. Gross was an astute and influential market analyst. So it was bad for us when he released a scathing report about GE. The report suggested that for decades, GE had merely purchased its vaunted growth and that we were overexposed in the credit market. GE, he said, "grows earnings not so much by the brilliance of management or the diversity of their operations, as Welch and Immelt claim, but through the acquisi-tion of companies—more than 100 companies in each of the last five years—using high-powered, high multiple GE stock or cheap near-Treasury Bill-yielding commercial paper." In the wake of Gross's attack, our stock price dropped by 6 percent.

While I disagreed with Gross—we'd done more than acquire assets—we had a problem, and not just of perception. This was part of the legacy I was inheriting. You could grow your earnings with acquisitions because nobody was really watching that closely. My problem was that while I wanted to operate differently, in the short term, GE Capital was our strategy. We had no other engines of growth. We had to keep our heads down and weather the scrutiny.

I asked Cassidy to give the top people at GE Capital a tutorial on how we funded ourselves, because even they were insufficiently aware of the specifics. Cassidy also devised a plan to reduce our debt. For the moment, she was keeping ahead of our critics.

But other problems were flaring. The Securities and Exchange Commission was looking into Welch's retirement package, which had been hammered out way back in 1996; it included use of a New York apartment for life, use of a company airplane, and payment of his country club membership dues. That didn't play well in the wake of Enron and WorldCom, and we unwound the package. Then on April 11, 2002, we reported earnings. Revenue was essentially flat, and net profit fell because of a change in accounting. Investors dumped the company's shares. Almost 79 million shares changed hands on the New York Stock Exchange, making ours the most active stock traded there that day. The stock price dropped more than 9 percent, slicing almost $35 billion from our market value.

Three days later, the *New York Times'* Gretchen Morgenson dropped a bomb, writing an analysis of GE Capital that sent the stock tumbling even further. The headline: "Wait a Second: What Devils Lurk in the Details?" She quoted a fund manager she described as "an expert in spotting accounting practices that burnish immediate results but that do not necessarily translate into long-term earnings growth." His con- clusion: GE was doing nothing improper. But he questioned the qual- ity of our earnings. Particularly troubling, the fund manager "estimated the entire gain shown by GE Capital, whose financing operations con- tributed 40 percent of GE profits in 2001, was a result of a significantly lower tax rate" that added five cents a share to GE's earnings.

When I sat down with GE Capital CEO Denis Nayden to talk about how we should respond to Moody's complaints, Gross's broad- side, and Morgenson's direct hit, he pushed back, basically telling me to mind my own business. "How about you take care of your stuff and I'll take care of mine," he asked me. I'd long known Nayden was a pit bull, but he'd crossed a line, and seemed determined to keep crossing it. Though not founded on hubris, GE Capital had become the tail wagging the dog, and that was the way its leaders liked it. I decided that GE Capital's corporate layer—Nayden himself—needed to go.

I felt shitty about that. Nayden believed he'd earned the right to run GE Capital his way, and I could see why. Over the previous decade, nobody had done more for GE than he had.

But he didn't think he needed a boss. And times were changing in a way that made his imperious attitude unworkable.

I called our HR guy, Bill Conaty. I had a nickname for Conaty— Mr. Wolf, after the fixer character played by Harvey Keitel in the Quen- tin Tarantino movie *Pulp Fiction*. I got Conaty on the line and said, "Mr. Wolf, I've got a job for you. I just eliminated Nayden's position." He said, "No way." I said: "Yep. Sorry." It was Conaty's job to figure out the details. We broke GE Capital into four separate businesses—GE Commercial Finance, GE Insurance, GE Consumer Finance, and GE Equipment Services—each of which had its own chief, who would now report to me. When we announced the reorganization in July 2002, the stock price went up 5 percent. Nayden, meanwhile, went to run a successful financial-services advisory firm. We'd work together again.

A TIME FOR CHANGE

In the wake of 9/11 and the meltdowns of Enron and WorldCom, cracks were showing in our most successful division, GE Capital. But that was just one of many challenges we faced. GE Power was dealing with the bubble I've already described, which accelerated fifteen years of demand for gas turbines in the United States. GE Aviation had been hard hit by the terrorist attacks and would soon be hit again, in November 2002, by an outbreak in China of severe acute respiratory syndrome (SARS), which closed air travel to Asia. We had underinvested in NBC, giving it no exposure in cable just as cable was about to take off, and also in Plastics, Appliances, and Lighting. GE Transportation was confronting engine failure issues, and customers were pissed. GEMS was doing fine, but it was a relatively small part of GE's portfolio. None of our businesses were truly world-class, by which I mean none of them demonstrated consistent technical, global, or cost leadership.

After just a few months in the job, I was surer than ever that we needed to make some bold investments—and quickly. Our growth rate was declining and some of our businesses were stale. To help guide this delicate series of deals, I brought in the best investment bankers and consulting firms. Some of their advice was helpful (invest in life sciences), some was contradictory (buy a bank), but none of it dictated a path forward. The truth of the matter was that if we did nothing, we could run our businesses exceptionally well and, nonetheless, our valuation would likely revert to the mean, and our stock price premium would erode.

I received no clear mandate from the board as to a future path for

GE. They liked what Jack Welch had delivered and wanted to see it continued. With a company as vast as GE, a new CEO doesn't come to the job with a ready-made plan. There are too many things he or she doesn't know, and it takes some time to prepare the team. But I did have a sense of direction. I wanted to build a company that was more technical, because I felt that was essential to shareholder value. I wanted GE to be more global, because our market share outside the US was half that in our home market. I wanted GE to be closer to the customer, offering services that made their businesses more profitable. And I wanted a company that was more diverse. In 2001, 85 percent of our leaders were white American males. There was a world of talent. In many ways, this sense of direction guided my action for most of my tenure.

We decided to invest massively in new technologies that could rejuvenate our industrial businesses. Next we needed to exit the insurance business, which was damaging our cash flow. Finally—and we did this intentionally—we would let the rest of GE Capital grow so that we could keep earnings on a steady path, while the industrial businesses could catch up. Like every CEO, I worried about our stock price. I sometimes laugh when people say, "Just do the right thing! Don't worry about the stock." Sorry, but that is naive. At the same time, though, I knew that we would never again have the lofty valuation, or PE ratio, we had when I became CEO. I thought the best we could do was steadily grow our earnings per share and GE's dividend. That was the only language our investors understood. With that as cover, I was hoping we could transform the portfolio at the same time. This was the proverbial "changing the tires on a moving car" situation.

Soon we would enter the life sciences, avionics, and renewable energy businesses. Undeterred by Bill Gross's critique, in 2003 alone we'd spend more money on acquisitions than in any year in GE history, with total commitments exceeding $30 billion. Some of our businesses weren't keeping up with the times. Some of our businesses didn't make the best use of our expertise. Even as we began to expand and absorb other companies, we also took a hard look at the businesses we were already in. Change was coming.

TECHNOLOGY FIRST

GE's research center was one of GE's most potent internal engines. Some within GE called it the House of Magic. And for good reason.

Founded in 1900 by Thomas Edison and others, the GE Research Laboratory was the first industrial research facility in the United States. The idea behind it was that GE would benefit not just from the commercial applications of scientific innovations but also from discovering those innovations first. Starting with its perfection of GE's earliest product, the incandescent light bulb, the Research Lab had for decades played a vital role in keeping GE ahead of the technological curve. In 1906, GE's Ernst Alexanderson, an electrical engineer from Sweden, invented the high-frequency alternator there, enabling the first radio broadcasts. In 1913, GE physicist William D. Coolidge invented an X-ray tube that included a tungsten filament that GE then used in its light bulbs. And in 1932, GE scientist Irving Langmuir would earn a Nobel Prize for his work in surface chemistry.

But in the decades before I became CEO, the research center—located in Niskayuna, New York, just outside of Schenectady—had lost some of its luster. In the 1950s, GE president Ralph Cordiner had turned away from basic science to focus more on scientific management—the inner workings of GE's own bureaucracy. By the time Jack Welch took over in 1981, that reliance on professional management was entrenched, and Welch would only build on that thinking. But that was accompanied by defunding basic research (Jack preferred to buy successful technologies that had been developed elsewhere). Many of GE's finest minds departed for academia or companies like Lockheed Martin and IBM. By the time I took the helm, even the research lab's appearance looked tired. It was more like a forgotten museum than a thriving think tank on science's cutting edge.

So one of my first acts as CEO was earmarking $100 million to enliven the place. GE had roughly fifty thousand engineers across all its divisions, but the majority of those people were focused on whatever assignment was in front of them. The engineers in Niskayuna—which

we would soon rename the Global Research Center, or the GRC—
served a different function. They were GE's institutional memory, yes,
but also the key to its future. They were the ones we relied on to imagine,
to improvise, to hypothesize, and to apply proven expertise to unsolved
problems. They were our resident geniuses, our noodlers in chief.

The GRC was home to specialists such as Bernard Bewlay, a
world-renowned expert in structure-processing-property relationships
in metals, ceramics, and coatings who held more than 110 patents,
and Pete Finnigan, who knew more than anyone about composite fan
blades. These guys were part of a cross-company technical community whose ideas made GE better. So did their devotion to GE. I've
always been struck by the salary gap between one of these scientists
and their counterpart working in finance. A loan originator at GE
Capital might make $2 million a year. A chemical engineer with a
PhD and thirty to forty patents would make maybe $250,000 a year.
But it wasn't about the money for them. It was about the mission.

Previously at GE, you could be viewed as a good manager even
if you cut research and development (R&D) and had lousy products. We changed that, making people more accountable for their
long-term results by measuring our leaders on market share and
innovation. We expected each business to find two or three technical breakthroughs a year, and they were held to that in their annual
reviews. I wanted our leaders to get good at picking products. Engineers began giving most of the presentations at corporate meetings.
When we began measuring product launches and new revenue from
innovation, we got results. In 2001, GE Power earned 90 percent of
its revenues from a single product. Several years later, it had seven
products that each had more than $500 million in sales.

Since leaving GE and becoming a venture capitalist, I have grown
more aware of the link between innovation and value creation inside
companies. I admire leaders such as Elon Musk, who has harnessed
the best technology to create great products across a multitude of
industries. But even in 2001 I knew that, particularly with private
equity on the rise, many industrial companies and their leaders would

merely get by without ever making a big technical bet. I sensed that GE couldn't afford that approach. Thus, my emphasis on the GRC.

There are three different types of technology: vertical, horizontal, and exponential. The GRC brought value to all three. Vertical technologies were right in the swim lanes of each of our businesses. Whatever the next product or next improvement or next problem we needed to solve in Aviation or Power or Transportation, the GRC was there to help. Horizontal technologies lifted all boats across the company, informing and improving all our products and processes. The GRC's work in these areas had multiple payoffs.

It behooved the GRC to pay attention to exponential technologies—developments such as artificial intelligence, virtual reality, and nanotech. Exponential technologies are called "exponential" because they expand in capability at a pace with or exceeding Moore's law, a computing term from the 1970s that held that the number of transistors on a microchip doubles every two years, while the cost of computers is halved. While GE wasn't in the computer business, at one point we would use AI to create "digital twins" for some of our core industrial products—locomotives and jet engines and MR scanners—as a way to predict failure.

Because the GRC was connected with academia and with government agencies, it was also the place for crystal-ball gazing—what I like to call "What If?" thinking. What if you could get anywhere in North America in under twenty minutes? That would require hypersonic speed, or planes that travel more than five times the speed of sound (a capability that doesn't exist today, though the Pentagon is working on hypersonic missile technology). As a manufacturer of jet engines, GE needed to at least be thinking about hypersonics as it related to mainstream air travel, and the GRC was the place for that kind of brainstorming. Even if there wasn't a product we could take to market anytime soon, having a handle on the technologies that might someday be needed by one of our core businesses was a way of staying competitive in the future.

Another example is ceramic matrix composites—a strong, lightweight material that we invented for use in engines and turbines.

CMCs were essential for some of GE's best-selling products—the LEAP engine and H System turbines, among them—because they increased fuel efficiency. From start to finish, they took us fifteen years to develop—a long time in a world beholden to quarterly earnings statements. But we never stopped investing.

| | | |

I wasn't an engineer, but my sales background gave me appreciation for what engineers do. This is how it should work: leaders fund technology and engineers make great products, and if you do both right, everybody thrives. When I'd meet with our sales teams, I'd joke, "The better our products are, the less I need you guys. I could sell them myself! You are here for when we have shitty products." I'd always get a laugh, but they knew what I meant. Engineers and salespeople were mutually accountable, and I wanted them to remember that.

I understood that GE made infrastructure products that our customers depended on, and you didn't sell infrastructure based on style. You sold them on economics: What kind of bang would customers get for their buck? The research center's job was to make sure our technology delivered a bigger bang.

The other initiative I felt was important was growing our global research presence. When I took over, GE had just launched a huge research center in Bangalore, India, that would grow to employ more than six thousand scientists. It was an awesome sight, with an amphitheater and stunning buildings, but the best part was that it began to provide GE with round-the-clock research coverage. You could email a query from Cincinnati at the end of your workday, and the folks in Bangalore could work on it while you slept. It made GE faster and more efficient and gave us access to a broader pool of talent.

When I became CEO, I decided to expand on that, using new research centers to enter new markets around the world. In 2004, we opened a research center in Munich, Germany. It wasn't long before our European sales grew; apparently, the new GRC hub had enhanced our brand. In South America, it was the same: we built a GRC in Brazil, and sales went up. In China and Saudi Arabia, too.

I saw the Niskayuna and Bangalore centers as the true cross-company research centers. Other GRC offices would be more narrowly focused. The Oil & Gas Technology Center, which we would later open in Oklahoma City, would zero in on unconventional gas extraction, or fracking. You would rarely hear talk of jet engines or MRI machines in that office. Similarly, after a couple of acquisitions of German companies, the Munich GRC would become GE's headquarters for additive manufacturing—3D printing, rapid prototyping, and other approaches that create lighter, stronger parts. We'd host other business gatherings there at times, but pound for pound, that office was focused on this kind of additive tech.

Some will ask the chicken-or-egg question: Were our GRCs around the world really such powerful revenue drivers, or were they merely the beneficiaries of rising globalization? I believe the former. Before we expanded the GRCs, our customers mostly interfaced with GE salesmen. Afterward, they had easier access to GE engineers, and that—in addition to the statement our local presence made—was great for business. I love salespeople, having been one, but the expertise of our engineers was more persuasive than any sales pitch could ever be. Our Healthcare business in Germany doubled its market share. Our locomotive sales in Brazil exploded.

In China, the GRC's office in Shanghai was the place we met with state-owned businesses and won their trust. (It wasn't uncommon, when Wen Jiabao was China's premier, for him to call and say something along the lines of, "I'd like to do a press conference at the GE tech center to talk about how much we welcome foreign investment and Western partners.") There, and everywhere, our investments in our GRC proved their worth.

PROTECT THE BUILDERS

Mark Little wouldn't shut up about the wind business. I liked Little, and I respected him. Not only did he hold three degrees in mechanical engineering but he had hard-won credibility: in the mid-nineties, he'd guided GE's power generation business through a rough patch when a new gas turbine required a lot of mechanical repairs. But at first I couldn't understand his fascination with wind.

He tried hard to explain it to me. The wind business, he said, was a natural outgrowth of our gas-turbine business, which was the market leader. Both turbines and windmills are machines whose spinning parts generate electricity. Why not use some of the expertise we'd gained making turbines, Little asked me, and apply it to wind? GE engineers knew a lot about the required rotors and gears; they understood how to build the complex control panels that manage such movement. GE made some of the lightest and best propeller blades for aircraft engines. What's more, the sales force at GE Power understood the customer base. Wind was the future, Little said again and again, and GE needed to get into it.

I must have hung up on Little three times before I began to agree with him. "This is a Hula-Hoop, a fad!" I told him more than once. I felt the wind business was overly reliant on government subsidies. It was a small industry made up of many small companies, none of whom had any technical differentiation to set them apart. Could GE apply its expertise in a way that would give us a meaningful advantage? And was it worth our time?

Ultimately, I decided the answer was yes. My confidence came from my faith in the folks at the Global Research Center. There was a chief engineer in Niskayuna, a guy in the Electrical & Electronic Technologies section, named Jim Lyons, who had long been gung ho about the potential of the wind business (he'd written his PhD thesis at Cornell on variable-speed wind turbine generators). Little later admitted that one of the reasons he'd been nagging me to see wind as an opportunity was that Lyons had long been nagging *him*.

The numbers made it an easier bet. The beleaguered Enron was selling its wind power assets at a fire sale price. Enron had run its wind business as more of a real estate development deal. They didn't aspire to building a better windmill, and it showed: two out of three wind turbines installed in the year 2000 wouldn't be working by 2005.

By contrast, GE was all about making surefire machines, so it stood to reason we could excel where Enron had not. In March 2002, I made Enron Wind one of my first acquisitions as CEO, paying $358 million.

It was not an immediate success. The business we bought had a lot of reliability issues, and the folks I initially put in charge of GE Wind Energy failed to solve the technical problems. When you're dealing with a field of windmills, size is everything. The smaller the windmill blades, the less cost effective the field can be, because you have to build and anchor and maintain and retrieve electricity from more devices. The answer to this problem, of course, was building bigger windmills—much bigger. But that had its challenges.

Imagine a windmill spinning twenty-five stories in the air, its blades as wide as a football field. If you can build such a contraption, that single windmill can power five thousand homes. But the blades must be strong enough to capture all that wind power without snapping off. The base—think of it as a massive tree trunk—must be strong enough not to keel over from all the torque. And you need to figure out a way to maximize how often that windmill is spinning. If it's facing east and the wind is coming from the south, it will sit idle until there's a change in the weather.

Before we figured out how to solve these issues, GE Wind lost money at a steady clip. We used to say it was as if we bought the business in 2002, then bought it again in 2003, and then again in 2004.

At the end of 2004, we convened a Future of Energy summit at Crotonville with the CEOs of all the major utilities. I wanted to sprinkle a few seeds about an idea that was percolating in my head that we'd eventually name Ecomagination (I'll talk more about that in the next chapter). But I also wanted to get all the CEOs' views on wind. I invited Jeffrey Sachs, then the director of the Earth Institute at Columbia University, to give the keynote: a talk about climate change. It wasn't hard to read the body language in the room. As Sachs spoke of the importance of sustainable development, the CEOs shuffled in their seats and glared at him, at least at first. But Sachs was so articulate and persuasive that I think many of them had to admit: he might be right.

On the topic of wind, there was something of a riotous debate. The CEOs from utilities in California, Minnesota, the Northeast, and even the Midwest were saying, "Hey, this is the future. It's going to be critical. Let's go." But those who hailed from the Southeast, the Southwest, and the mid-central states were adamant: "If GE gets so visibly involved in wind, it's going to hurt our business, because you'll be implying that coal is bad." David Ratcliffe, the CEO of Southern Company Energy Solutions, a huge customer of ours, argued that nuclear power was better than wind power. If we embraced wind, he warned, "You'll bankrupt us."

Ultimately, we staked out a position between the environmental camp and the utilities and tried to be a bridge between the two. In the meantime, we installed new management in our wind division. Mark Little and his team were now in charge, and he brought in Vic Abate, who was then Power's engineering vice president. They found ways to stabilize production and make technical fixes, drawing on the strengths of other divisions. Engineers at GE Aviation had developed lighter-weight products for turbine blades, while the folks at GE Transportation knew how to make gearing systems operate at peak efficiency. Little and Abate scrapped the 70-meter windmill we'd acquired from Enron and set about making one that was more than 150 meters in diameter. Their team improved the electrical control systems and devised ways to turn the windmill blades into and out of the wind, so they'd always be spinning.

GE Wind's motto, which they embroidered on jackets the team wore, was "98 Out of the Gate"—meaning that GE's windmills were reliable and available to start spinning 98 percent of the time. We also led in the technologies that allowed us to monitor and reset the windmills from afar, which, given how remote many wind fields are, was a major selling point.

The turnaround of GE Wind was also a result of good old-fashioned cost management. When you're dealing with products this huge, the logistics of getting them where they need to go is daunting and expensive. By partnering with other manufacturers who built tower sections and blades to GE's specs and delivered them on-site, we saved a lot of money. Our wind division also benefited from GE Capital's help.

At one point, GE Capital had financed $15 billion worth of wind power projects. So when we boosted prices—a move that startled but then reset the industry—we could reap the rewards. Within a period of about forty months, GE Wind went from a money loser to a tremendous winner. By improving both the technology and the business model, we created a $12 billion renewable wind business.

The GE Wind gamble was fundamentally a bet on the operational strength of GE. I admit we were lucky that the market also turned our way at the right time. But without our ability to differentiate and improve on what we bought from Enron Wind, we wouldn't have had any success.

FULFILLING THE DREAMLINER DREAM

An aircraft engine is a miracle. At once lightweight and strong, it must excel at two seemingly contradictory tasks: gunning it during takeoff to get up in the air and also cruising efficiently during flight. What's more, it must function at 40,000 feet, where the outside air is minus 40 degrees Fahrenheit or colder. All this while its combustion system produces a plasma whose temperature—2,400 degrees—is higher than the melting point of the fan blades just a few meters away. Only through the use of cooling air passages inside the engine—whose blades, by the way, are spinning at 16,000 RPMs—can it do its job and maintain its integrity (not break into pieces).

The aircraft engine business, meanwhile, is a bear. The payback is a super long cycle, by which I mean manufacturers generally make no money on the price of the engine itself, but they make up that shortfall over twenty or thirty years of maintenance and parts revenue. Before you can enjoy those revenues, meanwhile, you must compete to be chosen by the major airplane manufacturers—Boeing, Airbus—as one of the engines that will be available on any given aircraft. Whether or not your engine is chosen usually boils down to three factors: cost, performance, and weight.

In the wake of 9/11, we knew that to remain competitive on those three factors, we needed to invest significantly in aviation-related R&D. This was more than a single budget line; it was an existential decision about whether to stay in the business. Given what was going on in the world during my first years as CEO, there was always a reason to put the brakes on. Had we been looking to justify spending less money, my team and I could have easily found a way. But in Aviation, we knew that failure to take timely action would set us back twenty years. We couldn't afford to falter.

So in 2002, we increased our investment in Aviation research, spending more than $1 billion a year on commercial aviation alone. Our goal was to develop several new engines, but the biggest bet we made was on the GEnx engine, which would eventually be installed on a brand-new plane: Boeing's 787 Dreamliner.

Boeing's leadership team, led by its CEO of Boeing Commercial Airplanes Alan Mulally, imagined the Dreamliner as a way to accomplish two goals at once: developing a game-changing airplane while also rejuvenating the industry. (In a crisis, good leaders can hold two truths at the same time: they prepare for the worst while taking big swings to set the table for needed improvements.) The new long-haul, midsize, twin-engine wide-body would have room for hundreds of passengers and would be fuel efficient enough to travel very long distances. Instead of employing the old hub-and-spoke model of getting passengers around the world on different legs, this airplane would fly from point to point. It would get you from New York City to Sydney—formerly a two- or three-stop trip. If it could be built, it would be a godsend for many airlines, especially those in Asia and the Middle East. And it would make Boeing more competitive.

But here was the catch: Boeing's engineers didn't yet know how to make this transformative aircraft, and we had no idea how to build the engine it required. Boeing made clear from the get-go that the Dreamliner's engines would have to deliver an unprecedented level of fuel burn efficiency. They wanted a 15 percent improvement, a major stretch. To improve fuel burn efficiency just 1 percent requires significant design changes. We had no idea how we'd pull it off, but we committed to those specs, and GE Aviation—along with another engine maker, Rolls-Royce—won the engine contract.

The airline industry was on its ass after 9/11. Here was a proposal to change the industry's flight structure—an idea that could give the sector a much-needed boost. But for GE it meant committing a lot of money with no guarantees of a return.

At one point my CFO Keith Sherin and I had a meeting called an AR—appropriations request—with the guys in GE Aviation, a team then led by Dave Calhoun (who is now the CEO of Boeing). We were in Connecticut, they were in Cincinnati, and we were exchanging charts and graphs and other data via videoconference. The report we all were poring over was eighty pages long, and it promised a 12 percent return over thirty years on a $1.5 billion investment. It took us four straight hours to review. In the end, though, when we hung up, Sherin and I looked at each other and agreed that our decision came down to two questions: Did we want GE to lead in the industry? And: Did we trust our team? The answer to both questions was yes. As I told Sherin, "It's not like we can make this decision based on what's on page 20 or page 40 or page 60 of this report. It's more like: If we're in this business, we need to do this. If we trust the team, we need to do this." So we went for it.

I've said that Boeing ordered engines from two manufacturers: GE and Rolls-Royce. Down the road, when airlines ordered new Dreamliner 787s, they would have a choice of which manufacturer's engine they wanted installed. (Boeing had wanted to offer its customers three engine options, but Pratt & Whitney had decided to sit this round out.) We were happy to have the contract, but we knew we'd have to hustle to get our engines aboard those planes once they were sold. We also were relying on the airlines' survival, which was not a certainty. I remember a board meeting in 2003 at which we modeled the impact of four airlines going into bankruptcy. It was not a pretty picture.

For GE Aviation, the GEnx engine was a bet-the-farm, bet-the-reputation, if-you-miss-this-chance-there-won't-be-another-one-for-thirty-years kind of moment, and all of our people knew it. We needed to invent new ways of using new materials and to redesign whole systems, all on a deadline, while also keeping passenger safety paramount in our minds. You may have heard the line: the difference between doctors and engineers is that doctors bury their mistakes one by one. Whether they're designing a bridge or an aircraft engine, when an engineer makes an error, the potential tragedy is multiplied many times over. The stakes, as always, were high.

The development and testing of the GEnx engine took years. We experimented with removing parts to reduce cost, but we lost fuel efficiency. At one point we were way overweight. To solve these problems, our aviation engineers partnered with experts at the GRC. Whenever we identified a problem, the question was: Who's seen this problem before? We recruited those people, no matter where they worked. We even brought people out of retirement.

At engineering school, you learn that products are ideally designed using mature, ready technology. Not this time; we were developing new technology at the same time we were developing the GEnx engine. Days started early in Aviation, with 7 a.m. meetings to confirm what progress had been made. At end of day, there were more meetings laying out what needed doing the next day and what might be achieved overnight.

Ultimately, to reduce weight, the GEnx engine featured just eighteen composite fan blades, down from twenty-two on a previous engine, the GE90. We made our fuel efficiency specs, but we made mistakes along the way. The compressor we designed without a part-ner's help? We didn't get it right at first, and it took three iterations to fix it. But it was all worth it. Within the industry, the GEnx is a marvel of technology and engineering and determination. So when we pulled it off, it was a huge boost to morale, as well as to our bottom line. This is despite the fact that it had a cost overrun of $500 million. The story of our GEnx effort, then, is about what happens when your people commit themselves to success.

We could have easily sat out this engine development cycle. The airline industry was deeply shaken, and there were so many other decisions we needed to make at GE after the terrorist attacks. I could have argued that GE had too many other priorities that came before competing for the Dreamliner contract.

But that would have been shortsighted. Delaying your investment in the future looks good on the quarterly income statement for a while, but it eventually hurts you, and the costs of catching up are humongous. The day that Boeing announced the winners of the engine contracts, GE's stock went down (and the stock price for United Technologies Corporation, an engine maker that sat out the competition, went up). But we knew it would be harder to get the next engine contract if we were no longer seen as an innovator.

GE Aviation didn't only make engines on the Dreamliner. In 2007, we acquired a British company called Smiths Aerospace that made the core computing system for the plane, as well as avionics, electric power, and loading gear. The Boeing project gave GE the chance to build our content and capability for the next generation of aircraft.

I will always be especially proud of the GEnx. When it came time for the airlines that had ordered Dreamliners to decide on an engine, we would trounce the competition for years to come. In early 2018, of 1,277 orders for the B787, more than 53 percent selected the GEnx, as compared to just under 32 percent that opted for the Rolls-Royce Trent 1000 (about 14 percent hadn't yet decided). GE is still reaping the benefits of this effort.

As an ironic aside, we lost our first campaign to sell our engines onto the Dreamliner for reasons related to 9/11. Remember how, in the immediate wake of the attacks, Dennis Dammerman and I had to make those phone calls to countries that hadn't yet secured terrorism insurance, telling them they couldn't fly our planes? Well, Japan's All Nippon Airways, or ANA, had been among those affected. So years later, when our sales folks approached ANA, trying to get them to buy GE engines for their Dreamliners, Japan got its revenge. The engines on ANA's Dreamliners would all be made by Rolls-Royce.

DON'T FALL IN LOVE WITH AN IDEA

When Bill Woodburn first buttonholed me about adding water purification to GE's portfolio, I didn't argue. There was a growing awareness that water scarcity was the next catastrophe that was going to befall the earth. So finding ways to clean water seemed like a great business to be in.

I also liked the potential breadth of market. Industrial waste-water, where Woodburn suggested GE should focus its efforts, was ubiquitous. Imagine a factory that uses water as a coolant for its machinery. Inevitably, that water picks up particulates and other gunk as it does its work. To be both efficient and ecological, factories need ways to re-purify and reuse that water instead of jettisoning it after a single use.

In 2002, under a newly formed division called GE Water & Process Technologies, we began acquiring companies that had the expertise we needed. BetzDearborn, an industry leader in water services, and Osmonics, a fluid filtration equipment manufacturer, came first. Soon we'd buy Ionics Ultrapure Water Corporation, a global leader in desalination, and a membrane maker called Zenon that used microscopic pores to filter out contaminants. Soon our operation would be the second-biggest water-treatment company in the world.

We had high hopes. In our 2002 annual report, we predicted that GE Water would prove, yet again, how GE's people, technology, and experience translated into profits. "It is a $35 billion global industrial market, growing 8 percent a year with high margins," we said. "It's a fragmented industry whose customers are outsourcing more and more of their water requirements." Because of GE's technical, service, and globalization expertise, we thought we could grow this business "15% annually and, by 2005, have a $4 billion global business leader."

If only it had worked out that way. We never found a way to differentiate GE's water purification technology from everyone else's.

I've already described how, when GE entered the wind business, we used our know-how to set our products apart. We had similar success in the air purification business, where we were known for our superior technology. But in water? We just had what everyone else had.

The water industry operates differently than other regulated industries in which GE competes, such as healthcare and power. The reason: consumers viewed water as a basic right, and that put a limit on its price. Despite tremendous scarcity concerns, consumers will not pay more for innovation. As a result, the industry never grew faster than the Gross Domestic Product (GDP).

We had made a classic mistake, falling in love with an idea and letting our passion blind us to realities that, in retrospect, should have been obvious. We made a solid intellectual argument for why GE could rule this market, and we were so convinced by our own reasoning, and by our belief in GE's technological clout, that we failed to see the bigger picture. It didn't help that we overpaid for each constituent part. We sold GE Water to Suez in 2017 for a gain. But it was still a mistake.

PIVOT TO GROW

At a strategic meeting in 2001, I asked Joe Hogan at GE Medical Services, "If you had to pick just one company in the world to buy, which would it be?" Mike Jones, GEMS's business development manager, was there, too. They answered in unison, "Amersham."

I knew all about Amersham, a UK-based life sciences company. We'd had our eye on it for years. Amersham was a leader in what's called precision medicine. That involves the use of molecular imaging, which is the process of injecting agents that bind to certain molecules to enhance the resulting picture. This technology was new back then, and scientists were excited about what it would allow them to see. Up to this point, imaging equipment was mainly anatomical. You could see a static tumor or a black spot on a lung, but you wouldn't know precisely what it was unless you biopsied it. By contrast, molecular imaging promised in vivo biopsies; after you injected a radioactive isotope or some other imaging agent, you could watch it bind to the receptor cells on a tumor, say, and know whether or not it was cancer. The promise of this technology was that doctors would be able to spot disease earlier. Hogan and Jones were excited. "This is going to be the next step for imaging technology," they told me.

But the real hidden jewel of Amersham was a division that made systems for pharmaceutical manufacturing. It sold everything that a drug manufacturer would need to produce a drug, from processing equipment to chemicals. In 2004, this was a small business, but it was a great fit for GE in that it would enlarge our global footprint and servicing skills. Acquiring Amersham would expand our customer base to include biotech. As drug development exploded, so would our business.

Now we learned there might be an opening: the company's chairman and CEO, Sir William Castell, while not quite ready to retire, was looking to plan his exit.

We engaged Goldman Sachs to evaluate Amersham as a potential acquisition. Once they'd contacted Castell and found him amenable to a possible deal, I wanted to meet him. On October 23, 2001, just six weeks after 9/11, we sat down for our first get-acquainted session at NBC's 30 Rock building in New York City. A former accountant, Castell is a charming and visionary man, and he was well connected. I liked him right away. But this wouldn't be a quick negotiation. In the coming months, we'd have many conversations, a lot of them held on one of the GE jets. I'd fly into Biggin Hill, a regional airfield in the southeast suburbs of London, Sir William would come aboard, we'd spend a few hours chatting, and then he'd exit and I'd take off again.

These talks went on for nearly two years, but I had good reason to hang in there. I was convinced that diagnostics were changing in a way that would require us to have expertise in life sciences. More and more, capturing the best image of a patient's body would involve not just great machinery but also great chemistry.

I wanted to close the Amersham deal, though not at any price. Finally, in September 2003, Castell and I agreed to try one last time to come to terms. At 5 p.m. on a Thursday, a team of five colleagues and I boarded one of GE's two Boeing 737s for one more trip across the pond. The Boeing Business Jet, or BBJ, was a luxuriously reconfigured passenger plane. Instead of seats for 175 people, it had a conference room, a living room/office space with eight seats, and another space with a U-shaped banquette that sat about twenty people. Then there were two spacious bedrooms and bathrooms in the back of the plane. (These planes had been bought during Jack's tenure; I would sell them in 2005 to save money.)

On Friday morning, after six hours in the air, we landed at Luton Airport outside of London, and Castell and his bankers and advisers came on board. Pam Daley, who was GE's top lawyer on mergers and acquisitions (M&A), was my partner on these trips. She was whip smart, with unmatched focus—before joining GE in 1989, she'd graduated first in her class at the University of Pennsylvania Law School. With Daley at my side, I felt like whatever we did, we'd do it right. I also knew that Castell and his bankers liked her.

Initially, we all gathered in the plane's conference room, but it wasn't long before our two teams dispersed to caucus in private. More than once, Castell and his team headed to the front of the plane, while the GE team gathered at the back. If I remember correctly, Castell's daughter was getting married the next day, but that seemed to motivate, not distract, him. I don't even think we served him and his folks lunch. Five hours later, around 2 p.m., we were all exhausted. "That's as far as I can go," I said finally.

Castell put his head down. For what seemed like an eternity, but was probably only thirty seconds, he didn't move. Then he looked up, met my eyes, and said, "Let's do it." We shook hands on the price and the salient deal points. And soon our jet was in the air, headed for home. When the team and I landed back in Connecticut, it was just 4:45 p.m. on Friday. We'd been gone barely twenty-four hours.

Our Amersham acquisition surprised many people. The company

was high-tech, global, and expensive. When the deal was completed in April 2004, we paid $9.8 billion in an unusual equity swap—the largest all-share transaction ever to occur in Britain based on shares not quoted on the UK stock market.

My team and I took a lot of external criticism for the price tag. With our long history in financial services, we had trained our investors to value only low-multiple deals. In the past we'd used our high-multiple stock to buy low-multiple financial service businesses, which—once we absorbed them—were immediately valued more highly by the market. Now we were paying a value higher than our own multiple. Our stock price went down the day we announced the acquisition.

But I knew this was a key part of my plan to raise GE's growth rate. Our research suggested there was potential for Amersham's earnings to grow faster than GE's. As it turned out, Amersham would soon make us even more than we'd projected when we negotiated the deal. What initially looked, to the market, like an extravagance would prove to be a bargain. Not only did the math work, but Amersham further diversified our business and lessened our reliance on financial services. Had we waited, its price tag would only have gone up.

I made Castell the president and CEO of the new entity, which we renamed GE Healthcare, while keeping Hogan the president and CEO of all the elements he was already running, a group which was now renamed Healthcare Technologies. This move coincided with a shift in my thinking: after years of promoting generalists, I was beginning to believe that increasing specialization meant our leaders needed domain expertise. GE Healthcare was growing, and there were all the expected growing pains as we integrated the two businesses and cultures. Change is never easy, even when it's necessary.

When we agreed that Castell would be CEO, he worried a bit about leading "this beast called GE Healthcare," as he put it. But the might of GE would soon reassure him. When he took sixty or so of the top people from Milwaukee and England to Crotonville to develop a mutual vision, he was so struck by the creative thinking in the room that he casually remarked that he wished he'd thought to videotape the session. An hour later, an NBC camera crew arrived and began to tape it. "I realized then that I should no longer fret about coming to General Electric," he would recall, "because it had the power to deliver."

When markets mature, the best businesses pivot into new segments. GE had failed to do that in its Plastics division, sitting on the sidelines as its competitors—Dow, DuPont, and Monsanto—responded to stagnating markets by moving into the agriculture business. But in Healthcare, we did it right. Our Amersham acquisition wasn't a shiny new bauble. It enabled us to add complementary capability—what I call moving strength to strength—giving a strong core business a new leg of growth in an important market. In subsequent years, Amersham would become more valuable than the business it bolted onto, proving that you have to dare to invest in what's next.

SEIZE OPPORTUNITY

At the same time that we were negotiating the Amersham deal, more than one suitor had been sniffing around NBC. I wasn't eager to sell it. Jack Welch had bought the TV network in 1986 as a part of GE's acquisition of RCA, and I admired its leaders, who ran it well. But in 2003, as cable offerings were beginning to outshine traditional network fare, I'd concluded that GE either needed to grow and diversify NBC or sell it to someone who would.

Then Vivendi—the French company that had bought Universal Studios in 2000—announced that it was putting Universal's movie studio, theme parks, television business, and cable channels up for sale. Its CEO, Jean-Marie Messier, had resigned, leaving Barry Diller, the former studio chief and media mogul, and a Frenchman named Jean-René Fourtou in charge. NBC's CEO Bob Wright called me. Universal had the USA Network, Sci Fi, and a couple of other cable channels. Its movie studio churned out great content.

If we could make a deal, a merger would give NBC the breadth it needed.

I had long trusted Wright to steer NBC's course, and now I trusted him to oversee this negotiation, offering to help where I could. Fortuitously, while working in GE's Plastics division years before, I had gotten to know Fourtou when he ran RhônePoulenc, France's state-owned chemical company. That would give us an advantage over our rival bidders.

The Sunday night of Labor Day weekend 2003, the final bidders—about a hundred people in all—converged on the Fifth Avenue offices of the New York City law firm that Vivendi had hired to handle the sale. I was there with a team representing GE, and we were cordoned off from the other potential buyers—including Comcast and others—in the four corner offices of the firm. There's a lot of downtime in these kinds of marathon sessions, and at one point I was walking down a hallway to get a cup of coffee when I ran into Fourtou, who was also stretching his legs. I could tell by his body language that he liked GE's bid. Nothing overt was said. But when I returned to the conference room where my team was camping out, I shut the door and confided, "I think we've got a shot here."

In the coming days, Fourtou encouraged me to get the deal done. "Let's figure out a way to do this," he'd say. In the end, the new media venture between GE and Vivendi, named NBCUniversal, gave Vivendi cash and a 20 percent stake in NBCUniversal while GE retained 80 percent ownership. I agreed to this unique structure because I thought it was only a matter of time before we spun NBCU out.

The pieces of Universal's portfolio that I was least excited about were its theme parks. I saw only the downside in a business proposition that relied year-round on attracting tourists and retaining tens of thousands of minimum-wage workers. To me, that meant red flashing lights. My first concern: the push to unionize seemed likely. And then there was the possibility that a high-profile event—a roller-coaster injury, say—would reflect poorly on our other businesses. I could imagine customers who bought our highly technical machines asking, "How can I trust you to make a jet engine if you can't keep your roller coasters safe?" I could see only liability and risk.

But then I met Tom Williams, the chairman and CEO of Universal Parks & Resorts and one of the most competent managers I've ever known. Walking around one of the parks with him, I noticed how often cheerful employees came up to greet him. More important, he understood the economics of every facet of the experience, from the refreshments to the rides to the park's security and medical services. For years, I'd dismissed as wishful thinking the assertion that the theme parks were brand extensions of the movie studio. But Williams made me believe it. Today, the theme parks remain one of the company's most durable profit centers.

Of all the GE businesses, NBCUniversal was the outlier. It had few synergies with our other businesses, and it sold a product—filmed entertainment—that most GE managers, me included, didn't really understand. I couldn't go into a meeting and say, "You need to punch up the script, because it's boring!" What that meant was that during the six years we owned NBCU, I spent a lot of time searching out executives in Hollywood and in New York who I felt I could trust. To a one, they were scrappy and self-made, and I liked that. For a guy who came up inside an industrial conglomerate, the Industry, as Hollywood calls itself, can feel like a foreign land. But I found people within it to learn from.

I loved Ron Meyer, who ran Universal's movie studio, because he blended business savvy with pure creativity. The son of Jewish immigrant parents who'd escaped Nazi Germany, he'd dropped out of high school at fifteen, joined the Marine Corps, and then started at the bottom at a talent agency in Los Angeles. He helped found Creative Artists Agency, which today is one of the biggest and most respected talent representation firms, and went on to become the longest-serving chief of a major motion picture company.

In a town that seemed to run on air-kisses and subterfuge, Meyer was always surprisingly candid with me. Our first blockbuster movie after GE purchased Universal was *King Kong*, whose budget was way north of $200 million. For an industrial guy, that's a huge amount. I kept thinking: you could build a plastics plant for that! When Meyer came into GE headquarters to do a quarterly review of NBCU, he ticked off the business plans for upcoming releases. When he got to *King Kong*, he said, "It sucks! It's a real flop!" and kept right on going. I gasped. "Can't we do anything to help?" I asked. "Nope," he said. "We are toast. That's the movie business!" He never apologized or flinched or cast blame. He was impossible to dislike.

I'd known Lorne Michaels, the creator of *Saturday Night Live*, and NBC Entertainment president Jeff Zucker for years, but after we formed NBCU, it seems I interacted with the two of them even more. I would invite Michaels to dinner, sometimes with the impossibly tall, red-haired host of our *Late Night with Conan O'Brien*, and we'd talk about the future of the media business. I also liked talking to the cable exec Bonnie Hammer, who ran USA and Sci Fi, and *Meet the Press* host Tim Russert and his DC team.

I had to fight to make Zucker the CEO of NBCU. At the end of 2006, his predecessor, Bob Wright, looked around at the other aging media titans who dotted the landscape—Sumner Redstone was then eighty-three; Rupert Murdoch was seventy-five—and decided that, at a mere sixty-three years old, he didn't want to leave. He had already gotten rid of Andy Lack, the man Jack Welch had wanted to succeed him. Now he attempted an end run by orchestrating a gushing profile in the Sunday business pages of the *New York Times*. The November 19 story acknowledged that I was leaning toward replacing Wright with Zucker but said that Wright "hardly looks like someone on the brink of retirement." The piece went on: "Mr. Wright is such a large presence at NBC Universal that it is hard for many to imagine the place without him. Indeed, analysts and media insiders are raising fresh questions about Mr. Zucker's suitability to assume the reins."

Opening my newspaper that morning, I was pissed. Wright had broken with GE protocol in not telling anyone he was participating in a piece. So the next day, I told Wright I was accelerating the timeline:

Zucker would replace him in February. "It's over," I said. Wright tried to argue. "That's a big mistake," he warned. "Zucker can't do it. You have to run these places with a firm hand. We should just spin the business out! I've already worked up a deal with John Malone." But I didn't want to sell NBCU then because doing such a deal would've only inflated GE Capital's percentage of our earnings; this would put pressure on our valuation. Wright was desperate to keep his powerful position, but I was done with him. Wright had done a lot for GE, but it was time for change.

As for Zucker: he was famously brash but also supremely effective. While in high school in Florida, he was elected president of his sophomore, junior, and senior classes after he ran on the slogan "The little man with big ideas." (He is five foot six.) Nose to nose, I had a solid ten inches on him, but on matters of programming, I looked up to Zucker. When *Friends*—NBC's number one show—was coming to an end, he flew to New York and told me we needed to extend it one more year. Despite its astronomical price tag (Warner Bros. wanted $10 million per thirty-minute episode—then the highest price in TV history), I approved it. While NBC was unable to sell enough ads to cover those costs, *Friends* was central to the network's Thursday-night lineup, which we called "Must See TV," and helped cement NBC's place as the number one network for one more year. Extending *Friends* was the right call.

It was Zucker, too, who enlisted my help with a certain real estate tycoon he wanted to recruit to host a new reality show: Donald Trump. In 2004, the network was talking to Trump about hosting *The Apprentice*. After the finale of *Friends*, NBC was on its knees as a network. We needed a hit. Bob Wright and another NBC exec, Randy Falco, and I traveled to a golf course Trump owned in Belford, NY, and played a few rounds. Standing there with a five iron in one hand, the future president of the United States looked at the three of us and declared, "You realize, of course, I'm the richest golfer in the world?" Then he shot a hole in one.

It's not lost on me that NBC, and by extension GE, helped create the celebrity that would later catapult Trump into the White House. Through his shrewd charisma, he turned *The Apprentice* into a hit. And in the years since our golf game, Trump has called upon me more than once to tell the story of his hole in one in public—and then corrected my telling. "No, I actually said I was the best golfer of all the rich people, to be exact, and *then* I got a hole in one," he'll say. "So it was sort of cool." What he leaves out is that, right from the start, he informed me how his relationship with NBC was going to work. "You're great," he told me on the putting green. "I'll be talking directly to you. I'm not going to fuck around with Zucker. Only you."

Certain powerful men believe having direct access to the top is a measure of their importance. So with Trump, I played along. But I liked Zucker and tried to protect him. When we later sold NBCU to Comcast, Zucker's reputation got hammered, but he made many of the calls that still benefit NBCU today: nabbing *Sunday Night Football*, creating *The Voice*, building the Harry Potter theme park ride, green-lighting several animated hit movies.

When it came to running these businesses, I came over the top of the NBCU executives only a few times. In the spring of 2007, radio personality Don Imus described the Rutgers women's basketball team as "nappy-headed hoes" on his show *Imus in the Morning,* which was owned and produced by CBS but simulcast by MSNBC. It wasn't long before I heard from several African-American leaders within GE, including Deborah Elam, who I'd made GE's chief diversity officer five years earlier. "I have two black daughters and this is not okay," she said, her voice shaking. Then she reminded me that the annual meeting of GE's African American Forum—one of GE's many employee affinity groups—was coming up in July. "Every year, I stand up with you in front of thirteen hundred mostly black employees and say this company values diversity. If Imus's behavior is okay, I can't stand up with you." I called Zucker, then the president and CEO of NBCU. "You've got until eight a.m. tomorrow to fire Imus," I said, "or I will." Zucker ousted Imus, beating CBS's Les Moonves to the punch (the next day, Moonves canceled the show). Imus's racist, sexist rant had no place anywhere near GE.

DON'T BE AFRAID TO ACT

While investing to grow is great fun, I also had to do something harder: clean up existing messes. GE's biggest mess was insurance. Remember the harsh assessment we'd gotten from Moody's that I described at the beginning of this chapter? Well, if that had clarified anything for me, it was that we needed to exit insurance. It was the largest business in GE Capital, accounting for 40 percent of the division's earnings (and probably 20 percent of the company's earnings overall). But it was an over-levered mess.

There were many acquisitions we'd made in the late nineties—a collection of second-tier financial insurance products, the world's largest mortgage-insurance business, a high-risk bond-guarantee insurance arm, a collection of long-term care assets, pet insurance, and a broad assortment of property-reinsurance assets—that were albatrosses around GE's neck. When the Capital team had first proposed these deals, there were many people within GE who thought they were crazy (including Bob Nardelli, Jim McNerney, and me). But none of us had spoken up. Then, having paid too much for these businesses, GE ran them poorly. This was a highly regulated industry with low returns. It was clear to me that we needed to get out.

So we embarked on a series of transactions, the biggest of which was Genworth Financial Inc. We were creating and spinning out a new company for the first time ever at GE. With the help of some great advisers—Goldman Sachs's David Solomon and John Weinberg, Morgan Stanley's Stephen Crawford and Ruth Porat, and a great team of lawyers from Weil, Gotshal & Manges—we launched an IPO for Genworth Financial in May 2004. (Here is a good rule: the quality of an asset is inversely proportional to the amount of talent it takes to sell it.)

I remember our advisers said we had to hit a minimum threshold of 8 percent return on equity, or ROE. We struggled to do so. When you divided Genworth's net income by our shareholder's equity, we barely squeaked to that number. So we priced the shares at $18.50—16 percent below our $22 target. At first, we could barely get them to trade. Finally, the bankers were able to stabilize the stock, and we raised $2.83 billion for about 30 percent of Genworth. GE would soon move to divest the rest of the shares.

I've said that analysts and investors really didn't understand what we had in GE Capital. That was our dilemma as we began dismantling the Blob. When we sold insurance, we were selling $2 billion of earnings—probably $40 billion in market cap at the time. As a freestanding company, Genworth was worth $10 billion in 2005. In subsequent years that dropped to just $2 billion. So even before the financial crisis, these assets were worth a fraction of what they'd been worth within GE—simply because they now existed outside the GE umbrella. This trade was difficult for investors.

At the last minute, we included our profitable mortgage-insurance business in Genworth. I would always be grateful that we did. This business would be hard hit during the financial crisis due to its sensitivity to housing prices. Around the same time, we sold the Financial Guaranty Insurance Company, our bond guarantee business, to a consortium of investors that included the Blackstone Group. FGIC provided financial guarantee policies for public finance and structured finance obligations issued by clients in both the public and private sectors. I didn't like the business. It required taking a huge risk to insure against outcomes that would almost never happen, but for a minimal fee. It didn't seem worth it to me. This business also would soon get crushed in the financial crisis as well, as bonds defaulted. If we hadn't sold mortgage and bond insurance when we did, I believe GE wouldn't have survived 2008 and 2009.

Also around this time, I made another difficult decision: I asked Ken Langone, a founder of the Home Depot and Jack Welch's best friend, to leave the GE board. I had several reasons for doing so. First, it was awkward that under Nardelli, the Home Depot had eliminated most of GE's business there. (Imagine doing a town hall and having an employee ask, "We have a board member who founded the Home Depot and we still are losing business there? How is that possible?" That actually happened.) Second, I was disappointed that despite his deep financial expertise, Langone had approved all of the disastrous insurance acquisitions made by my predecessor. Finally, Langone was in a very public fight with then New York Attorney General Eliot Spitzer over the salary paid to former New York Stock Exchange chief Dick Grasso. Hank Paulson, who was then Goldman Sachs's CEO, and others thought it was too high. It didn't help GE to have one of our directors arguing so publicly with Spitzer, who was riding high at the time as the new "Sheriff of Wall Street." Beyond that, we were dependent on bankers like Paulson and Bill Harrison, who was also on the NYSE board, to help execute our portfolio strategy. (Ever profane, Langone had told *Fortune*, "Paulson is the guy that's going to have not only egg, but shit on his face . . . When I get through with these fucking captains of industry, they're going to wish they were in a Cuisinart—at high speed.") We were attempting to execute a very difficult portfolio transformation. We needed to build trust with the banks at this time and our board knew it. I knew I was turning Langone into a lifelong enemy, but it was the right thing to do.

Finally, we sold our reinsurance business to Swiss Re Group. I remember Swiss Re's CEO Jacques Aigrain met with Dammerman and me at 30 Rock to discuss acquiring GE Insurance Solutions, as we called it. I remember I almost tackled Aigrain on the way to the elevator, I was so desperate for him to take it off our hands. He agreed to a $6.8 billion deal, announced in December 2005, for most of the division, which meant a $3 billion loss for us. I couldn't have been happier.

In recent years, these many insurance divestments have gotten less attention than the parts of the insurance business we held on to—in particular, parts of the long-term care and structured-settlement business. Our decision to hold on to those remnants, which was approved by our board and disclosed to investors, was necessary to get the Genworth deal done. As was common at GE Capital when retaining stubs of businesses we had exited, we would wind these businesses down without writing any new policies. In retrospect, through a 2020 prism, it would have been better to attempt to dump LTC in 2004 even at what everyone would have regarded as a stiff and unfavorable price. Despite extensive oversight, none of us saw then, or over the intervening years, how toxic the investments GE had made in the late 1990s would eventually become. Had Keith Sherin or Sandy Warner or Dennis Dammerman walked into my office and told me to get out of long-term care, we would've. But none of us saw what the future held.

Because the insurance industry is so highly regulated, we felt comfortable that our liabilities were subject to enough internal and external scrutiny that we had a good handle on the risks associated with them. We also hired the Genworth controller to do the same job at GE. She was an insurance pro, and she gave me confidence we were managing LTC well. Beyond that, I knew that our insurance reserves would be reviewed every year by our auditors and regulators.

In the end, we had the unanimous support of both the GE Capital board and the GE board. The core insurance business works this way: insurers take customers' money, guarantee them an outcome, and then invest the money in the hopes of generating returns that are higher than what they've promised to pay out. But decades of low interest rates had made it difficult to generate those higher returns. The Genworth spin-off was among the more important deals I did as CEO. In hindsight, it would have been even better if we could have included LTC, but LTC difficulties that surfaced in 2018 have overshadowed how much worse it could have been for GE had we stayed in the insurance businesses acquired by Jack Welch.

All this proves the adage: opportunity often comes at inconvenient times. In 2004, our stock was struggling. Nonetheless, between Genworth, Amersham, and NBCUniversal, we made several multibillion-dollar decisions within six months. My team and I couldn't have made those calls if a few organizing principles hadn't guided us: win in the marketplace, find out what's next, invest in technology, and sell around the world. Still, there's no easy formula for decision making—no perfect amount of data that will guarantee success.

Knowing what to do is often easier than knowing when to do it. Leaders can't afford to be indecisive. There is nothing more frustrating to a team than when its leader thinks out loud but cites caution as a reason not to act. That kind of dithering causes companies to fail. Making imperfect decisions in the pursuit of progress always beats the alternative: letting fear of blame stop you cold.

CHAPTER 4

Leaders Are Systems Thinkers

My wife and I love to binge murder mysteries. Whether it's the cable TV adaptation of my all-time favorite movie (the Coen brothers' *Fargo*) or *The Bridge*, a Scandinavian series we stream on Netflix, we'll plow through several episodes at a time. Without fail, during the first or second episode of each newly discovered show, Andy will turn to me on the couch and ask, "Who do you think did it?"

"Honey," I'll reply, "just let it come to you." That's just how I'm wired: I'm relatively comfortable amid uncertainty. I've learned from experience that sometimes you have to stick around till the eighth or ninth episode before the answer starts to become clear. I think I developed that kind of patience while pursuing a math major in college. My professors helped me understand that it was okay—necessary, even—not to know right away how to solve a problem. I suppose that training helped me embrace the discipline known as "systems thinking."

Systems thinking can sound a little abstract at first, but it's worth the effort it requires. Basically, it analyzes the complexity of your markets and your organization by paying attention to how the component parts interrelate. Traditional linear analysis breaks down systems into separate elements, searching for cause and effect. But when a system's many segments are all interdependent and commingled, such as the businesses within a conglomerate like GE, you must think in two dimensions: vertical (in a single market) and horizontal (across multiple markets).

Let's pick a market like Aviation. Here is a vertical question: Will outsourcing the making of precision castings (a key engine component) imperil our service business by enabling a third party to sell our parts directly to our customers? If the answer is yes, we should make the part ourselves. Here is a horizontal question: If GE Capital lends Boeing money to make its 787, will that help us place more GE products on that plane, beating out our competitors? To answer both questions requires considering the many constituencies within GE's complex system and breaking down the silos that separate them. That's systems thinking.

More than a buzz phrase, systems thinking helps leaders see what others don't see (and, ideally, identify opportunities before others do). Can you recognize a sea change as it's happening and then be bold enough to take action? With the help of systems thinking, GE often could. In 1997, we created a division that did backroom processing—billing, receivables, collection management, customer service, IT help desks, and the like—for all our businesses. We based it in India because wages were lower there (you could hire a person with a PhD for a quarter of the cost of a far less educated person in the United States), and from the start, we ran it as a separate operation. By centralizing these functions, we needed fewer people than we would have if each of our divisions had their own billing and collections staffs. It was a win-win-win for GE: higher efficiency, fewer employees, and lower salaries.

Eight years later, though, we examined several factors—GE's

breadth, GE's respected brand name, GE's international footprint—and realized we were uniquely positioned to create more value for our investors by spinning the division out. By stepping back and looking at the business holistically (and not merely as a part of GE's bureaucracy), we could see how it might serve customers outside GE. (Besides, we knew that building a business purely around wage arbitrage would hurt the brand.) In January 2005, the company—now named Genpact—became independent and began to serve clients outside of GE. Genpact now has about eighty thousand employees and nearly $3 billion in revenues. Without systems thinking, it would still be an internal division of GE.

So how does one "do" systems thinking? For starters, you must push beyond merely observing events or data to another level of inquiry: identifying patterns of behavior and the structures that drive those patterns. Inside GE, I looked at what behaviors our divisions had in common. Then I looked outside GE, at factors that were changing not just our business landscape but everyone's. Think about the impact China's growth, say—or the emergence of cloud computing—has had on multiple industries. Or, to cite a more recent example, think about the COVID-19 pandemic and the ripples it has caused throughout the world's economy. Whatever the cause of such market changes, leaders need to pay close attention to them, assess their impacts, and make decisions accordingly.

For me and my team, systems thinking always started with listening to GE's customers. More than any other group, they provided the insights and data that led to some of our best ideas. The other group I relied on was scientists inside and outside the company. They were good at seeing the efficiency of an entire system instead of obsessing over a single module within it. What you want when you own airplanes is to maximize their "time on wing," and there are many factors that determine that. To focus too narrowly on any one factor is to miss the point. Scientists have to think systematically to do their jobs. Increasingly, I did, too.

What did that mean in practice? I had regular dinners with a group of CEOs I trusted and respected: Ken Chenault of American Express, Johnson & Johnson's Bill Weldon, IBM's Sam Palmisano, PepsiCo's Steve Reinemund (and, later, Indra Nooyi). I read fifty to sixty annual reports a year. I was trying to put myself in the way of new ideas.

During my time as CEO, there were many instances in which systems thinking helped me see the need to pivot, sometimes in a radical way. I could write a whole book about those, but I'm going to limit myself to two: Ecomagination, which we launched in 2005, and the formation, in 2011, of GE Digital and its platform Predix. Both were a response to our customers' needs and to the broader atmosphere—economic, environmental, scientific, technological. Both got major pushback, and later jump-started vast cultural change, within GE.

COMMUNICATING WITH THE WORLD

In 1998, Jack Welch asked Beth Comstock to leave NBC, where she was a senior vice president of corporate communication, to become GE's chief communicator. It wasn't long before Comstock came to visit me at GE Medical Systems in Wisconsin. I liked her sensibility. GEMS had made a lot of breakthroughs in mammography and ultrasound, and we'd launched a women's health initiative. Comstock felt passionately that the world should know about those efforts and about the women GE was helping. She understood it made for powerful marketing, of course: most consumers didn't associate GE with fighting cancer. But I was struck most by her curiosity and the ease with which she connected with engineers and executives alike.

In 2002, as I finished my first year as CEO, I was thinking a lot about how the role of business leaders was changing. In the past, GE's top brass could afford to adopt a closed-door, "don't ask questions" stance when it came to the outside world. But in the wake of 9/11 and Enron, and the increasing demand for transparency, I could see that GE needed a more outward-facing posture. GE was so multifaceted that it was difficult for customers and investors to feel they knew it. I needed someone to figure out how to explain the role GE played in a way people could understand. I made Comstock GE's chief marketing officer.

Comstock was an unlikely choice for the job. A self-described introvert, she grew up in a small town in Virginia and stayed close to home for college, attending William & Mary. She'd majored in biology, not math or economics, and she hadn't gone to business school. But I'd been impressed by how she threw herself into problems, no matter how intractable. And I had a couple of big problems for her to solve: while GE had a big sales force, we had trouble using them to drive new revenue from new sources. And since GE didn't sell directly to consumers, it had used marketing as a way to launch products. I wanted to see if we could be more creative and more proactive than that.

I asked Comstock to rethink GE's motto, "We Bring Good Things to Life," which we'd used since 1979. The phrase had been terrific for its time. But increasingly, I saw we needed to go from being a consumer and financial-services company to a technology and innovation-based company. We didn't need rebranding, exactly; we needed to express ourselves in a new way for a new century. We wanted our people at GE to dare to imagine the future, every single day, when they came to work. We wanted our customers and investors to have faith in GE's innovative excellence.

Working with BBDO, the ad agency, we settled on a new slogan, which we debuted in a TV ad during the Golden Globe Awards show in January 2003. As Johnny Cash sang "Come Take a Trip in my Airship," viewers saw grainy images of the Wright brothers readying a new airplane prototype for their first powered flight at Kitty Hawk, in 1903.

"One hundred years ago, the Wright brothers had the inspiration to make a brilliant idea take flight," a voice-over said. "And although GE wasn't there on that remarkable day, we'd like to feel we were there in spirit." Suddenly, the biplane transformed: it was now strapped to a modern GE engine. The engine roared, blowing the roof off a nearby shed, and as the plane rose into the air, the flickering archival footage changed to full color. "GE aircraft engines and our aviation partners are proud to have helped take Orville and Wilbur Wright's invention to heights they themselves might never have imagined," the voice-over continued, before introducing our new slogan: "GE: Imagination at Work."

New mottos and witty TV commercials weren't all I wanted from Comstock, though. I gave her a broader mandate: creating teams that could help find gaps in the market and then imagine what GE could do to fill them. Together we launched something called Imagination Breakthroughs, or IBs. In just six weeks, each GE business had to come up with two or three ideas for new revenue sources—whether they were products, applications, geographic areas, or previously unserved customers. Within five years, each business had to generate substantial growth.

Soon, the Imagination Breakthrough proposals started to come in, and Comstock and I spent a day a month going over them. The idea was to cultivate ideas that were not quite ready for prime time— to give them not just funding but also a little protection. I knew that in a large company, ideas were particularly vulnerable when in a nascent stage. My hope was that the IB program would help the best new ideas survive.

When people came in to champion their proposals, I told them I didn't want long-winded PowerPoint presentations. I wanted a short summary and a willingness to answer my questions. I usually started with three: What is the biggest *internal* barrier you face? What is the biggest *external* barrier you face? What is the revenue flow? A year into the program, we'd given the green light to eighty IBs. By 2005, twenty-five IBs were generating revenue, and I was proud of every one.

Yet I was struck more than ever by the pushback to new ideas within GE. In September 2003, I gave a speech at MIT in which I talked about that explicitly. "If I were to give you a chapter of my business book," I said (even though I had no plans at that point to ever write one), "it would be called, 'Two Million Dollars from Greatness.' I can't tell you how many GE leaders give me the excuse, 'I could fund new innovations but I can't afford it. I can't fit it into my budget.' These are from leaders that have a billion-dollar base-cost budget! Investors expect companies to take risk."

It's funny to me, looking back on that statement today. Consciously or not, I was laying the groundwork for something not just risky but audacious. Within a year, we were going to commit to a company-wide initiative that was truly countercultural: Ecomagination.

GREEN IS GREEN

In 2004, GE had the biggest Superfund site in history. Two of our factories had dumped PCBs into New York's upper Hudson River for thirty years, from 1947 to 1977. We'd done everything legally, but after the factories closed, and some scientific studies indicated PCBs caused cancer in rats, the EPA said we had to clean it all up. We'd been fighting that order—the testing was thin and never conclusive about danger to humans, and the river was already much cleaner. At one point, at the National Governors Association conference in 2008, I went so far as to suggest to New York's governor Eliot Spitzer that the public would be better served if GE took the money we were about to spend dredging the Hudson River and used it to build a bunch of elementary schools instead. (He declined my offer, saying the politics were too complicated.)

But the whole situation got me thinking. We were already in the wind business. We were implementing new energy-saving standards for GE refrigerators. Now we were being forced to address GE's past history as a polluter. Was there something positive we could do that would tie all these pieces together?

Around this time, GE customers were thinking about the environment, too. Enhanced regulatory standards in the United States and the European Union were putting pressure on our customers to lower all kinds of pollution, but they dreaded how expensive it would be to convert their old technologies to cleaner new ones. When the topic would come up, some of our customers were more motivated by being good corporate citizens; others were focused on protecting their balance sheets. What they had in common, though, was anxiety about the future. And many wanted GE's help.

I told Beth Comstock I had what I liked to call "half an idea." This was something I did often as CEO: tossing a trusted leader an undeveloped theory or proposition and asking them to run it to ground. Truth be told, sometimes "half an idea" was an exaggeration—what I was thinking was a quarter baked at best. But getting fresh eyes on something I'd been noodling over helped me in three ways: it gave me valued feedback on whether the idea was worth more of our time; it told my people that I trusted them; and it usually resulted in something better than what I'd given them in the first place.

Comstock knew I always had my eye out for internal innovations that could be implemented horizontally, across GE's businesses. I put the question to her: Was there a way to craft a message aimed not just at ourselves but simultaneously at our customers? Environmental concerns were top of mind for business, and certainly for GE. GE had deep knowledge of environmental policy, a university's worth of talented scientists, and relationships with every customer in the world. Could we use all that, and our vast technological resources, to create a groundswell of positive action, while at the same time boosting revenues?

My motivations were many. First, I wanted to grow the company. Second, I was always searching for ways to make this 120-plus-year-old company look and act younger, and I knew from talking to my seventeen-year-old daughter and her friends that teens and millennials cared more about the planet than their fuddy-duddy parents ever had. I had paid attention when Vic Abate, who was running our Wind division, described what he called its culture of "renewitude"—the swagger employees felt because they were addressing an important world problem.

Third, I'd always believed in leading by example. When it came to improving GE's environmental reputation, I didn't think adding my signature to a list of, say, a hundred pro-environment CEOs would do anything. There was nothing wrong with such solidarity. But I felt to make real change, GE should commit to doing something on its own. Finally, I knew that being one of the world's biggest polluters was not a good look for GE. Without question, we needed to change our image. And yet, I made clear to Comstock that mere greenwashing wouldn't pass muster with me. Unless we could do something with measurable outcomes that could be scrutinized by the public, I wasn't interested.

Comstock soon convened a working group to hammer out ideas. They surveyed the effects of environmental regulations on business, and studied companies such as Toyota, to see how it had handled its successful hybrid, the Prius. They surveyed all of GE's business leaders and talked to customers as well.

The company's view (and mine) was that climate change is real and caused by man. We believed that the United States needed to join global agreements. We believed that addressing this challenge would require technical, policy, and financial solutions. At the same time, we firmly believed that transitioning legacy technologies to make them more efficient was a key to building broad support. Today, California and Germany make headlines for being pro-environment, but no one follows their lead. They offer solutions for the elite—ones that are expensive and uneven.

From the start, we stressed that improving legacy technologies was as important as inventing new tech, such as LED lighting, hybrid locomotives, and durable, lightweight materials. Even amid a push for renewable energy, we knew that most of the world would continue using coal and natural gas to generate power for a long time. So if we could launch products and services that reduced pollution from fossil fuels, that could have a huge impact on global warming. Meanwhile, GE would commit to reducing its own carbon footprint as well. Our working catchphrase was "Green is green."

It's difficult to remember now, with climate change on more and more people's lips, but this work was bold for its time—and not particularly popular. In the beginning, even within GE, few people thought it was a good idea. At Crotonville, in late 2004, when Comstock first pre-

sented the Ecomagination initiative to GE's Corporate Executive Council—the top thirty people in the company—she ticked off the pros and
cons, the myths and potential payoffs, and she unveiled a new TV ad
that had been created to announce Ecomagination to the world. BBDO
called this one "Dancing Elephant" because it featured a young pachy-
derm re-creating Gene Kelly's iconic dance moves to the tune of "Singin'
in the Rain." A voice-over explained: "Water that's more pure. Jet engines,
trains, and power plants that run dramatically cleaner. At GE, we're using
what we call Ecomagination to create technology that's right in step with
nature." The spot finished with a succession of GE images: the iconic
light bulb, a wind turbine, a molecule, an X-rayed hand, a power plant,
a jet engine, the Ecomagination green leaf, and the GE logo.

When the lights came up, there was near pandemonium. "You're
going to make us look like idiots," someone yelled from the back row.
There were countless objections, many of which had merit. Wouldn't
we look like hypocrites, given our Hudson River problems? What if we
didn't have the technology to deliver on our promises? Some feared we
would scare our customers away by seeming to encourage more regulation. Others wondered about the logistics: because Ecomagination
was a program that set new goals for all GE divisions (but wasn't a
business to itself), it was unclear how much each division would have
to pay to participate. There were only two people in the room who
wanted to give Ecomagination a chance: Comstock and me.

I wasn't an environmentalist, per se. I like looking at a pristine
beach as much as the next guy, but I wasn't coming at this from a
tree-hugging perspective. Instead, Ecomagination was a response to
global trends that I believed were creating demand for new products
and services. I felt that Ecomagination was the right initiative for that
particular moment, both for the environment and for GE's business
strategy. (We would soon tell the EPA we'd pay $3 billion over ten
years to begin dredging the Hudson.)

I reached out to Jonathan Lash, president of the World Resources
Institute. Lash was one of a few environmental leaders who were
looking to collaborate with the private sector in the hopes of forging

stronger policies and better performance. Still, when I first invited him to meet with me at Rockefeller Center, his staff advised him to say no. They feared he would be seen as in cahoots with GE.

But Lash and I hit it off. He believed that my motives were in earnest, not just about burnishing our image, and he agreed to appear at our Ecomagination kickoff event: a news conference that was beamed live to all GE employees. I spoke first, announcing that GE would double its research budget for energy and environmental technologies to $1.5 billion. I pledged that over seven years, GE's own energy efficiency would improve by 30 percent and our worldwide greenhouse gas emissions would decrease by 1 percent (they would have increased by 40 percent otherwise). Then Lash delivered an impassioned speech made more meaningful, to me at least, because we hadn't required him to vet it with us beforehand. Addressing GE's people, he urged them to work hard to make Ecomagination succeed. "This is a big, big deal," he said.

I knew that to make Ecomagination a big deal would be difficult. Crucially, we needed grassroots support from inside the company. To drum that up, I needed to bring a strong leader on board, someone who had worked in GE's businesses and could sell Ecomagination both inside and outside the company. There was only one person, I felt, who had the technical chops and the required horse-trading skills (she knew how to move her peers).

Lorraine Bolsinger, who at that time was the chief marketing officer at GE Aviation, was an engineer by training; she'd majored in biochemical engineering at Penn and had worked in GE Power before heading to Cincinnati to work in GE's marine and industrial engines business. I'd seen her in action as a saleswoman, so I knew she was always prepared, determined to have all the answers for customers. She was a straight talker, but also a master of persuasion. Once, she got the Museum of Modern Art in New York to accept a fan blade from the GE90 engine into its permanent collection. She could charm the bark off a tree.

When I got Bolsinger on the phone and admitted that Ecomagination was a work in progress with no guaranteed pathway to success, she was skeptical. She loved the job she had, for starters. But

I'm pretty persuasive, too. "I want you to make Ecomagination what you think it should be," I said. "I need one part engineer, one part marketer, one part salesman. That's why I'm coming to you. I don't have another one of those."

Finally, I told her that her skepticism was an asset. If she took the job, she would face at least a few cynics. It would help if she was a little bit cynical herself. Why? Because if we didn't make good on our promises, we'd be tarred in the court of public opinion. And if, conversely, we innovated to solve environmental problems but didn't make money doing so, Ecomagination would be denigrated as do-goodism. To the extent that it ever sounded like that, I wanted Bolsinger to call bullshit. Any time we missed our commitments I wanted her to push back on me. I wanted her to think like a critic, even though I'd assigned her to be Ecomagination's biggest booster, because her straight talk would make it succeed.

Bolsinger told me she wanted to think about it, but I hung up pretty sure that I'd piqued her interest. When she called me the following Monday, she had a few conditions. First, she said she needed some "walking around money."

"Walking around money?" I asked.

"Yeah," she said. "Everyone at GE is one million dollars from greatness, and when I ask them to do things, they're going to say if they only had fifty thousand to do a little market study or run a little test, maybe they could help me out. I can't come to you every time someone asks me for fifty thousand dollars. You know I'm the cheapest person in the world, so I probably won't spend it, but give me a few million bucks I can walk around with, greasing the wheels."

Done, I said, surer than ever that I'd tapped the right person. Anything else? "Metrics," she said. "That's the only thing that GE people really respond to. So I need clear metrics to tell the businesses what's expected, so they understand it's not just greenwashing—it's important."

"You got it," I said. At the end of the phone call, Ecomagination had its new ambassador.

For the next two years, when Bolsinger called, I answered. She kept me apprised of the customers she met with, the deals that were getting done. She regaled me with tales about how we were improving GE's greenhouse gas emissions and its energy efficiency. The story of how she replaced a rotten old water tower at GE Aviation is a great example of how she worked. After begging executives there to improve water quality by replacing the system (and being told no, it was too expensive), Bolsinger got creative. She happened to know that the leader of the supply chain responsible for facilities was eager to get his hands on some SEROs, or special early retirement options, which the company had stopped offering. So she went to Shane Fitzsimons, GE's vice president for financial planning and analysis, and asked him for fifty of them. Fitzsimons balked at first, but Bolsinger made the case that every dollar spent on SEROs was worth ten dollars in terms of meeting Aviation's Ecomagination targets. Ultimately, Fitzsimons coughed up the SEROs and the facilities guy installed a new, efficient water tower. That was classic Bolsinger. She was great at her job because she instinctually grasped people's needs and motivations—or, in her words, "I knew where everybody's goat was tied."

Throughout, Bolsinger ran Ecomagination like a business, even though it wasn't technically a business. I remember she and I traveling to Bentonville, Arkansas, for an important negotiation with Walmart, where GE had long enjoyed the best shelf space for light bulbs. When they told us that unless we shifted our inventory from LEDs to compact fluorescent lamps, they would give our shelf space to Sylvania, Bolsinger didn't flinch. Not to worry, she said, it would be done.

I wish we'd been as successful in our attempts to affect public policy. A group of twenty companies including GE tried to create a groundswell behind the American Clean Energy and Security Act in 2009. The bill, which would have set emissions standards to curb the heat-trapping gasses scientists have linked to climate change, passed the House by seven votes but was never brought to the floor of the Senate. Make no mistake: the dearth of consistent policies has made clean investing difficult. The nuclear industry has had a rough forty years, and tens of billions of dollars' worth of investments in solar batteries, clean coal, and other ideas have been written off. GE's Ecomagination fared better than most.

Of course, we got pilloried by everyone from Fox News to the Green Party. As I told *Vanity Fair* in a lengthy 2006 article about Ecomagination: "I know I'm doing something right when I have the left saying it's not good enough and the right saying this is Communist corporate do-goodism bullshit." But notably, our critics did not include the leading environmental groups. They lauded us for taking, as the president of the Pew Center on Global Climate Change put it, "a gutsy stand." At one point, *New York Times* columnist Thomas Friedman even went so far as to recommend that President George Bush replace Vice President Dick Cheney with someone with the vision to reshape America's energy landscape: me.

Those who'd worried about how Ecomagination would impact GE weren't all wrong. We did lose some business. When John Wilder, who ran the energy company TXU, heard about the initiative, he called me to say he was taking $100 million of his business elsewhere. (He'd ordered coal plants; in the end, they didn't get built at all, but at the time it stung.)

For every critic who weighed in, however, it seemed we heard from two supporters—some of them unexpected. I remember getting a call from the gentleman who ran the National Development and Reform Commission, China's infrastructure agency. "Next time you're in China, I want to meet," he said, saying that advancing clean technology was among his top priorities. This official was high up in China's leadership structure. Hearing from him told me Ecomagination was changing the dialogue about GE.

Was Ecomagination a marketing ploy? Absolutely. We wanted to change our image, but we wanted to earn that shift. It wasn't long before we could show real, measurable impact. Sure, some of the seventeen technologies we listed under the new Ecomagination umbrella had been in use for years. There was the H System gas turbine, which produced more electricity from a thousand cubic feet of gas than any competitor when it was introduced in 2000, and of course the GEnx engine for Boeing's 787 Dreamliner, with 15 percent less fuel per seat-mile. But I didn't buy the logic of dinging GE for already being eco-conscious.

Did Ecomagination do everything perfectly? Of course not. But it was one of the most successful commercial efforts in GE's history. The new green products we brought to market included everything from halogen lamps to biogas engines. We invested heavily: after an initial commitment of $700 million in 2008, we committed another $1.4 billion to R&D, and in 2010, we added another $10 billion to Ecomagination's budget over the next five years. Over a dozen years, Ecomagination generated $270 billion in revenues.

THE DIGITAL FUTURE

In 2009, a group of scientists at the Global Research Center in Niska-yuna made a prediction. "You know how our new GE jet engines are equipped with sensors that collect enormous amounts of data?" they asked me. "Well, someday, that data will be as valuable as the machines themselves, if not more so." I took a mental note.

A few months later, I was at Crotonville for a meeting of the GE Service Council, a quarterly gathering of the leaders of GE's various service departments—the people who executed the contracts we had to fix the engines and turbines and imaging devices we'd made. We often invited customers to these events. The folks from Burlington Northern, who bought our diesel locomotive engines, were there. And they had a complaint.

For decades, we'd been saying to them, "Here's our engine, here's what it costs, here's how much oil it consumes." We were focused on fuel efficiency. Now they told us: "Thanks, but what we actually need to know is where our locomotives are and how fast they are moving at any given time. We need to be able to do computer-aided dispatch"—basically matching customers' needs with vehicle availability—"and in order to do that, we need GPS input and loads of data. And we need to be able to predict failure."

Meanwhile, the healthcare business—an early adopter of digital technologies in patient record keeping—was now shifting toward using machine learning to improve diagnostics. I visited Sam Gambhir, the chairman of radiology at Stanford, who showed me the potential to improve drug staging using artificial intelligence. In the past, an MR or CT was the primary diagnostic tool in medicine. Radiologists who read those scans functioned as interpreters. In the future, Gambhir told me, those interpreters would rely not just on their eyes but on supplementary data stored in the cloud. GE needed to lead in this area, just as we had in imaging. It was that or get marginalized.

In 2020, it seems everyone is talking about the importance of "digital transformation." But a decade ago, I wasn't thinking about fancy words. Instead, I wanted to develop a technology that could change the nature of our relationship with customers and differentiate GE. For a century, GE had sold a suite of complicated machines. On the industrial side, our business model had been to sell hardware for little more than cost, and make money fixing the hardware when it broke. Now I sensed we needed to move toward a different model: selling not just hardware but customized, performance-enhancing, software-enabled solutions. For industrial companies, especially, there was an urgent need to figure out the so-called Internet of Things, or IoT, which allowed machines to increase efficiency by sharing data.

We knew that data-driven service was a way to grow our service business. But if we failed to act, it would become an existential threat. If GE didn't do it, someone else would. I asked the Global Research Center, which Mark Little was running, to sketch out the parameters of a potential digital initiative. In addition, I asked several classes of leaders who were studying at Crotonville to do some homework for me. One of them stumbled on an alarming fact: IBM and several high-tech start-ups were gathering data from GE's customers to develop data-based services in sectors such as aviation and power.

Already, our rivals were using data we were collecting with the aim of disrupting our businesses.

I could see that it wouldn't be long before someone like Accenture or IBM or Google would be offering airframe manufacturers and other customers essential data about our GE aircraft engines that promised cost-saving efficiencies. If we didn't do something, not only would our competitors soon encroach on our service business, but they'd use data from GE-made machines to do it.

This was a dilemma. GE, like most legacy companies, had outsourced our digital capability twenty years before. Enterprise tech companies like Oracle told us what to do and our BPO, or business process outsourcing, partners in India helped us execute. Our IT leaders weren't really technologists; they were program managers. It was fine in theory to outsource administrative software, but that left us with a talent gap for artificial intelligence and data analytics. These two things would be the guts of our products and services in the future.

In past years, when we had business reviews, IT may have had a seat at the table, but they rarely had a speaking part. More broadly, if you read the annual reports of major companies before 2015, IT was rarely mentioned. Now, though, the digital revolution was finally coming to the industrial world. I always had believed that GE could do anything. But what we resolved to do next—launching GE Digital—would test that belief.

When my team and I went to the GE board for seed money in 2010, our thinking was informed by a past mistake. Back when I was CEO of GE Medical Systems, we'd entered the medical IT business and had some success, but I'd always regretted what I felt was a missed opportunity. When it came to expanding into enterprise software, I felt we'd half-assed it. Later, in 2006, we'd acquired IDX Systems, one of the top five healthcare software companies in the United States but we'd failed to capitalize on the $1.2 billion deal. While we said we were going for excellence, we let GE people who lacked the necessary expertise run that new initiative, and we lost our market position while also losing many of its best people. I knew then that if we were ever going to attempt something in the digital space again, we would have to launch it outside of GE proper, locating it in or near California's Silicon Valley and staffing it with leaders from outside GE.

When we created GE Digital in 2011 we opened a software center in San Ramon, California, in the San Francisco Bay Area. And then we hired Bill Ruh, a global strategist with a zeal for implementing the IoT, away from Cisco to run it. Ruh remembers that when he and I first sat down, my proposition to him was a bit fuzzy. I knew we needed to do something, but because we lacked expertise, I wasn't quite sure what. I asked him to assemble a team of talented people who could help us define GE Digital's business proposition. Starting with an investment of $200 million over a few years, Ruh set out to embed sensors and instrumentation into GE machines, capture and study customer data, and develop software applications for all of GE's businesses.

There were three areas where we knew the use of data could help our customers. First, data would help optimize the performance of each machine—making GE's jet engines, say, burn less fuel during landing. Second, data-crunching software would allow GE to predict when a machine would need repairs, helping minimize costly downtime by identifying early warning signals before a breakdown. And third, GE software could enhance the overall performance of any system in which a machine operates—a railroad like Burlington Northern, say, or an oil field or a wind farm.

Building GE Digital took some time, but by 2012, I thought we were onto something. GE kicked off a new annual event that year for customers and software developers called Minds + Machines. The first gathering was small—about four hundred people—but many of those who attended soon became customers, mainstreaming GE analytics into their operations. Little by little, we were beginning to get people inside and outside GE to understand that data could make our machines work better and last longer.

While Google and Facebook had created platforms for consumers—and Microsoft had created a platform for the office—there was no platform to link complex machines. We thought GE could create these digital commercial links with our industrial customers. GE Digital was trying to use analytics to improve the performance of machines. And Predix was a cloud-based platform that enabled industrial-scale computing for use inside and outside GE. Predix worked by creating a computerized model, or "digital twin," of each machine that showed in real time how it was performing and when its parts were wearing out. The system also created a "digital thread" that logged, like a medical record, every aspect of a machine's life—from initial assembly to repairs to replacement parts.

We liked to say that, at any given moment, Predix could monitor performance while a jet engine was in the air, or tilt turbine blades to increase power output while they were spinning. We knew that, given the huge costs of our machines, even tiny efficiency gains could be hugely valuable to GE customers (and to us, as we were asking to be paid a portion of any cost-savings our tools enabled).

There are two ways companies can pivot into new markets and remain relevant: by buying existing businesses or by building them from scratch. I've discussed the acquisition of Amersham, which positioned us to grow in healthcare. That was risky, but it made sense because it built on top of an already successful business. With GE Digital, that wasn't possible.

For a big, public company, investing organically is a hundred times harder than doing an acquisition. Here, we had to recruit new talent, reallocate funds, create and integrate a new culture, and build new processes—all at the same time. I had to convince my team that they should bet on digital with me. It would be an uphill fight, so I enlisted the aid of three GE veterans to help Ruh navigate GE. Jennifer Waldo, who'd been at GE Aviation, would run human relations. Jim Fowler would move from GE Capital to become GE Digital's CIO. And I thought Khozema Shipchandler, who I made CFO, could do for GE Digital what Lorraine Bolsinger had done for Ecomagination. All three were seen as comers within GE. Their presence bestowed credibility.

COMPETING FOR TALENT

We had a difficult time hiring top-flight software engineers. And we needed them. That's the problem with outsourcing a key part of your infrastructure: it creates an expertise deficit. As we sought to change that, we were competing with companies like Google and Apple whose innovative reputations made them more alluring. Despite GE's long-standing prowess making complex machinery, the best candidates for digital didn't initially see us as having tech expertise. Having a Silicon Valley headquarters and hiring a proven performer like Ruh went a long way to countering that misperception. But we also needed to get the word out: we made products that helped people. Especially the younger candidates we talked to were excited about the idea that their work would have tangible benefits in healthcare and in industry. Working on coding a game like Candy Crush can be fun, I'm sure, but it couldn't be as fulfilling as doing something that saved lives or made the world a better place.

I turned to Comstock for help, and she and I met with Waldo, of HR. Waldo said a GE Digital employee had told her of attending a neighborhood barbecue where—when he revealed he worked at GE—someone responded quizzically, "I thought you worked in tech." Comstock, a big believer in what she called "mindshare before market share," knew right away that the germ of a great idea was there. She worked with the advertising agency BBDO to make a series of cleverly self-deprecating TV ads that introduced the idea that, yes, GE was in the software business (and that working for GE could be satisfying). The commercials featured a gangly, bespectacled computer engineer named Owen as he tried to explain his new job at GE to confused family members and friends. In one ad, an exuberant Owen announces, "I'll be writing a new language for machines so planes, trains, even hospitals can work better!" To which one of his buddies replies disappointedly: "So you're going to work on a train? You're not going to develop stuff anymore?"

The ad that garnered the most attention, though, spoofed the tech industry even as it acknowledged GE's fledgling digital status. A programmer friend of Owen's has just gotten a job at "Zazzies, the app where you put fruit hats on animals." Owen counters that at GE, "I'm going to transform the way the world works." But his friends are more interested in a photo of a cat with a casaba melon on its head. "I can do dogs, hamsters, guinea pigs, you name it," Owen's friend brags. The ad ends with this directive: "Get yourself a world-changing job."

Within a month of the ads' debut, there was a 66 percent increase in visits to GE's online recruiting site. Half a year later, the number of applications to work at GE had gone up eightfold. If you were a young engineer who loved data science, and you were designing emojis, say, or coding at a dog-walking app, this campaign let you know: at GE, you could use your talents to invent solutions to vital problems.

BRINGING THE TEAM ALONG

Predix would be my first experience with the phenomenon of the Innovator's Dilemma—a term made popular by the 1997 book of that title by Harvard professor Clayton Christensen. Christensen argued that established firms face a dilemma when they try to innovate because doing so can mean cannibalizing their existing markets, at least in the short term. But in the long term, not innovating could mean something far worse: obsolescence and, ultimately, extinction.

Say you work in the GE Oil & Gas business. You make little to no money when you sell a customer a compressor, but you make up for it in the coming years by selling the parts to maintain and fix it. Now here comes a new GE division whose main product—Predix—promises to help customers buy fewer spare parts. It's easy to see how, for GE Oil & Gas execs focused on making their quarterly numbers, this arrangement could sound like bad news.

Of course, we tried to counter that viewpoint by providing a longer-range context. We repeated until we were hoarse some version of: "Hey, this change is going to happen! If GE Digital doesn't do it, one of our competitors will capture all these revenues. Yes, Predix will hurt short-term. But long-term, it's our only chance." But still, there were many naysayers within GE. Shipchandler, the CFO, even coined a name for them: "GE antibodies."

These antibodies rejected GE Digital, at least at first. There was, without question, an us-versus-them mentality. As we hired new people, GE's existing IT teams felt threatened (and resented that their new colleagues were paid higher-than-standard GE salaries as an incentive to join a manufacturing giant).

But the GE antibodies weren't only people who worked in IT. Because our investments in Predix inevitably cut into the funding of other GE businesses, there was a rivalry between the incumbent businesses and the new digital one (especially since, in Predix's nascent stages, the incumbents were generating all the capital). When, as a way to save money, I tried to give Ruh more input into the budgets of each business's IT department, the CEOs of those businesses hated it. And I'll admit that I was asking people to support uncertain, long-term innovation while also making their short-term numbers.

We had one other challenge that many big companies face when making change: Do you move centrally, creating one entity to work across the company, or do you let each of your businesses do their own thing within their own digital departments? We chose to move centrally, as GE Digital, because I felt we were mostly solving a single, multi-business problem (improving services for our customers). Moreover, having GE Digital stand alone helped us recruit talent. However, this approach put a limit on experimentation within each business; had we gone the other way, it could have created more buy-in.

There was also the problem of Digital's burn rate, which didn't match GE's culture. Many faulted us for spending too much money on GE Digital, but I felt that criticism didn't acknowledge how other start-up software companies behaved. A start-up like Splunk (which produces software for searching, monitoring, and analyzing machine-generated big data) tears through a lot of money initially, before it gets to break even. Tech start-ups define success, especially in the first decade, on how well they acquire customers, build capability, and penetrate their emerging markets. That wasn't how GE had traditionally defined success. We were about increasing revenues and making our numbers. Analyzed by that metric, this little start-up within a big parent company was seen by many as a disappointment.

So in addition to building the Predix platform itself, we also spent a lot of energy building support for it in-house. Shipchandler remembers going to Crotonville repeatedly to try to persuade his fellow executives that GE Digital wasn't the enemy. A small-town kid from Indiana, Shipchandler could be a poster boy for GE. He likes to say that GE opened his eyes to life's possibilities: the satisfaction of working on something that mattered. By the time he got to Digital, he'd been at the company almost twenty years, in Plastics, in Aviation, in Corporate Audit, at home and abroad in the Middle East. So he had credibility with his peers.

"Look," he remembers telling critics, "I'm not a GE Digital native. So I understand your reluctance to buy in. But GE has always been a company that helped invent the future. GE Digital is part of that tradition. And we need it to succeed. I'm one of you, and I'm out there rooting for your businesses to be successful. Why won't you do the same for me?"

More often than not, that changed the tenor of the conversation. Shipchandler recalls how people would follow up with him afterward, curious what they could do to figure out digital synergies in their businesses. But progress was slow, especially because at times, some of the digital folks who were new to GE got turfy and alienated their colleagues in other businesses. Some people felt Ruh was too enamored with empire building and tried to do too much at once.

But I knew about the role the antibodies played in that assessment, so I protected him.

In 2013, a great entrepreneur in the digital space, Tom Siebel, the founder of the artificial intelligence software platform and applications company C3.ai, had said of our GE Digital effort, "Jeff, you are aiming at the right target here. But you will never be able to do this inside a big company. Your company won't let you." I couldn't yet see how right he was.

NOT FINISHING THE JOB

In 2016, we held our fourth Minds + Machines conference, and the number of attendees—including customers and employees across all GE businesses—was ten times bigger than in 2012. In a series of panels, we asked our customers to talk about how Predix was helping them meet their goals. Again and again, they affirmed that we were onto something. One by one, as each speaker rose to describe their particular experience, I felt they were giving GE permission to be a digital company. Recently, the IT consulting firm Gartner had named GE Digital a leader in its Magic Quadrant series, which validated us. So I felt good when I took the podium and introduced a new rallying cry: "Why not us?" Why couldn't GE be the company whose digital platform served the Industrial Internet?

We weren't imagining the importance of the Internet of Things. Customer after customer told us they needed help. And other industries needed it, too. Think about any CEO of a legacy automotive company. All of their options are bad right now, what with the coming age of not just electric vehicles but autonomous ones. As we march through this era of technical change, leaders must dare to invest despite uncertain returns.

In big companies, it is said that you are either moving forward or moving backward. You're never idling. So momentum really matters. You can spend seven years building something, but it only takes a minute to kill it. When a leader of a big organization says, "I'm not sure," people within that organization feel that vacuum. That's the reason I was always out front as CEO, pushing us to stretch our capabilities. I had learned this from my predecessor. When Jack Welch started Six Sigma, no one thought it was a good idea. But he wouldn't listen to those who didn't embrace it. I was the same way with GE Digital.

Despite the undeniable strategic promise, much of what we built at GE Digital has been dismantled since I left. In 2017, several companies wanted to invest in Predix, which they valued at more than $5 billion. Instead, it seemed to me that the new GE leadership was unclear and inconsistent about its digital strategy for more than a year. Most of the best talent left and got great jobs in the tech sector. Today, Khozema Shipchandler is CFO of Twilio, a cloud communications platform; Jen Waldo is a top HR leader at Apple; Jim Fowler is the chief technology officer at Nationwide. Kate Johnson, a digital native we recruited from Oracle, is now a senior leader at Microsoft.

Today, I see dozens of disruptors—backed by billions of dollars in investment—that are all targeting the industrial-services market Predix was designed to address. None of these platforms have the advantages Predix had. Transforming a big legacy company requires persistence. It is difficult to please everyone. When we invested in digital, I mostly closed my ears to the critics, and I believe I was right to do so. You can criticize me for overspending on GE Digital or for failing to take on an established partner, like Microsoft, to buoy the effort. I see those flaws. But I was right to drive GE into that business. Remember Tom Siebel, who warned me I couldn't create a start-up inside a legacy company? I ran into him the other day, and his company is pulling data from GE turbines, executing on what Predix started.

In legacy companies, new leaders can't change everything. Sometimes you have to run your leg of the race, by which I mean: take something you didn't start and make it better. In that vein, I had

hoped that the next generation of GE leaders would make GE's digital strategy better, not shut it down. By choosing not to lead, GE has
become less relevant in what is inarguably a digital future. For industrial companies, the next decade will be about integrating physical
assets with digital technologies to create new pockets of value. The
coronavirus pandemic will only accelerate that trend.

I played a role in that failure. I probably underestimated GE's
digital deficit from years of outsourcing. And we didn't create enough
digital migrants—by which I mean GE veterans willing to actively
embrace the digital future. We tried our damnedest, offering training
that we hoped would bridge the cultural divide between the established parts of GE and the fledgling upstart in California. In so many
ways, industrial and digital had opposite norms (slow vs. fast, deliber-
ate vs. agile, risk averse vs. risk taking). But I wish I could have artic-
ulated more clearly how essential GE Digital was to GE's survival.

Since leaving GE, I've been working in Silicon Valley at a
venture-capital firm. Recently, I took Jeff Lawson, the founder of
Twilio (on whose board I serve), around to meet with a few of my old
contacts. We visited twenty legacy companies, from JPMorgan to
Delta Airlines to Marriott. It was like déjà vu for me as, one by one,
each CEO told us they believed digital innovation would be central
to their companies' success. Just as they'd told us ten years ago.

Moreover, the COVID crisis has demonstrated the digital divide
in a profound way. Digital companies are thriving as they promote
remote work. Industrial companies are suffering due to their need
for proximity. At GE's 2012 Minds + Machines conference, I
interviewed Marc Andreessen on stage alongside a jet engine. He
had just written a much-talked-about essay in the *Wall Street Journal*
titled "Why Software is Eating the World." I dared to argue, telling
Andreessen, "Software will never eat this engine!" I was wrong.
During the pandemic of 2020, Zoom is booming and commercial
aviation is getting crushed.

CHAPTER 5

Leaders Persevere in a Crisis

I 've never been much for nostalgia. I think of my childhood as happy, and I have given money over the years to the public high school I attended in Finneytown, outside of Cincinnati. But while my framed football jersey is still displayed, under Plexiglas, on a cinder-block wall outside the Wildcats' gym, I don't yearn to live those days over again. That was then; this is now.

That unsentimental outlook was helpful at the end of 2006, when I sat down to do a business review with the folks at GE Plastics. They were missing their numbers, and at the end of the meeting, a guy I respected—Brian Gladden, who was then the division's chief financial officer—pulled me aside and asked if he could level with me. "I know the way you remember Plastics," he said, "but those days are over. This will never again be the business you want it to be." I respected Gladden and I knew he was right.

I've already acknowledged how we failed to invest in the future of Plastics. As DuPont, one of our main rivals, had expanded into agricultural chemicals, buying the seed corn company Pioneer, other companies like Monsanto, Bayer, Dow, and BASF had done the same. But GE Plastics had stuck to the status quo. Now that lack of diversification had left us vulnerable. Rising oil and benzene prices meant our plastics cost more to make than they once had. And because we weren't backward integrated—we didn't own any oil wells—we had no control over our supply chain. As important as "Mad Dog" Plastics had been to my own career, and as fond as I was of many people who worked there, I could see it was part of GE's past, not its future.

In May 2007, we agreed to sell GE Plastics to the Riyadh-based chemicals company Saudi Basic Industries. They *did* own oil wells, so the acquisition made sense for them. The price SABIC paid—$11.6 billion in cash—was far more than analysts inside or outside GE had expected, so after the deal closed, about forty of GE Plastics' top managers held a dinner where they gave me a couple of sleeves of Titleist golf balls, each emblazoned with the GE logo and "$11.6 billion," and a bronze sculpture: a sack of money that resembled what you might find on a Wells Fargo coach. It was mounted on a marble base whose nameplate read: "Congratulations, Jeff. $11.6 billion. From your friends at GE Plastics."

Little did I know that bronzed memento, complete with etched dollar signs, would soon provide my team and me with an ironic visual counterpoint. Sitting on a shelf in my conference room in 2008, that faux bag of money would preside over some of the most intense, gut-wrenching, high-stakes meetings any of us ever hope to attend.

Before I tell the story of how the worldwide financial crisis shook GE and the American economy to its core, it's important to remember how much GE Capital's business model differed from that of a bank. Banks take deposits and then lend money based on those deposits. More important, those deposits are insured by the federal government. GE Capital, by contrast, borrowed money inexpensively (because of its rare AAA rating) and loaned it out at a higher rate. In 2008, GE Capital was the largest nonbank finance company in the world, with assets of $696 billion and $545 billion in debt. If it had been a bank, it would have ranked as the nation's fifth largest. For decades, we'd enjoyed many advantages over banks—crucially, lower funding costs and less regulation. But just as crucially, because we weren't a bank, we could not rely on the government to bail us out.

The GE Capital team, led by Mike Neal, was fantastic. Neal was a graduate of Georgia Tech who'd grown up in the Peach State, and he liked to portray himself as a country bumpkin—he said his grandmother told him to prepare for the apocalypse by stocking up on ammunition, canned ham, and gold (to bribe border guards). But I wasn't fooled. He was one of the smartest guys I ever worked with. Because of him, GE Capital excelled at commercial lending, an area where most banks struggled.

There's a great story about Neal traveling to Bangkok in the late 1990s to bid on a portfolio of Thai auto loans. Heading to his meeting, he mistakenly walked into an office full of Goldman Sachs bankers who were working to win the same deal. "You never have a grenade when you need one," Neal joked as he backed out of the room. That was him: quick on his feet and competitive to the core. And he built a cadre of colleagues with the same traits.

BUNDLE AT YOUR PERIL

Heading into the crisis, GE Capital had one thing in common with many banks: too much mortgage lending. In hindsight, I see we'd gotten our first inkling of trouble in 2006, when WMC, a subprime mortgage broker that GE Capital had purchased for $500 million in 2004, started feeling the pinch. The short version of this story is: we bought into a business that many were entering at the time, and we learned the hard way that we'd made a mistake.

WMC would originate mortgages and resell them to banks that bundled them into mortgage-backed securities known as collateralized mortgage obligations, or CMOs. WMC made money by selling the banks as many mortgages as WMC could originate. But in 2006, the residential retail market began a sharp reversal as the holders of mortgages originated by WMC—which by then was the nation's fifth-largest issuer of subprime mortgages—began to default at an alarming rate. That diminished the value of the bonds for which the mortgages served as collateral and also exposed WMC to claims that the quality of the mortgages was deficient.

My team did several reviews, and by the first quarter of 2007, we'd decided we were done with WMC. We would not originate another mortgage, and we would focus on finding buyers for the $3.5 billion in mortgages we already had. In the end, we took a substantial loss to unwind WMC (and later, in 2019, we agreed to a $1.5 billion settlement with the Justice Department as part of an industry-wide investigation of the subprime mortgage industry). I wish we'd never gotten into the business.

Around the same time, however, we did something that we'd soon look back on with relief: we reduced our exposure to what's called leverage lending. In those years, GE loaned a lot of money to companies that had a lot of debt (or leverage). We never kept 100 percent of the loans; we might keep 20 percent and sell the balance to other financial institutions. Between the time we originated a loan and when we sold it, however, we'd park it in an entity we called "the warehouse." Sometimes, our warehouse contained as much as $25 billion. No more, we decided. By early 2007, we'd whittled our warehouse down to about $5 billion.

In general, I thought I was keeping a close eye on GE Capital. In the buoyant years before the credit crisis, it had contributed about half of GE's overall profits. My goal from the start had been to reevaluate GE Capital's role as our growth engine, but six years into my tenure, its dominance within GE had stayed about the same.

Partly that was because our Power division had cratered. We were letting Power and Aviation recover before restructuring more of GE Capital, and—since we were still trading at a premium to the sum of our parts—investors were supporting our approach. In the summer of 2007, we traded at $42 a share—a 19 PE—with 50 percent of our earnings in financial services.

During this period, we made GE Capital smaller. But we didn't do enough and didn't move as quickly as we could've. In the fall of 2006, a few of my deputies had recommended selling our commercial real estate business, for example, but I'd said no because I felt we had a strong team and could guarantee exceptional returns. In 2007, we stopped making any new deals, and there were many who wanted to spin the division out, so it could grow. But we were in the process of replacing the leader of the business, so again I said no. That was a mistake. I viewed commercial real estate as a core platform for GE Capital. But we let it get too big.

In our defense, the coming storm was not yet visible. In mid-2007, determined to monitor GE Capital's risks, I'd commissioned a study by the consulting firm McKinsey & Company. Sixty days later, McKinsey told us that money from nations with a trade surplus, like China, and sovereign wealth funds, among other investors, would provide enough liquidity to fuel GE Capital's lending and leverage for the foreseeable future. According to McKinsey, we were okay.

BEWARE A COLD SNAP

For a little while, it looked as if McKinsey was right. In February 2008, we released our annual report looking back on the company's previous year. It was titled "Invest and Deliver Every Day," and I felt confident that we would do both.

Determined to reach the 2 million shareholders—about 40 percent of our investor base—who were rarely invited to GE investor relations events, we put out the word that we'd be accepting questions online. More than six thousand investors sent in their queries, and on the afternoon of March 13, 2008, I participated in a live webcast to provide answers and reassurance. I had good news: GE had averaged double-digit earnings and revenue growth over the previous five years, and our robust overseas sales would more than make up for the economic slowdown in the United States. As for GE Capital, I said what I knew to be true: it was strong and profitable. The turmoil in the financial markets, I said, wasn't cause for concern at GE. Instead, it was an opportunity to buy businesses on sale that would add value to GE's financial portfolio.

Just thinking about what happened next makes my stomach clench. Three days after my webcast, on March 16, the global investment bank Bear Stearns collapsed, overwhelmed by its exposure to mortgage-backed assets. The credit markets froze, and that would hurt GE.

GE Capital had been our most reliable performer for decades. Since financial assets are, under normal conditions, far more liquid than tangible assets, GE Capital could opportunistically sell them at a profit. But now its business model was under duress. Losses were growing, and it was harder to sell assets at a gain, which had been a normal practice for years.

In the wake of Bear Stearns's failure, finding willing buyers for those assets was nearly impossible. We lowered our earnings forecasts, but not enough. The result: when we announced first-quarter earnings on April 11, we fell short of expectations by $700 million. It was an unthinkable miss for GE, but—truth be told—the miss would've been even bigger if not for the hard work of our GE Capital team. They hustled to minimize our shortfall. That's why I can still smile when I think about arriving at a meeting soon after our earnings miss, only to discover that Jeff Bornstein, GE Capital's CFO, had strapped a football helmet to his head for protection.

Bornstein could be cantankerous—some felt he was blunt to a

fault—but I knew he was all in for GE. Born in a gritty mill town in Maine that was covered in snow for too much of the year, he'd joined the company right after graduating from Northeastern University, and he loved GE fiercely. Since I'm several inches taller, some people called us "Big Jeff" and "Little Jeff" (although Bornstein, who's ten years my junior, preferred "Jeff the Older" and "Jeff the Younger").

Anyway, when I walked in and saw Little Jeff girded for battle, I couldn't help but chuckle, and the whole room exploded in laughter. For a moment, it took the edge off. Bornstein's willingness to don headgear to poke fun at himself helped everyone remember that we were sticking together.

In contrast, I had a harder time chuckling six days later when we failed to deliver on those first-quarter forecasts, and Jack Welch went on CNBC, the GE-owned cable network, and threatened to kill me. I'm not kidding. Asked what he thought would happen if I ever missed our earnings again, he said, "I'd be shocked beyond belief, and I'd get a gun out and shoot him . . . Just deliver the earnings," he continued, aiming his comments directly at me. "Tell them you're going to grow twelve percent and deliver twelve percent."

Over more than a quarter century at GE, I'd been reamed countless times by Jack, but this time it really hurt. When you lead an organization the size of GE, you accumulate a lot of "friends in name only," but I hadn't thought Jack Welch was one of them. I remember Chad Holliday, the CEO of DuPont, called to offer me support during this period, as did others. Jack chose not to be a true friend.

I remember Jack's explosion on CNBC was on a Thursday. The next day, he called me, and for the first time ever, I addressed his less-than-perfect legacy head-on. "Following you has been no fun," I said. "I've kept my mouth shut about the problems you left me. I bolstered your legacy, when I could easily have shot it full of holes. And because I've done so, you are still 'Jack Welch, CEO of the Century.' But now, when I need your help, you stab me in the back? I just don't get it."

Jack was contrite in his way. "Look, I'm sorry," he said. "You fucked up, but I shouldn't have said what I said on air." I understood Jack's frustration—hell, I shared it. And I couldn't dispute another point he made on CNBC: that I had "a credibility issue." Missing your numbers three weeks after promising to make them was confusing to most people. No one wanted to hear technical jargon about the unforeseen vagaries in the credit market. But still, this felt personal to me. Jack knew better than anyone what a "bag of shit," as Sir George Simpson had put it, he'd given me to clean up. Jack also knew I'd never once pointed a finger at him, even when it would have made my life a lot easier. He later walked back his comments, calling me a "helluva CEO," but the damage had been done. This essentially ended our relationship because I'd finally realized that he was using his criticisms of me to promote his own brand. In the sixteen years I was CEO, Jack would appear on CNBC more than fifty times.

DARKNESS VISIBLE

The fact was, we had missed our numbers. The context, which had not yet become apparent, was that we were witnessing the dawn of the financial crisis. The truth was our liquidity problems were about to get much worse.

In April 2008, we got another inkling of darkness ahead. Lehman Brothers called, asking if GE might be interested in buying the global financial-services firm. I asked Jeff Bornstein and Mike Neal to take a look. They were unenthused. Nobody had forgotten what had happed in 1986, when Jack Welch bought the securities firm Kidder Peabody. Six years and two high-profile trading scandals later, GE couldn't wait to unload it, selling to Paine Webber. We weren't going to do that again.

Not long after we passed, though, the folks at Lehman called back, saying they were raising capital and wanted to issue some preferred equity. That meant they were selling a class of stock that promises a higher claim to dividends or asset distribution than common stock does. They were in trouble, though none of us at GE suspected how much. Again, there was no real reason for GE to get involved, but Lehman had been a longtime partner to us, and I wanted to help. In early summer, we bought $250 million of preferred stock from Lehman. Three weeks later, we sold it at a 20 percent markup. We are probably among the last entities to put money with Lehman that didn't come out the poorer for it.

By August 2008, the capital markets were schizophrenic. And then came September. The first week, the Treasury Department and the Federal Reserve decided to put Freddie Mac and Fannie Mae— the Federal Home Loan Mortgage Corporation and the Federal National Mortgage Association—into conservatorship. The second week, the Big Three automakers—GM, Chrysler, and Ford—asked Congress for a $50 billion bailout, and the Fed, worried that Merrill Lynch didn't have the liquidity to operate, pushed Bank of America to buy the struggling retail brokerage.

That merger was announced on Sunday, September 14. Inconveniently, Sherin had scheduled a leadership conference to begin that same evening. This was a gathering of GE's top three hundred finance leaders. We considered canceling—people were afraid—but I said no. Nothing says, "Time to panic!" more loudly than a canceled meeting. Besides, we felt safer together.

On Monday, September 15, Lehman Brothers filed for bankruptcy. The Dow Jones Industrial Average dropped 504 points. The insurance giant AIG's stock dropped 66 percent. Soon, the American economy would be in free fall.

As it happened, I was in Treasury Secretary Hank Paulson's office that Monday afternoon to talk about something else: GE's desire to repatriate cash reserves overseas without paying high penalties. Corporate tax rates in the United States, which were higher than those of other countries, had led global companies to stockpile profits abroad. But that effectively trapped it there, because to bring it back required paying the substantial difference between the foreign and US tax rates. I knew Paulson pretty well—we had both played football at Dartmouth, though ten years apart—and I knew that with a recession on the horizon, he'd see the benefit of encouraging US companies to bring home as much cash as they could. But that day, when I raised the issue, I found him understandably distracted.

"We're just going to let AIG go," he said at one point, meaning he intended not to bail out the insurance company. But crises breed pragmatism. Just a few hours later, Paulson changed his mind. He announced an $85 billion AIG bailout the very next day. I believe society benefited from that course correction, but my point is: these were days in which very little was certain, and circumstances were changing minute to minute.

An important aside: Later, Paulson wrote a memoir in which he erroneously stated that I had called on September 8 to tell him that GE's commercial paper operation was having trouble selling short-term debt and that I reiterated this point during our meeting on September 15. But Paulson, who had cautioned in his book that he was relying on date books that listed the participants in calls and meetings but not their subject matter, was mistaken. GE was not having any such problems at the time. My communications with Paulson in early to mid-September were about tax reform, which is why our tax director accompanied me to the latter meeting.

Paulson's mistake—which has been repeated in published accounts as recently as 2020—caused the US Securities and Exchange Commission to investigate a September 14 investor blast about GE's CP program. To set the record straight, our lawyers created a huge, multicolor exhibit laying out exactly what happened and when during the remarkable month of September 2008. The SEC subsequently closed the investigation without taking any action against GE.

SEPTEMBER 2008

SUNDAY	MONDAY	TUESDAY	WEDNESDAY	THURSDAY	FRIDAY	SATURDAY
	1	**2** WAM: 56.5 O/N LIBOR -8 CP Isc(d: 12.38b(O/N) + 1.6B(T)) = 13.9B	**3** WAM: 58.2 O/N LIBOR -9 CP Isc(d: 9.9B(O/N) + 1.0B(T)) = 10.9B · Central banks of industrialized nations on three continents cut interest rates and inject more than US $200B into global financial system	**4** WAM: 58.3 O/N LIBOR -9 CP Isc(d: 9.9B(O/N) + 0.6B(T)) = 10.6B · Treas and Fed decide to put Fannie and Freddie into Conservatorship	**5** WAM: 59.1 O/N LIBOR -10 CP Isc(d: 10.0B(O/N) + 1.4B(T)) = 11.4B · Meetings with OFHEO	**6** · Fannie and Freddie told that being put into Conservatorship
7 · Announcement of Conservatorship	**8** WAM: 57.4 O/N LIBOR -11 CP Isc(d: 9.6B(O/N) + 1.5B(T)) = 11.1B · Big 3 Autos seek $50B bailout · Paulson / Immelt Call	**9** WAM: 57.3 O/N LIBOR -10 CP Isc(d: 9.5B(O/N) + 0.9B(T)) = 10.5B · LB $3.9B 3Q loss	**10** WAM: 58.2 O/N LIBOR -10 CP Isc(d: 8.1B(O/N) + 1.3B(T)) = 9.8B · LB ↓ 45% · WaMu ↓ 20%	**11** WAM: 60.9 O/N LIBOR -9 CP Isc(d: 7.4B(O/N) + 3.0B(T)) = 10.5B · LB & AIG liquidity rumors	**12** WAM: 62.2 O/N LIBOR -9 CP Isc(d: 7.1B(O/N) + 1.5B(T)) = 8.6B	**13** · All day emergency at Fed · LB Firesale negotiations; Merrill Lynch under duress · Rumors about AIG & Morgan Stanley
14 · LB rescue efforts fail · BofA Merrill Lynch deal · GE Investor Blast; CP program "robust"	**15** WAM: 58.3 O/N LIBOR -34 CP Isc(d: 10.1B(O/N) + 1.4B(T)) = 11.5B · LB files for BK · Dow ↓ 504pts · AIG ↓ 66% · Paulson / Immelt meeting	**16** WAM: 59.6 O/N LIBOR -324 CP Isc(d: 13.5B(O/N) + 2.9B(T)) = 16.4B · $85B bailout of AIG · Reserve Fund "breaks buck"	**17** WAM: 60 O/N LIBOR -186 CP Isc(d: 11.3B(O/N) + 0.7B(T)) = 12.0B · Dow ↓ 449pts · Gold historic 1-day gain · 3-mo. T-bill goes negative · SEC bans naked shorts · MS ↓ 24% · GS ↓ 14% · MS & Wachovia start merger negotiations	**18** WAM: 58.3 O/N LIBOR -99 CP Isc(d: 12.1B(O/N) + 0.9B(T)) = 12.9B · UK & US ban short-selling financials · Paulson proposes TARP	**19** WAM: 61 O/N LIBOR -97 CP Isc(d: 9.8B(O/N) + 0.8B(T)) = 10.5B · AMLF announced · Treas guarantees money-market funds · US bans short-selling of 799 stocks	**20** · Bush proposes fund to buy $700B of toxic MBS
21 · GS & MS become bank holding companies	**22** WAM: 60.8 O/N LIBOR -62 CP Isc(d: 6.8B(O/N) + 1.0B(T)) = 9.8B	**23** WAM: 60.9 O/N LIBOR -86 CP Isc(d: 6.8B(O/N) + 0.8B(T)) = 9.5B · Goldman announces $5B Buffett infusion and equity offering	**24** WAM: 60.8 O/N LIBOR -115 CP Isc(d: 7.5B(O/N) + 0.4B(T)) = 7.9B	**25** WAM: 63 O/N LIBOR -104 CP Isc(d: 4.8B(O/N) + 2.5B(T)) = 7.3B · 8:30am - GE investor update · 3:15pm - WaMu seized; JP Morgan buys WaMu assets, $30B in debt wiped out · White House economic summit goes poorly; TARP in doubt · 8:51pm email: GE debtholders questioning if GE has done enough · LIBOR-OIS spreads ↑ 300bps	**26** WAM: 59.6 O/N LIBOR -73 CP Isc(d: 6.2B(O/N) + 1.0B(T)) = 7.2B · WaMu files Chapter 11 · $5B run on Wachovia; shares ↓ 27%; CDS doubles to 1560bps · MS CDS >1000bps · Wachovia ↓ 27%	**27** · Citigroup and Wells Fargo compete in firesale negotiations for Wachovia
28 · $16.3B bailout of Fortis in Belgium	**29** WAM: 57.3 O/N LIBOR -14 CP Isc(d: 9.2B(O/N) + 0.9B(T)) = 9.6B · UK seizes Bradford & Bingley · $50B bailout for Hypo Real Estate in Germany · Citigroup announces Wachovia deal · House votes down TARP · Dow ↓ >700pts, largest ever 1-day decline; $1T in market cap evaporates	**30** WAM: 55 O/N LIBOR -277 CP Isc(d: 11.4B(O/N) + 1.1B(T)) = 12.4B				

When I look at the calendar on page 129, I'm reminded of the debt that we owe Paulson, Geithner, Bernanke, and their teams for keeping it together through such a trying period to pull the world's economy back from the precipice. I use this calendar to give students in my business school classes a sense of the extraordinary, and unrelenting, events my colleagues and I were dealing with during this period.

| | | |

On September 16, I'd committed to be on a panel with former vice president Al Gore at Google's annual Zeitgeist conference, a two-day think-fest about global issues, whose guests included movie star Leonardo DiCaprio and Mexican businessman Carlos Slim. Early that Tuesday morning, my top communications guy, Gary Sheffer, and I flew out to Silicon Valley, and I was preparing to give my remarks when we got word that a multibillion money-market fund called the Reserve Primary Fund had "broken the buck"—that is, reported that a share's value was less than a dollar.

Money-market funds had long been considered as risk free as a bank savings account. But the Reserve Primary Fund, like many others, had a stake in debt securities issued by Lehman that were now essentially worthless. Dominos were starting to topple.

I'd been invited to Google to talk about GE's Ecomagination initiative, which I loved doing. Now, though, I was overcome by the need to get back to GE headquarters. Though we'd already flown three thousand miles, I told Sheffer we needed to cancel my speech and fly home. After some quick apologies, we flagged down our driver. But on the way to the airport, Sheffer wasn't happy. "You should not leave," he kept saying. "This isn't a meeting of some local chamber of commerce. This is Google. Lots of media. If you leave, people will know that you're terrified."

Our plane was readying for takeoff, and I was eager to get

going. But Sheffer was adamant that we should go back to Google. He called the conference organizers to ask if they could move my panel a few hours earlier. They said they could. At the same time, I called Keith Sherin, my CFO, who was trying to move his son into a dormitory at Northwestern University. I was only the latest person to blow up his phone. We commiserated briefly—the world was going crazy!—and then I asked Sherin: Should I stay or should I go?

"Stay put," he told me. "Exude calm." Even between trips hauling stuff to his son's new room, Sherin was doing just that, fielding calls from his own team, trying to steady their nerves. I wanted to argue that carrying luggage was easier than what he was urging me to do: delivering a speech about green business while the financial markets exploded. Sherin could hear how rattled I was.

Finally, I hung up and turned to Sheffer, who looked so tense he could've bitten a pencil in half. "You're right," I said. "I should stay and do this." And with that, Sheffer and I stepped off the plane, got into the car again, and drove back to Google.

A few hours later, when we were headed home to Connecticut, the television was tuned, as always, to CNBC. I asked the flight crew to turn it off. I couldn't bear to listen. Instead, I called Paulson and Tim Geithner, then the head of the Federal Reserve Bank of New York. Both said they were very worried about the commercial paper market. I told them GE wasn't seeing any cracks in its ability to sell its commercial paper, or CP.

When we touched down on the East Coast around 9 p.m., Sheffer and I headed straight to the office. Sherin and GE treasurer Kathy Cassidy were there, waiting for us. Between them, these two had better analytical abilities than the folks running many small countries, and a larger budget to crunch. If Cassidy was my rock, Sherin was GE's Swiss Army knife. He could get anything done.

"Okay," I asked the two of them, "what CP do we have to roll tomorrow?"

ROLLING PAPER

Rolling commercial paper was a key engine that enabled GE Capital's profit-making machine. We had a large CP program that averaged sixty-plus days maturity. We used this type of funding, along with some short-term one-year and two-year debt, to finance consumer credit cards and other receivables, dealer inventories, and assets that repriced frequently and had balances that could go up or down every day. As I've made clear, our triple-A rating enabled us to borrow money in all markets, both short-term and long-term, at very attractive rates—often nearly at the federal funds rate, which at that point was about 2 percent.

That wasn't the only borrowing GE Capital did. Our goal was to have our assets and our liabilities be "matched funded" to avoid taking interest rate risk. Here's what that meant: Unlike the banks, the majority of our debt was long-term. As we originated and held long-term, fixed-rate aircraft leases, or commercial real estate loans, or real estate equity, for example, we borrowed money in the long-term debt markets for three, five, ten, and even thirty years. That meant that overall, when you put our short- and long-term borrowing together, our interest rate margins—or the difference between what we charged borrowers versus what we paid to borrow money—were very stable and predictable.

But now the seizing up of the credit markets had begun to raise our borrowing costs. Over the next two weeks, instead of paying 2 percent on the commercial paper we issued, we would pay as much as 3.5 percent to borrow beyond sixty days. People still wanted to lend to us—to buy our CP—because GE was triple-A rated, and the banks were just single-A. Still, it was becoming clear we had way too much short-term debt: $90 billion.

During this time, we were all working weekends, and every Sunday, a guy named H. Rodgin Cohen would come to the GE offices in Fairfield to sit down at our big round conference table with us, spitballing various options for our survival. "Rodge," as we called him, was a corporate lawyer known for his command of banking law. We saw him as our resident wise man—at once wonky and creative. At one point, we batted around the idea of selling our private-label credit card business—which served customers who shopped at stores like Walmart and JCPenney—to JPMorgan for $3 billion. (Thankfully, that idea fell through; we'd later spin it off into something called Synchrony Financial, which now has a $30 billion market cap.) We talked about cutting loose GE Capital from GE, but that would have risked putting the finance arm, which relied on Big GE for funding, into bankruptcy. We also spent many an hour with Rodge considering the pros and cons of GE becoming a bank holding company, but the Fed shot that down. Again, that was probably for the best.

We had often discussed how big we should let our commercial paper program get. When making acquisitions, it's easy to let that part of your finance structure grow, because you need the money. But CP is supposed to be a safe investment. When people got worried about liquidity, even GE's CP seemed vulnerable. Looking back, I realize we'd made a mistake in the way we were looking at the CP issue overall. We were pleased that our CP was just 15 percent of our debt load, which was exactly what the ratings agencies wanted it to be to maintain our triple-A rating. But 15 percent of a very large number is a very large number. At times, we'd failed to contextualize our own aggregate size.

"LET'S GET THE MONEY"

Throughout all this, I felt lucky to have Kathy Cassidy in her position. Since I'd promoted her in 2001, she'd proven herself a strong leader with great relationships inside and outside the company. Thanks to her prodding, I'd forged inroads with the ratings agencies we depended on for our AAA status, and even before the crisis, she'd lobbied to rein in our CP. She was smart, strategic, and dedicated. In July 2008, just two months before Lehman's fall, her husband had died of an aneurysm at just fifty-four years old. The youngest of their three sons was still a junior in high school. And yet she committed herself to handling GE's crisis alongside her family's own.

Every morning during this period, Cassidy was in the office at 7 a.m. to meet with her team. Their goal was to track precisely which of our debts were maturing and what debts needed extending that day. At 7:30 a.m., like clockwork, she'd get a call from Jimmy Lee, the influential vice chairman at JPMorgan Chase, fishing for information. In his pin-striped suits and cuff links, Lee was a throwback—more consigliere than banker—whose deep relationships fueled his deal making. But he was also hugely creative, and he saw GE Capital, the largest CP issuer in the market, as a leading indicator.

"Are you going to have a problem in the CP market today?" he'd ask, to which Cassidy would reply: "No, Jimmy, we're fine. Don't worry."

Then the CP markets would open, and she'd roll GE's paper, trading our money-market securities for cash that we'd then use to meet our short-term debt obligations. Several hours later, she'd call to tell me how we'd done. Each day, that call felt like being granted a twenty-four-hour stay of execution. Never did I hang up thinking, "We're out of the woods for good." I knew this was a day-by-day endeavor. To calm myself, I began taking showers in the little bathroom attached to my office. At some point every single day, I'd tell my secretary to hold my calls so I could stand under the pounding hot water, trying to relax.

On the morning of September 25, Sherin and I did an investor update. "Are you going to do an equity raise?" someone asked. I believed that we were in good shape. We had a lot of cash. Our CP was trading. So I answered: "We don't think so. We feel very secure." But our institutional investors weren't reassured. That night, Cassidy forwarded me an email from one of them, sent at 8:51 p.m. "What you guys announced has not put out the fire," it said. "Our bondholders are freaking out."

The next day—Friday, September 26—Washington Mutual, which had been placed into receivership the previous day, filed for bankruptcy, and Morgan Stanley looked like it might have to do the same. To me, this was the most catastrophic day—the one that made clear how huge a crisis we were in. After WaMu's bankruptcy filing, there was a $5 billion run on Wachovia Bank, whose shares dropped 27 percent. This was terrible news for us. Entities that owned GE's debt tended to buy insurance in the form of credit default swaps. Now our credit default swaps were blowing out—when the owners of our CP tried to buy insurance, it was either unavailable or very expensive.

That's when Goldman Sachs called Sherin. They wanted to meet that night, they said, to urge us to consider doing something that, less than twenty-four hours earlier, I'd said we wouldn't do: a public offering.

I'll never forget the look on Sherin's face when he came into my office around 5 p.m. to tell me what the folks at Goldman had just said: that we needed to raise equity. I pushed back, but Sherin was insistent, and I had to listen to him. Sherin had a "true voice," by which I mean he always put the company first, without regard to his own ego. If he was concerned, I knew I needed to be, too. A few hours later, we met with the Goldman team and sketched out a plan.

On Saturday morning, I headed to the office and got the members of GE's board on a conference call. As best I could, I summarized how treacherous and unknowable the environment had suddenly become for GE. We needed to raise at least $15 billion, I told the board, and we needed to start right away. There was dead silence on the other end of the phone that felt like it would never end. Finally, Roger Penske—the auto racing magnate who was always one of my favorite GE board members—spoke. "Let's go get the money," he said, and the rest of the board quickly agreed. How audacious was the task we were about to undertake? Here's some context: Just a few months before, in March 2008, Visa had staged the largest stock offering in history, raising $18 billion. But they'd spent months preparing for that equity raise. We didn't have months. We had days.

FISHING FOR AN ANCHOR

We needed an anchor investor, someone whose participation would encourage others to follow suit. Ideally, we needed Warren Buffett, the legendary stock-picker from Omaha. I'd met Buffett several times, but I didn't reach out to him myself because I knew he preferred to do business through the one banker he trusted—Byron Trott, Goldman's vice chairman of investment banking. The previous week, Trott, who shared Buffett's Midwestern roots and no-nonsense affect, had gotten Buffett to bolster a struggling Goldman Sachs with a $5 billion infusion. Now we asked if he would approach Buffett on behalf of GE.

Initially, we'd planned to launch our equity raise with or without Buffett on a Sunday night, September 28. So all that day, my team had been at work in Fairfield, meeting with our lawyers and others to get ready. We had to launch at 7 p.m. (Monday morning Asia time), but at about six thirty, I told everyone I needed a moment to think. Exiting the first-floor auditorium, where fifty or so internal GE folks and external advisers gathered, I headed to my third-floor office and reviewed what we knew. There were rumblings that the proposed Troubled Asset Relief Program, or TARP, was facing congressional opposition. That would make it hard to raise equity. It seemed risky. But delaying felt dangerous, too.

I knew everyone was waiting for me to give the green light, so I headed back downstairs. Passing a restroom along the way, all I wanted to do was slip inside, lock myself in a stall, and never come out. But I kept walking, and by the time I rejoined my colleagues, I'd decided: we would delay our launch.

The next day—Monday, September 29—the House refused to pass TARP, and the Dow dropped more than seven hundred points, which was then the largest-ever one-day decline. Seven European banks announced they were going into bankruptcy. Had we launched as planned, we would have gotten crushed.

On Tuesday, September 30, Trott was working on Buffett, laying out what we were hoping for and how Buffett stood to gain, but it was unclear whether he would agree. Early the next morning, October 1, my team gathered in the conference room that adjoined my office— the one where that bronzed bag of money that the Plastics team had given me sat on a shelf. Trott was due to call Buffett at his Omaha home at 8 a.m. our time. All we could do was hope.

The mood was tense as we waited for word. "If Buffett says no, we're fucked," Sherin said, resting his forehead on his arms on the table in front of him. Sheffer would later recall the scene in equally graphic terms: "Everybody in the room needed a new set of pants."

Finally, at 8:30 a.m., my phone rang. It was John Weinberg, a Goldman Sachs executive who worked with Trott, with good news: Buffett had agreed to invest $3 billion of Berkshire Hathaway money in return for a new issue of preferred stock and warrants allowing Berkshire to buy an equal amount of common stock over the next five years. I took a deep breath, got up from the table, and stepped next door into my office. I wanted to thank Buffett personally. When I got him on the phone, I kept it short. "Thanks, Warren," I said. "We won't let you down."

It's amazing how many competing sensations and emotions you can feel in a single moment. Gratitude. Weariness. And yes, fear. As we prepared to announce Buffett's investment, hurriedly writing a press release, there was another setback. Before 11 a.m., an analyst at Deutsche Bank announced he was sharply cutting his forecast for GE's 2008 profits. Our stock dropped 9 percent in a flash.

Just before two o'clock that day, we released the news of Buffett's support and said we'd sell $12 billion of common stock to the public, beginning right away. "I am confident that GE will continue to be successful in the years to come," Buffett said in a statement. Now we just had to get a lot of others to agree with him. The rest of Wednesday was spent running from office to office, calling sovereign wealth funds like the United Arab Emirates's Mubadala and mutual funds like Fidelity, talking to anyone who might be willing to buy. It was like an extended episode of *Dialing for Dollars*.

I'll never forget the conference call in the wee hours of Thursday morning, October 2, between my team and Weinberg and David Solomon of Goldman Sachs, who'd orchestrated the raise for us. "Hey, guys, we made it," Solomon said. "We got the money we needed," added Weinberg. We'd raised $15 billion in a little more than twenty-four hours.

The next day, President George W. Bush signed TARP, which had finally been passed by Congress, into law. Maybe, I thought, we'd get a little break. I was right, but it wouldn't last long.

THE KILLER CHART

Mid-October, I was in Crotonville for a GE officers meeting. As people found their seats, TVs around the room blared the headlines on CNBC. That's when everyone learned that the FDIC was going to launch something called the Temporary Liquidity Guarantee Program. The idea was to create an insurance policy, in effect, to allow banks to issue debt and raise cash. There would now be a commercial paper buyback facility, also guaranteed by the federal government. You might think this had nothing to do with GE. As I've said, our finance arm, GE Capital, wasn't a bank, so it didn't fall under FDIC's purview. And besides, up to that point, we'd had no problem selling our CP.

Now that the TLGP was a reality, though, the costs to GE became clear: by leaving us out of the program, the government effectively made our long-term debt worthless. It's not that anyone thought GE couldn't make good on its debts. It's that no one in their right mind would buy GE's debt when the debt being sold by banks had a government guarantee (and GE's didn't). Two things began to happen: (1) it became harder to get anyone to lend us money, and (2) our borrowing costs began to skyrocket. While GE didn't have a liquidity crisis, it looked as if these new programs were about to cause one for us.

The ramifications for us were frightening. We needed to make a strong case that GE Capital, though not a bank, should be covered under the new federal facilities that protected banks. It was that, or we'd be out of business. The message we needed to convey was simple: we're bigger, and more essential to the US economy, than most of the banks you're trying to protect.

Jeff Bornstein and a few others composed a one-page document that we nicknamed "the Killer Chart." It gave a snapshot of the critical lending segments in which GE Capital did business and showed its market position in each. Aircraft Financing? Number one. Equipment Lending/Leasing? Number one. Fleet Leasing, Healthcare Financing, Private-Label Credit Cards? All number one. The list went on and on. GE Capital was among the top-three commercial real estate lenders in the country. It was a leader in bankruptcy financing and energy infrastructure. GE Capital was also the largest lender for farm machinery and for trucking. These were Main Street, mom-and-pop businesses. "GE CAPITAL," the Killer Chart declared in big bold letters. "Continuing to provide liquidity to critical areas of the economy."

I had this ammunition in my pocket when I got on a plane for Washington, DC. GE's general counsel Brackett Denniston came with me. Our first stop: Paulson's office on the third floor of the Treasury's Fifteenth Street headquarters. I knew Hank was impatient by nature, and I knew how exhausted he must be. He had just ten minutes for us, but he listened closely to my pitch.

"I know you've got a thousand shit burgers on your hands, but you've got to think about the customers of the products we finance," I said. "We keep everyone from airlines to small business owners in business." When I handed him a copy of the Killer Chart, he read it over and nodded like he understood. I was heartened when he offered to place a call to Sheila Bair, the head of the FDIC, asking her to meet with us.

A few minutes later, we were heading down to the first floor of the Treasury to visit David Nason, Paulson's assistant secretary for Treasury Financial Institutions, when Denniston spotted Paulson in the hallway. He had the Killer Chart in his hand. Another good sign.

Right away we headed over to visit Bair at the FDIC, which occupies a mausoleum-like building on Seventeenth Street, just a few blocks away. It was late—almost eight o'clock at night—but she was still there. When we presented ourselves at her office, however, a deputy came out and said she had no time for us.

"We're not going anywhere," I said. "We'll wait." With a glance, the deputy sized me up: the look on my face said I wasn't leaving voluntarily, and at 240 pounds, I'd be difficult to force out the door. So he let us stay.

For more than an hour, we scuffed our shoes in the FDIC lobby. There was a janitor buffing the floor nearby, and the sound echoed through the hallways of that old Washington tomb. When Bair finally invited us in, it was clear she wasn't wild about GE's proposal. But we made our best case. Our argument wasn't that Bair should feel sorry for us. It was that punishing us would prove disastrous for the economy.

"The banks aren't going to tell you this, because they'd love to see us go away, but GE keeps the economy moving," I said. When Bair asked hard questions, I just kept stressing the broad role GE Capital played in the day-to-day business of innumerable companies, large and small, all over the nation. I explained that we'd been helping Big GE investors with their cash flow, even allowing them to redeem their CP early at times. But the government's new programs were making it impossible for us to continue these buybacks.

"People are coming to us," I said, "because there's nobody else out there who can help. If you don't help us continue to do it, how are these guys going to survive?"

The meeting was over quickly, and we left unsure where we stood. But on our way back to the airport, Paulson called. "We're going to get this done," he said. Hank understood that it was in nobody's interest for GE to falter.

Over the coming days, we did a bit of horse-trading, telling federal regulators, "Look, since we are one of the biggest issuers of CP, if we say we're going to use this facility that you're creating, that will be a powerful endorsement. No one will be afraid to use it." In other words, GE could give the TLGP instant credibility. It took three weeks, but eventually, the FDIC modified the program to crack the door for us.

I'm really proud to be able to say that GE kept its word to the regulators, and then some. And in contrast to some banks, which reneged on commitments to mid-market private-equity firms during the financial crisis, we funded every commitment and met every obligation. We were tough lenders, but reliable. I like to tell the story of Elkhart, Indiana, which is the center of the country's mobile home industry. Throughout the crisis, we were the only lender that kept financing mobile homes, and Elkhart never forgot it. Years later, they even threw a party to thank GE for keeping their business alive. I was invited, and I happily went. These kinds of heartland businesses were a key part of what GE was about, and we were honored to have played a role in their survival.

STEPPING INTO LIQUID

As we'd promised we would, we used the TLGP a lot—I think in all we tapped $130 billion of loan guarantees. This is often mischaracterized, though, in the retelling. Just the other day, I read an article that said GE Capital was so strapped during this period that we had to borrow money from the Fed. That's become the narrative (despite the fact that GE Capital never had an unprofitable quarter). But that narrative is wrong. The Fed never handed us any money. When we funded debt, they offered a backstop (and charged us a fee). We used those backstops in part to help ourselves, yes, but also to legitimize the programs they'd created that we believed would get America back on solid footing. And here's a little-reported fact: GE was also the first to exit those programs.

The architects of the TLGP and other monetary policies put in place during this period—Paulson, Bair, Geithner, and his soon-to-be successor Bill Dudley, who would become president of the Federal

Reserve Bank of New York in January 2009, and Ben Bernanke, the chairman of the US Federal Reserve—deserve a lot of credit. The programs were genius because they provided an incentive for entities to lend money to people who needed it, and that incentive validated the capital markets. That, in turn, enabled GE Capital to do its part. I remember a deal we did in January 2009—a thirty-year financing for $5 billion—that effectively reopened the markets for everybody. Frankly, we shamed the banks into getting back into the lending business. So we kept our promise to the Fed.

Still, for anyone in finance, living through the global financial crisis was like having the stomach flu for eighteen straight months. At GE, it was even worse. No team had ever taken a financial-industrial conglomerate through anything like 2008 and 2009. Like the banks, we were facing an existential threat. But unlike the banks, GE also had a lot of other pressing issues that could not be ignored or delayed. We had to fund the next generation of jet engines, for example. We had to reposition our power business in the Middle East and Asia. We had to get NBC News ready to cover a new administration, as President Barack Obama took office. We had to sell gas turbines in Iraq. We had to continue supporting our customers all over the world and to invest in our Healthcare, Renewable Energy, and Oil & Gas businesses to prepare them for the future.

In 2008, I'd committed to take six trips to meet customers with Nabil Habayeb, who runs GE's division in the Middle East, North Africa, and Turkey. Even amid the chaos I've just described, I took those trips. My reasoning was that the best way to counter bad news is to create good news. At one point I remember telling Gary Sheffer, my communications chief, that I wanted GE to be issuing at least one press release every day. If GE sold an ultrasound machine in Qatar, I wanted the world to know. Even as the globe's financial underpinnings threatened to crumble, we were trying to create our own momentum. Between September 2001 and the end of 2008, my team had managed to reshape GE's business portfolio, changing what we owned by almost 40 percent as we continued to try to build value. We were making progress, against all odds.

CUTTING THE DIVIDEND

As the calendar turned to 2009, the focus turned to GE Capital's balance sheet, which many felt needed to shrink (translation: we still had too much debt). The ratings agencies were considering downgrading us. And there was something else, too: I was completely fried. Every day on the business pages of the nation's newspapers, GE Capital and its impact on the parent company was being analyzed like bacteria under a microscope. Would we cut GE's dividend? Or would we pay it, and risk losing our coveted AAA rating, which required a significant amount of cash on hand to maintain? Everyone had an opinion. The scrutiny was no more intense than usual, probably. But I was exhausted, so my tolerance for it was waning. I'm a stress eater—salty, crunchy snacks give me comfort. Now, months of eating too many cheddar Goldfish crackers had made me heavier than ever. I remember opening my closet one morning to find just one suit I could squeeze into.

At the end of 2008, we'd built a business plan, approved by the GE board, that allowed us to maintain its annual dividend in 2009. On January 24, I announced that plan: GE would pay $1.24 a share. If necessary, we'd cut the dividend in 2010, but I hoped it wouldn't come to that. The retirees who relied on GE dividend payments weren't an abstraction to me—my parents were among them. I couldn't bear the idea that a dividend cut would happen on my watch. We'd paid a stock dividend since 1899 and cut it only once, in 1938.

In February, however, when I met again with the GE board, they weren't happy. Our stock, which had been at forty dollars the previous summer, had fallen to just over nine dollars. Our stock had become a favorite for hedge funds, and that was causing wild swings in our share price. Every day, the noise around the company got louder: Would this be the day the dividend would get cut? It was killing us.

There was much discussion around the boardroom table. After about forty-five minutes of spirited debate, Ralph Larsen, our presiding director, turned to me. "We're going to cut the dividend. We're going to do it now," he said gravely. "If we don't, it'll be in the press every day: 'Will they or won't they?' We have to cut the dividend. That's just the way it is."

I'd been overruled, and I remember feeling an odd combination of disappointment and gratitude. I respected Larsen, who'd built Johnson & Johnson into a multinational giant. He had all the wisdom and leadership traits of Jack Welch, but he was low ego. Hearing his decision, I was like a cub getting my ears boxed by an elder lion. I knew Larsen was right. Unwittingly, I had been fighting to protect my own ego. No matter how dire the extenuating circumstances, no matter how much people kept telling me it wasn't my fault, I didn't want to be the CEO who cut GE's storied dividend for the first time since the Great Depression.

Sometime in this period, I reached out to Dennis "Triple D" Dammerman, the former CFO who'd recruited me to GE and who'd been such a rock for me during 9/11. He'd retired in 2005, but we'd kept in touch, and now I just needed someone to talk to. A few minutes into the call, however, Triple D abruptly interjected, "This reminds me of Mexico's 1994 currency crisis." I was stunned. The Mexican central bank's sudden decision to devalue the peso and raise interest rates had serious consequences, for sure, but it was a walk in the park compared to what we were dealing with. I realized that even my smartest friends couldn't relate to what we were going through because they hadn't seen tail risk before. I hung up feeling lonelier than ever.

I'm glad to say that my next call for help yielded better results. Despite Jack Welch's public excoriation of me on CNBC a year earlier, I felt this was a time to seek his guidance. I didn't have the luxury of holding a grudge. We chewed on the issues together, weighing the potential fallout of me reversing myself for the second time in six months. Finally, Jack said something classically Welchian: "Jeff, you can go back on your word and be a smart guy or be a consistent dumb guy, okay?"

So I did the "smart" thing. But I felt like the company's pride—and my own—had been shattered. The three years from 2006 through 2008 had been a record for GE's industrial businesses, whose performance had been through the roof. Nonetheless, I announced in February that I was declining my bonus—more than $12 million. I'd always said that my compensation should reflect the financial performance of the company, and I'd meant it.

I also considered resigning.

I remember Gary Sheffer and I were in a cab in New York City when I told him. It was unseasonably hot, and the taxi had its windows down—the driver said they were broken and couldn't be rolled up. "I want you to get ready," I said, as the air whipped around us. "Once we cut the dividend, I'm stepping down." I was just so shaken by the feeling of failure. But Sheffer wasn't having it. "This isn't your fault," he said flatly. "You're not resigning. And don't ever say that again to anybody."

On February 27, 2009, before the stock market opened, we had a call with the entire GE board to approve cutting the dividend to ten cents from thirty-one cents. The market looked choppy, so the board wanted to wait to announce the decision. Unfortunately, someone leaked the news that we were considering the cut to David Faber, the cohost of CNBC's morning show *Squawk on the Street*, who posted a story midmorning. Now we had the worst of both worlds: we were paying the price for doing something we had yet to even do. I pushed the board, and they voted to approve the cut that day. The decision would save us nearly $9 billion.

But even that wouldn't be enough to preserve our rating. Just two weeks later, Standard & Poor's downgraded us one notch, to AA+. In March, the stock closed at a low of $6.66 a share. We knew we had to fight back in public.

Communication at this level, in these kinds of crises, is rarely easy. The media covered the tragedy of 9/11 respectfully and accu-

rately. But by the time the global financial crisis occurred, specula-
tors were manipulating the media to make money. Here's how: they
were shorting our stock, buying credit default swaps, and then calling
CNBC or Fox Business to float the notion that our company was in
trouble. I knew that during a crisis, the media will sometimes get it
wrong. I also knew we couldn't counter inaccuracies—neither fac-
tual errors nor contextual ones—with silence. We had to seize our
own narrative.

First, I did a grueling interview with Charlie Rose at a CEO conference hosted by JPMorgan. He showed up with several clips from
the *Wall Street Journal* that were saturated with yellow highlighter,
and he put me through my paces, but I think I held my own.

On the same day, Keith Sherin did a forty-five-minute interview
on CNBC to dispel false rumors that some of the more unscrupulous
hedge funds were spreading about GE Capital. He nailed it. Finally,
Mike Neal and Jeff Bornstein led a megameeting for investors and
analysts to try to calm the panic. Neal carefully laid out where we
were—and what we were doing about it—before a live audience of
about 250, with 300 more listening via telephone. It took eight hours.

Together, these three back-to-back performances put us on
firmer footing. It was a triumph of transparency.

I often have noted that when 9/11 happened, as awful as it was,
you knew all the key facts more or less by noon: how many people
had died, how many buildings were destroyed, even who did it. During the financial crisis, by contrast, it often felt like you knew nothing
about anything. And that not-knowing lasted for years. By the end,
we had all learned what tail risk looked like.

This wouldn't be my last tail-risk event. Just one year later, during the BP oil spill, I'd draw on some of the lessons I'd learned in
2008 and 2009. And in 2011, after the Tohoku earthquake let loose
a tsunami upon Japan that overtopped the seawall at the Fukushima
Daiichi nuclear plant, whose six active reactors had been designed by
GE, I would do so again. But looking back on these events, I see the
financial crisis as the most challenging, in part because it demanded

such a sustained response. I'm gratified to be able to say our best teamwork happened then, in the eight or so months after Lehman Brothers went bankrupt. Why? Because every decision had huge consequences. And because we had to act decisively, often without a clear picture of what was going on.

Here's what the financial crisis taught me: some people point fingers in a crisis, others solve problems, and there's very little overlap between these two groups. In a blaming culture, people stop working in order to cover their own asses. If you can nurture an ethos of "all for one and one for all," it can save your bacon. Good people will stand alongside you in a righteous fight. When you have a strong team, you can weather any crisis. Without that, you are lost.

I learned that in a crisis, leaders must fight for their companies' reputations. Sometimes lawyers and publicists will warn a CEO, "Don't sound defensive! Don't listen to your critics!" Leaders can't let lies and half-truths calcify, and they shouldn't let their team's narrative be irreversibly tarnished. There are plenty of people who can profit from a bad story about you. Leaders own their truth, particularly in a crisis.

Many people will compare the global financial crisis to the COVID-19 pandemic of 2020. But to my mind, the events of September 2008 will always take the prize for sheer economic intensity. In 2020, the government rolled out several relief programs quickly. Not so twelve years earlier, when the federal response was slower because the role of the government in backstopping the economy was being completely redefined, one day at a time. Moreover, the entire global financial-services sector was restructured, leaving no institution untouched.

And then there was this: in the financial crisis, anyone in the financial-services sector was seen as the villain. So if you did business there, you were fighting for your company's survival while also being flogged in the court of public opinion. By contrast, during the pandemic, people had their choice of villains—President Xi? President Trump? The World Health Organization?—but no one blamed any one sector of the economy for the world's suffering.

CHAPTER 6

Leaders Make Big Companies Small

"Does Tina Fey care about this?"

It was 2006 when I put that question to Lorne Michaels. The longtime producer and creator of *Saturday Night Live* had called to seek my support for a new series he was executive producing called *30 Rock*. That year NBC was launching not one but two new programs focusing on the off-camera lives of the people who run a live sketch-comedy show. The one Michaels was backing starred and was written by Fey, who was just coming off a terrific run on SNL. But the other show—a drama called *Studio 60 on the Sunset Strip*—was more highly anticipated because its creator was Aaron Sorkin, the man who'd made the Oval Office sexy on *The West Wing*.

I remember *Studio 60* debuted with a brilliant pilot that featured an homage to Sidney Lumet's film *Network*—an embattled showrunner melting down on live television. *Studio 60* had strong ratings out of the gate, while *30 Rock* gained fans slowly. Michaels rarely lobbied me on programming decisions. But now he told me that if NBC didn't give *30 Rock* the time it needed to build an audience, we'd regret it. "Tina is fully committed," he told me. "This is going to be a showcase for her. I promise you: GE will always be proud of this show."

To this day, on the rare occasions that I see Michaels, we laugh about what happened next. In 2007, after *Studio 60*'s ratings plummeted (and its production budgets soared), NBC made the decision to cancel it. By contrast, *30 Rock* would stay on the air for seven seasons, winning eleven Primetime Emmy Awards. Michaels had been right: GE was and will always be proud that one of its subsidiaries put *30 Rock* on the air. The reason we laugh, though, is that from the get-go, Fey's alter ego Liz Lemon and her fictional colleagues mercilessly mocked GE.

The show loved to make fun of GE's reliance on acronyms (a side effect of our Six Sigma processes) and of Six Sigma itself (they mocked its key tenets as "teamwork, insight, brutality, male enhancement, hand-shakefulness, and play hard.") At one point, Jack Donaghy, the GE vice president of East Coast Television and Microwave Oven Programming, played by Alec Baldwin, explained that when seeking employees to mentor, he looked for "the Drive and ambition to be worth my time, the Intelligence to understand the challenges they're going to face, the Humility to accept my help, and, finally, a life that is a bottomless swamp of Chaos." In other words: DIHC (pronounced, well, you get the idea).

No matter how innovative or forward-looking, no GE initiative was ever safe from *30 Rock*. Just as we were launching Ecomagination, Baldwin's character announced a company-wide environmental initiative complete with a spandex-clad green mascot named Greenzo. ("Saving the earth while maintaining profitability! The free market will solve global warming—if that even exists!" Greenzo, played by *Friends'* David Schwimmer, proclaimed proudly, describing GE as "America's first non-judgmental business-friendly environmental advocate.")

GE not only endured the ribbing; we welcomed it. Sometimes the show's writers would even reach out to my communications team for help identifying obscure products they could write jokes about. I've said that I always looked for ways to make GE seem younger and less uptight. In 2013, when *30 Rock* went off the air in a double-episode finale, GE created a TV ad to air during the show. "GE thanks *30 Rock* for seven years of making us laugh," the voice-over said.

The ad was especially notable because by then GE no longer owned NBCUniversal. In 2011, we'd sold 51 percent to Comcast, the nation's largest cable provider (which *30 Rock* would also mock, calling it Kabletown). For GE to raise the cash it needed to emerge— not unscathed, but still standing—from the financial crisis, I felt I had no choice but to sell the Peacock network, its sister movie studio, and everything that went with it.

FACING REALITY

After Lehman Brothers went bankrupt, I knew it presaged not just the beginning of a down cycle for GE but the destruction of our business model. GE Capital was a large, debt-funded finance company whose need for a cash buffer was a serious drag on Big GE. More and more, I realized that we needed to unwind GE Capital, which might take a decade. However long it took, we'd surely be second-guessed.

The criticism started right away. The US Treasury Department was hammering out new rules for financial institutions that would eventually become the Dodd-Frank Wall Street Reform and Consumer Protection Act. In May or June 2009, Tim Geithner, President Barack Obama's new Treasury secretary, released his first draft, and it contained directives that—while they didn't mention GE by name—seemed aimed straight at us. Geithner strongly implied that going forward, big financial institutions would not be allowed to have an industrial arm. Well, there were no big financial-services companies, other than GE, that had industrial arms. He was describing an island of one! It would have been funny, except for the fear Geithner's words instilled in me. Our stock dropped 7 percent.

Why was this so chilling? Because it indicated that the government might seriously seek to force GE to carve out GE Capital into a separate business. Early 2009 had felt like a near-death experience. But this latest scenario, as hinted at by Geithner, truly threatened our future. To spin GE Capital off, we'd need to back it up with $30 or $40 billion in cash (that, or not honor our debt, forcing bondholders to restructure their debt into equity).

Nobody wants to burn the furniture to heat the house. But in the dead of winter, even a favorite armchair starts to look like kindling. NBCU had always been an outlier within GE. For as long as we'd owned the TV network (and, later, the movie studio and parks), there were those who felt that alongside our industrial core, our entertainment holdings brought to mind that song the Muppets sang on *Sesame Street*—"One of these things is not like the others. One of these things just doesn't belong." I'd always enjoyed the people at NBCU, and for years, that had made up for the lack of many obvious synergies. But the financial crisis made NBCU a luxury we could no longer afford.

Ever since I'd become CEO, I'd fielded offers for our entertainment assets, but I'd been disinclined to sell them because doing so would have shrunk our industrial base, making financial services an even bigger gorilla within GE. Now, though, we put out the word that NBCU was for sale. We attracted several suitors, including News Corp and Time Warner. Because I knew the media industry revolved around pricing, however, I believed the cable operators, who controlled distribution, had the most leverage. So I favored the biggest one: Comcast. In December 2009, we announced we would sell them the company. The deal, which would play out in two transactions over four years, valued NBCU at $30 billion. When the first phase of the deal closed, GE pocketed $16 billion.

Many critics would say that Comcast got the better of the deal. In retrospect, I agree with them. But back then, it was all about protecting the future—we needed more cash. As I've said, NBCU under GE had a deep bench of talented executives, and I'm proud to say that many of them are still running media companies. Today Donna Langley is still at NBCUniversal, as chairperson, as are most other members of the film division brain trust that was there in our day. On the TV side, Randy Falco went on to run AOL and Univision, David Zaslav became CEO of Discovery, Inc., and Zucker is president of CNN Worldwide and chairman of WarnerMedia News & Sports.

RETAINING THE BEST

As we sold NBCU to raise cash, I was worried GE might be vulnerable in another way. Could we lose our best employees? Our reputation had been dinged. Our stock price had hit bottom, and it would be a long way back. It would take a while to reposition GE Capital and we needed everyone to hang in there. Now more than ever, we needed our employees to feel connected to one another, and to GE.

But when I reflected on the financial meltdown, I began to wonder if GE's connectivity was on the fritz. Was there something in the way we'd managed our people that had caused us to miss warning signs? What if there were GE people who could've helped us avoid disaster, but who didn't have the opportunities (or the personalities) to share it with me or with my leadership team? Was there someone in the company who was thinking, "You know, Jeff, we have way too much debt," but couldn't find the right forum to express it?

My team and I decided to take action to rebuild what you might call GE's psychic momentum. One goal, which we worked hard on, was to reduce the complexity of our bureaucracy. Another was to expand our education curriculum, designing training programs for our uppermost executives to reinvigorate them, and to make it easier for them to lean on one another. In these dark days, I believed that if we invested in our people, and made them feel valued, they would continue to give us their all.

I knew that the higher you rise within a company, the more difficult it is to see what's going on beneath you. People don't like to tell their boss terrible news. They don't want to complain or to look bad. They don't want to risk seeming stupid by asking what may be perceived to be ignorant questions. Especially at big companies, CEOs can easily live in a bubble. The best managers figure out ways to draw the truth out of those who report to them. One thing I found always worked well was to bring in outside speakers—business leaders like Ken Chenault from American Express or Marc Benioff from Salesforce.com, politicians like Rahm Emanuel, military commanders like Stanley McChrystal— and then throw out a general query: "Okay, what did we learn tonight?

What did you all think of what he or she said?" It sounds simple, but the introduction of an outside voice got people talking.

There was something else on my mind, too. The financial crisis had reminded me how wrenchingly lonely the job of leadership is. Feeling responsible for the livelihoods of three hundred thousand people and their families could be overwhelming. Seeing the company get trashed in the media really hurt. I was mentally exhausted and needed to get energized again.

So I decided to spend more time connecting one-on-one to our senior leaders. Once a month, on a Friday, I'd invite one of GE's senior leaders and his or her spouse or partner to come have dinner with me and Andy in New Canaan, Connecticut, where we lived. The idea was to break the ice with a good meal just as two couples, raising a glass together at the end of a long week. We always went to the same restaurant, Cava, a casual Italian place about ten minutes from our house. We'd order pappardelle and salmon and get to know each other a bit through organic conversation about hobbies, travel, children, world events—anything but GE.

Then on Saturday morning, the leader and I would reconvene just the two of us at my office to talk for four or five hours about their careers, their insights into their businesses, their aspirations, their thoughts about GE. There was no strict format. I wanted to hear their voices, their ideas, their dissent.

IT STARTS WITH YOU

Monish Patolawala was a brilliant finance guy from India. He'd graduated from college in Bangalore, then did a stint at the accounting giant KPMG before joining GE. When we had our weekend together, he was the CFO of a GE locomotive production plant in Erie, Pennsylvania. Before we sat down, I remember being struck that the feedback from his colleagues was resoundingly negative. People described Patolawala as a hammer—way too demanding. "He's setting standards that are too high," read a typical note. But halfway through our Saturday morning together, I couldn't find any evidence to support what I'd read in the briefing packet my HR folks had provided. Patolawala was thoughtful, unselfish, and hardworking. I thought I knew what the problem was.

"You know what, Monish? Just rip up all the shit people have written about you. They're wrong," I said. "The feedback you're getting is cultural bias. And it's not appropriate." He looked stunned, and I saw tears fill his eyes. While he was surely aware that some of his white employees had trouble being graded by an Indian executive, he would never have mentioned that to me. Soon, we'd promote him more than once; in 2015, we made him the CFO of GE Healthcare. (In 2020, he left GE to become the CFO of the multinational conglomerate 3M.)

Colleen Athans was the supply-chain leader in Aviation. She had eighty factories and probably thirty thousand people reporting to her. Sitting across from her during our weekend together, I thought, "This woman is amazingly competent, and she has zero ego." I liked to say that GE was a "we" company, not a "me" company, but I'd never seen that idea so fully realized until I spent time with Athans. As she described how she managed an incredible set of challenges, she wasn't self-aggrandizing. She was methodical and devoted. We both knew that GE was in the process of launching six new jet engines, representing billions of dollars' worth of investment, so at the end of our session, I was honest: "You're never getting promoted. This is your perfect job and we need you to keep doing it." Her face lit up with obvious relief. "Thank you," she said, exhaling deeply. "I love what I do."

Patolawala and Athans had something in common: they brought pure joy to their work. The both did difficult jobs, but they viewed them through a prism of opportunity. They thought they were changing the world. This is what these weekends, at their best, were about.

My memories from my early jobs helped shape these weekend meetings. You don't have to work long on a Ford assembly line or in a warehouse, like I did during college summers, to know that your colleagues feel respected when you understand what they do. It's not about being egalitarian (though that doesn't hurt). It's about looking past the job titles to delve into workers' day-to-day experiences.

I believed that if I got my colleagues talking, I'd learn how to keep them happy and make GE better.

I held about ninety weekend meetings, and every one taught me enormous amounts about the company and the people who worked there. My HR leader, a Scotsman named John Lynch, and I would choose the attendees carefully. I wanted to use the time with people who had clear potential, especially those who were at critical points in their careers. My hope was that our conversation would be as useful to them as it was to me.

Building a strong connection to the people you work with is about two things: time and truth. You've got to spend the time, and you've got to tell the truth. Dedicating a weekend to each of these leader's development demonstrated my commitment to them. And I made a point of offering very detailed evaluations and career guidance. I could engage with them with specificity and thoughtfulness. The best coaching sessions are equal parts constructive criticism and advocacy. That is what I strived to deliver.

Usually I'd start our session off by saying, "Tell me something about GE that I don't know." Then I had several go-to questions that I relied on to tease out not just facts but context. "Who is your favorite boss you've had at GE?" I'd ask, and the answers revealed so much. (The people who loved bosses who pushed them hard impressed me most.) "How did you solve a problem you created?" (Being able to identify and acknowledge a mistake is difficult but essential. A lot of people had trouble with this one.) "Why is your business important to GE?" (Could they see how they fit into the bigger whole?) "What detail do you track?" (Picking the right metric is a rare skill.) "Name an investment you've led." (In a big company, it's easier to not take risks. I wanted to see who had guts—who stood apart from the groupthink.)

Then I'd ask several questions to suss out how they were working to create the next generation of GE leaders. "Who are you developing?" (Could the person in front of me spot talent?) "Who do you want to promote? Why? Who are you doing executive assessments on? Who are you sending to study at Crotonville?" (I wanted to make sure our top leaders were taking chances on those below them.) The answers to these questions were every bit as important to me as what the person's revenue or operating income numbers were (and that was saying something, because I was a stickler for numbers). If you didn't show commitment to helping find your own successors, you weren't going to be in a leadership role for long.

The weekends were like job reviews on steroids. Thanks to our HR folks, I always arrived immensely well prepared. I'd review each person's history at GE in advance. I'd deliver my frank assessments of the person's strengths and weaknesses, and of how I thought they could best serve the company in the future. But my hopes for the weekends went beyond that. By the end, I wanted for us to have broken through some of the rigidity of the boss-employee/CEO-officer hierarchy, opening up opportunities to be candid going forward.

These people were often startlingly straightforward. Heiner Markhoff, the general manager of GE Water, told me that we weren't making enough progress in that business (so we sold it). Jamie Miller, then GE's controller, demonstrated in remarkable detail how our system's complexity was creating compliance and business risk. (I immediately made her GE's chief information officer.) Bill Fitzgerald, GE Aviation's general manager of commercial engines, laid out the risks associated with the LEAP engine launch. (I changed the compensation plan to focus on engine costs.) Kieran Murphy, GE Healthcare's general manager of life sciences, convinced me that his failure to grow revenues was an organizational, not a technical, problem. (We replaced the business CEO.) Kate Johnson, who we'd hired from Oracle to be GE Digital's chief commercial officer, alerted me to just how much talent we needed to add (and how much we'd have to pay them) to grow our Predix effort.

I remember my weekend with Rafael Santana, a Brazilian engineer who was running a small distributed-power business for us in Austria. I was completely blown away by how much he knew about his business and by how insightful he was. He had a humility about him, I noticed; he could delineate, in great detail, who he'd learned from and why. He was articulate but was also an active listener. After our weekend together, we didn't waste time promoting him to run a

big piece of the Oil & Gas business—a division called Turbomachinery and Process Solutions—and later he became CEO of GE Latin
America and then of GE Transportation. (He is now the CEO of a
public locomotive manufacturer called Wabtec.)

Some of my weekends got contentious. (One meeting I kicked off by
telling the leader in front of me, "You know, I should have fired you a year
ago.") A rare few were boring. There are some people who, when they
don't have a good answer, simply deliver a long one instead. Sometimes I'd
joke with my HR leader that I'd been tempted to cut off my little finger,
just so I could claim a workplace medical emergency and flee the room.
Other times I'd meet an employee's spouse or partner and think, "I wish
they were working at GE instead." And then there was this: some people
were terrific employees but needed to lose their know-it-all arrogance.
Sometimes they heard me when I delivered that critique; other times not.
Sometimes I could see that the person sitting in front of me was better
than the leader for whom they worked. The absolute worst were the people who had talent but were lazy. They had given up on themselves.

But it's funny. Andy reminds me that there were many Fridays
where I'd come home from work, grumbling that eating dinner with
a senior leader was the last thing I wanted to do. And then, almost
always, I'd emerge invigorated a few hours later. There was the
soft-spoken GE Lighting CEO who, when I told her she needed to
speak up more in meetings, turned it back on me: "You could really
help me by calling on me more." (She was right. I tried to remember
that, going forward, not just with her, but with other more reticent
leaders.) There was the GE Capital Real Estate executive who, when
we began cutting back his division, told me that it hurt, but he understood it was necessary. I appreciated his selflessness and his candor.

I didn't spend much time thinking about what I gained from the
weekends. At least not consciously. But at the end of my weekend with
Steve Sargent, the extraordinary Australian who ran GE Capital Asia
Pacific out of Tokyo, he put it to me bluntly: "Why do you do this?" Without thinking, I said something I hadn't before put into words: "I get my
energy from GE people." That was it: the weekends literally refueled me.

They also revealed to me some of the unsung heroes of GE—people like Dan Heintzelman. Multiple leaders I met with said he was their favorite boss. Beyond being a fantastic operator in Aviation, Power, and Oil & Gas, he was great at developing the next generation of talent. I had worked hard to get more technical and market innovators in the company. But I still appreciated hard-core operating leaders like Heintzelman. He was rare in that he was both a learner and a teacher. I valued that.

When I'd ask Heintzelman who he was developing—"Who's in your family tree?"—he always had a long list; he was a great recruiter and mentor. But he also had three other qualities I always looked for: he was an analyst who could see the big picture, knew the important metrics, and could set priorities; he was a master operator, calm and disciplined, who helped build accountability; and he was a creative innovator who was willing to take risks.

The weekends clued me in, as well, to the existence of a less impressive group I would come to call the "quiet caucus." These were the leaders who held others down with their selfishness or laziness or devotion to bureaucracy. The worst mistakes you can make as a leader are about people. We needed to eliminate the people who were hurting our culture and the weekends helped me see more clearly who they were.

People told me later that the weekends had a ripple effect as each leader I'd met went back to their team and talked about the experience. One leader described the message she took home in very simple terms: "I've talked to Jeff. He knows us. He cares about us. He supports us." I couldn't meet with every employee, but this was almost as good. People seemed to feel more valued when they knew their boss, or their boss's boss, had access to me. And that made them more committed to GE.

No one can manage three hundred thousand people all by themselves. My goal was to manage the people who managed our people. I often told our top officers: "If you value integrity, performance, and change, your people will, too. If you have ambition, if you're able to create excellence, if you can do four things—Imagine. Solve. Build. Lead.—then this is going to be a great company." My point was unwavering: it starts with you.

THE SOUL OF GE

Was GE training its leaders to succeed in this volatile modern world? This question was top of mind for me in 2009. My weekends with GE leaders gave a glimpse into the answer, but I felt we needed to do more. It was time to get creative, and I encouraged my team to try all sorts of new approaches.

We began holding once-a-month dinners to debate leadership with ten GE executives and one external thought leader—people such as the Harvard sociologist Rakesh Khurana and Herminia Ibarra, the Cuba-born organizational behaviorist. We launched a pilot program to pair high-potential employees with personal coaches—a practice that had previously been used only with employees in need of remedial help. And we took a hard look at the John F. Welch Leadership Development Center in Ossining, New York—the place everyone called Crotonville.

GE had always invested heavily in training. At this point, we were pouring more than $1 billion into corporate and compliance training and professional development a year (even during recession years), a figure believed unequaled by any corporation in the world. If you'd asked our top 185 executives how much of the last decade they'd spent in leadership training, the average answer was twelve months. Now I decided to make sure that time and money was being spent productively. I wanted to guarantee we were using Crotonville to make our leaders as competitive—and accountable—as possible. When it came to developing people who could innovate, execute, and drive change, I had a hunch we could improve.

Susan Peters, whom I'd known since the 1980s, was responsible for organizing and developing GE talent. Her title: chief learning officer. She had started in labor relations, but she had worked in multiple businesses: Plastics, NBC, Appliances. And she had lived outside of the United States. That gave her an edge in HR. She could give frank feedback—she'd certainly given me some—but people also confided in her. She was trusted.

Right after getting the job, Peters had upgraded the guest rooms at

Crotonville, which at that point had a Motel 6 kind of vibe: shiny floral bedspreads and the like. In 2007, it had been twenty-one years since the place had been renovated, so some basic improvements were overdue. But now, in the spring of 2009, I asked Peters to take a critical look at the content we were teaching, the environment in which we taught it, and the experiences that defined the learning process. Was Crotonville's curriculum doing what we needed it to do to make GE stronger? I also charged her with analyzing whether we were sufficiently using the jewel that was Crotonville to engage with our customers.

REIMAGINING CROTONVILLE

For years I'd made it my business to show my face at Crotonville several times a month, engaging with the leaders enrolled there about the challenges facing GE. It gave me a chance to listen to their ideas and concerns without a filter. I spent roughly a third of my time as CEO on improving GE's human capital—our employees. If the Global Research Center was GE's brain, I saw Crotonville as its heart and soul.

GE's growth made Crotonville even more important. When you acquire new businesses by the dozen, it is essential to get every employee, new and old, to share a general vision of where the company is going and how it plans to get there. Similarly, when you do business around the world, having Crotonville as a constant provides cultural continuity, even across international borders. By 2009, our research centers in Shanghai or Munich or Bangalore taught some of its curriculum. And its reach was extensive, with fifty thousand GE employees participating in on-demand curriculum via their laptops, thirty-five thousand people taking Crotonville's essential-skills course at their place of work, and about nine thousand people each year completing lengthier courses that involved living briefly at Crotonville.

Peters hired two professional provocateurs who ran a marketing company in Richmond, Virginia, that more than lived up to its name: Play. Andy Stefanovich and Barry Saunders urged Peters and her team to start by taking a walking tour of Crotonville. Here were a few of the observations the team came back with: Of the campus's fifty-nine acres, only about twenty were in use. And Crotonville's design made more sense to the people who were there every day than to the temporary visitors who were its main constituency—the reason it existed. There was no GE signage at the entrance, so when someone arrived from the airport in a cab, it took them a while to figure out where they were. Was that the experience we wanted people to have?

The classrooms and gathering areas felt tired and outdated—more like museums than hubs of active learning. Research into how people learn has shown that windowed classrooms encourage more creative thinking, but most of the places where GE's trainees worked together (including the most famous of those, the amphitheater known as "the Pit") were window free. High on the list of priorities that emerged from the team's notebooks: more windows (the Pit now has one), and more nonrectangular, nontraditional spaces to connect in groups of all sizes (outdoor firepits and hiking trails would soon be added, and an old barn on the property—built in 1909, complete with horse stalls— would be renovated to host discussions in a more casual setting).

When it came to studying Crotonville's curriculum, Peters's team convened a "What If?" session with historian Doris Kearns Goodwin and futurist Edie Weiner. The organizing theme: "What fundamentals should we be thinking about as we develop our leaders?" Much scholarship was done to identify new challenges that modern leaders would increasingly encounter—what West Point calls VUCA (volatility, uncertainty, complexity, and ambiguity). If we were going to inspire, connect, and develop the leaders of today and tomorrow, we needed to prepare them for those and other stressors.

The work of Peter Senge, the systems scientist from MIT Sloan School of Management, was an inspiration. Early on, we'd identified that our people needed to get more comfortable with something Senge calls dynamic complexity. In situations of dynamic complexity, the effect of a leader's action or decision is not immediately obvious, but only becomes clear over time. That, in turn, means conventional methods of forecasting and planning don't work. In the midst of turbulent change—in the months after 9/11, say—creating a twelve-month plan and requiring everyone to stick to it might be precisely the wrong move. Increasingly, we needed our leaders to get better at enduring ambiguity and being flexible as new data arose. Only then could they be as nimble as we needed them to be.

So we made big changes in the way we taught our leaders. Our Executive Development Course, which typically included fifteen of GE's top people, had long been taught in a classroom. Not anymore. Now, whenever possible, EDC participants would learn through experience. If the theme was "Leading in Geopolitical Uncertainty," for example, our people might be asked to sleep in tents at the Dead Sea, where an Israeli military team would rouse them each morning at six. They'd visit Egyptian government officials and have a meal with one of our field engineers and his family near a GE power plant in Cairo. The goal was to get people out of their comfort zones, to put them in new environments where they would learn through experience about one another and themselves.

This wasn't just about learning new facts. As I've said, fostering connection between leaders was a primary goal. At the end of the session, each participant was asked to give each of his or her colleagues very specific feedback: "Here's one thing I've observed about you that you should continue doing. Here's one thing that you should consider changing about your leadership style." But our hope was that this kind of frank talk was just the beginning—that these leaders would continue to solve problems together long after the session was over.

Some will see this as gimmicky. To me, it was anything but. More and more, I believed that GE's success depended on fostering a culture of mutual accountability. It wasn't enough for me to meet one-on-one with senior leaders. I wanted GE people to have a horizontal bond—to connect to (and root for) one another.

LEADERSHIP EXPLORATIONS

Modernizing Crotonville's general curriculum improved our training of young and mid-career leaders immeasurably. But as we thought

about retaining our most senior leaders—GE's 180 vice presidents—
we realized we had a curriculum gap there, too. Many of them had
been as young as their late thirties or early forties when they'd last
had any significant training. If we hoped for them to spend twenty
more years with the company, we needed them to feel committed
to GE. The best way to inspire that feeling, I felt, was to show how
committed GE was to them.

GE made products that couldn't fail. If an aircraft engine or an
MRI machine glitched, lives could be lost. This was why the organizational theory of Six Sigma made so much sense at GE: it was
all about enhancing quality and eliminating errors. But now, to be
more innovative, we needed to find ways to maintain that ethos
while underscoring another vital idea: creativity was impossible if
you feared failure. We needed to communicate clearly to our top people that we needed them to stretch, to risk, to go for it.

The people in the group we were targeting—the top .06 percent of
our workforce—were busy with a lot of responsibilities. We knew we
couldn't take them away from their jobs for weeks at a time. We needed
to invent something shorter than our other immersion curricula but
just as impactful. Moreover, we wanted a mechanism to throw people
together who didn't know one another well. Some top leaders lacked
peers in their particular businesses, so if we could connect those VPs
to others at their level across the company, that'd be a bonus.

Peters and her team came up with a four-day program that did all
these things and more. It was called Leadership Explorations. One
iteration, called "The Longest Day," was organized around the query
"Do I trust my team? Really?" It took place in Normandy, France.
On day one, twenty or so participants arrived around noon at Pointe
du Hoc, a promontory overlooking the English Channel. From there,
they could easily see the beaches where American soldiers landed on
D-Day, June 6, 1944. As they ate lunch—a military MRE, or meal
ready to eat—a historian and US Army veteran summarized the valiant
efforts of our troops and commanders on Omaha and Utah Beaches.
Were there any parallels, he asked, to modern business leadership?

Later, while walking together across La Fière bridge, where a key battle was fought, the group was asked to imagine staring down their enemy on this lovely village road, or stepping over fallen comrades on the way into battle. ("Everything was a metaphor in these classes," Kimberly Kleiman-Lee, the architect of this program, told me.) Participants then gathered to debrief in a church that still bore the scars of gunfire inflicted during World War II. Sitting together in the ten pews, they were asked to describe the toughest obstacle they'd ever overcome as a leader. These sessions could get emotional, but that was part of the point. Vulnerability builds connection, we believed.

The trips were varied. One took participants to an ashram in India, another to Silicon Valley, California, to get a crash course in venture capital. One took our people to Africa to live briefly with the Maasai people; another had two comedians teach GE people how to do stand-up comedy on a rented Broadway stage, and then perform live in New York City's Times Square. (That one's query: "Am I willing to experiment, fail, pivot, refocus, realign, and learn in the name of progress?")

We wanted to build global entrepreneurs. And we wanted to retain them. These trips helped us do that, but not because they were lavish junkets (they were anything but). Instead, Leadership Explorations gave senior leaders a way to become mentors for one another. Somehow, by focusing on an activity that wasn't purely business-related, they found it easier to forge connections that would serve GE's interests for years to come. Our retention at senior levels during these years was amazing (we lost just 3 percent of the people we wanted to keep).

Some people will read this and label these programs frivolous, particularly given GE's current troubles. But remember the problem I was trying to solve: namely, to retain a strong leadership team, and foster their sense of mutual accountability, as we were recovering from a near fatal blow. Every GE team had financial commitments it needed to hit. But in a conglomerate, a misstep by one business or leader could screw it up for everyone else. The leadership programs we developed at Crotonville helped protect us from such a worst-case scenario because our top leaders got a chance to know and like their peers. They wanted to compete not just for their own good but for one another's. My hope was that if they developed respect and empathy for one another, they would be better able to push back on me—to make me better.

Many of our top people could have made more money elsewhere. They stayed at GE because they cared about one another and believed in GE's purpose—and because they felt invested in it. One top executive told me his trip to Normandy was the most amazing week of his life. Through these development programs, we formed a compact of trust with our people. It was hard to put a price tag on that.

VALUING EVERYONE

When I became CEO, GE was an extremely male-dominated place. "Where GE Falls Short: Diversity at the Top," read a *New York Times* headline in September 2000. The story noted that just 6.4 percent of our corporate officers were female, as compared with an average of 11.9 percent for all Fortune 500 companies. That didn't mean women didn't work there—many did, and they did their jobs very well. But the culture valued a certain kind of contrived toughness. GE's narrative about itself was that we were badasses who could do anything. I believed that we could, but I also understood that too often, that self-image tended to glorify a sort of tough-guy attitude.

How did that impact female employees? In myriad ways. I remember when I was working in Appliances, Jack Welch told the guy who ran product placement that he should make a woman the product manager of the range stovetop business because women understood cooking better than any man ever could. His statement was not mean-spirited, just outdated. But at least that was an instance of a stereotype creating opportunity for a woman employee. More often, that kind of thinking held women back.

I've always believed that merit has no gender or race or sexual orientation. Promoting the best people was good for GE. So was enabling the best people to do their best work. Back when I was running GE Healthcare, Welch initially shot down my request to put a day-care center inside our headquarters. He worried that if we did it there, GE would have to do it everywhere. But I explained that because Healthcare was located outside Milwaukee in the isolated town of Wauwatosa, its location made it difficult for employees who were parents to do their best for GE. I won that battle and the day-care center still exists to this day.

During that same period in Wisconsin, meanwhile, I was fortunate to attend a dinner that would expand my understanding of what it was like to be a person of color at GE. The dinner was the idea of one of our HR leaders, Ernest Marshall, who at that point was heading Healthcare's African American Forum, which was part of GE's system of internal affinity networks designed to demystify our personnel policies, to provide a setting in which black employees could meet and support one another, and to develop a formal mentoring program.

Marshall was a real talent (he's gone on to be the HR leader at Eaton, a large industrial company run by Craig Arnold, another black GE alum). One day, he called my assistant Kathy and asked if she thought I'd be open to having a conversation with a half dozen black employees. He was concerned about the lack of black women managers in our division, so he led with that, but he's told me since that his broader goal was to clue me in more generally to the day-to-day experiences of black workers at GE.

I remember when Kathy brought the proposal to me, she said Marshall didn't want the dinner to be at the Westmoor Country Club, where we held many events. "I want it to be like a casual sit-down dinner with your family," he'd told her, explaining why we'd be eating at the home of another colleague. I talked to my human resources leader about the invite, and he discouraged me from accepting. Weren't there sufficient mechanisms for employees to air their concerns? But that didn't sit right with me. "People are frustrated," I said. "I want to understand why."

On the appointed evening, I arrived at the host's home and was greeted warmly by the group. I'd met all six of them before, but I knew some better than others. We sat down at the dining room table, and each person told me a little bit about themselves: where they'd grown up and how they'd come to GE. Then we headed to the kitchen to get food (Marshall is still proud of the menu, which he told me was intentionally "our food": fried chicken, macaroni and cheese, and collard greens). When we returned to the table with heaping plates, the talk became more emotional. One person described, through tears, how it felt to never be invited to lunch with her white colleagues. Several shared the reasons they'd been given for being passed over for promotions. It seemed to them that a quality such as confidence, which was seen as positive in a white candidate, was often deemed "arrogance" in a black candidate. One described what that does to your psyche—to not know whether you are imagining a slight (or being naive when you try to ignore it). I tried to ask good questions, but mostly I listened.

Three hours later, after a round of handshakes and hugs, I walked out the door—winded, but grateful they'd trusted me enough to level with me. In the car on the way home, I called my HR leader. It was time to create a position at GE Healthcare to focus on inclusion and diversity, I said. I wanted the job to be posted ASAP.

Three years later, in 2002, I would continue this intensified effort from the CEO's chair, appointing Deborah Elam—a fifteen-year GE veteran who was then managing director of human resources at GE Capital Commercial Finance—to head the company's diversity and inclusion leadership program. (Four years after that, I'd make Elam GE's chief diversity officer.) I charged Elam with aligning GE's domestic diversity initiatives (which by this point had expanded to include affinity networks for women, Hispanic, Asian-American, and gay and lesbian employees) with GE's global business strategy.

I wanted Elam to create what we called an "operating system" around diversity. In other words, we needed to build both capability and metrics. Elam helped us focus on recruitment, retention, and promotion. We held our leaders accountable for making improvements in each.

When we recruited on college campuses, our people knew that the ideal was to hire an equal number of men and women. We didn't always meet that, but we used every technique we had to show that this old industrial company was a great place for women to work. We changed our maternity and paternity leaves to be as good as those at tech companies. To encourage interest in STEM, in 2011 we founded a GE camp for middle-school-age girls that continues to this day. Finally, in my last year as CEO, we launched an initiative to build a female workforce of twenty thousand in engineering and tech jobs.

All along, in our TV advertisements, we communicated our belief in equality to the world. In 2014, we unveiled what came to be known as the "My Mom" ad during the winter Olympics. "My mom?" a little brown-eyed girl narrates. "She makes underwater fans that are powered by the moon. My mom makes airplane engines that can talk. My mom makes hospitals you can hold in your hand. My mom can print amazing things right from her computer. My mom makes trains that are friends with trees. My mom works at GE."

To recruit more talented African Americans, we reached beyond college campuses and into the fraternity and sorority system. This was a huge network, and we found that going beyond traditional recruitment channels paid off.

As for retaining the diverse leaders we already had, Elam and I relied on those affinity networks I've mentioned to give each community an identity and support system. I saw my role as not dictating the activities of these networks, but instead acting as a catalyst. I always attended each group's once-a-year symposiums, usually giving the keynote speech. I'll never forget one year, when a young man got up at the annual meeting of GE's Gay, Lesbian, Bisexual, Transgender & Ally Alliance and asked me, somewhat bluntly, why I was there. The room went quiet as I answered. "It's important for you to know," I said, "that GE is everyone's company."

More than recruitment and retention, though, I saw promotion as the place I could make the most impact. Because when you're diverse at the top, not only do non-white/non-male leaders recruit and promote others like them, but their very existence sends a powerful message. I ran a quarterly pipeline review with each business CEO and his or her HR leaders. We would examine each level of the company with the goal of identifying the three or four diverse "best bets"—people who the team felt were capable of thriving at the next level up. Once that "best bets" list existed, I would turn to it when our diversification numbers stalled, urging my business leaders to promote a best bet in whatever group was underrepresented. This made some top executives uncomfortable, but I got the point across: I want to see swift, measurable improvement.

That's why we made our leaders commit to what some wrongly viewed as a paradox: they had to sustain a meritocracy while at the same time expanding the numbers of diverse leaders. Anyone who complained that was too difficult was given no quarter. I knew terrific diverse individuals around the company, and I knew they could be developed anywhere. My message to my team was: just do it.

Promoting women was a particular goal of mine. I'm the son of one brilliant woman and the husband and father of two more. I learned from all of them, and from many great GE women, several of whom I've already called out in these pages. As CEO I specifically championed, promoted, and recruited women. I believed—and often told interviewers—that women were more loyal than men and more willing to try new approaches to solving problems. Sometimes that loyalty comment got misconstrued to mean that I valued women because I thought they were more obedient. That wasn't how I felt at all. Instead, I believed women were better able than men to devote themselves to a shared vision. They had an easier time managing their egos.

On my watch, we strived to make GE a place where women employees not only got a fair shake but also received mentoring and advancement. I'm proud, for example, that at one point, 80 percent of the employees in GE Aviation worked for a woman, which in such a male-dominated, engineering-driven division was almost unheard of. Our head of supply chain and our head of engineering were women, as were two-thirds of the leadership team.

GE set a strong example in this area, and others followed our lead, both at home and around the world. Often when our teams met with international customers, the GE delegation would be heavily female, while the people they were meeting were all male. Whether this impressed our clients or merely embarrassed them, it seemed to have an impact. More than once, I heard from GE executives that the next time they paid certain customers a visit, a woman was present on the other side of the table.

Rachel Duan is a great example of how GE built leaders from the ground up. A Shanghai native and the daughter of two engineers, Duan first joined GE for a summer internship at GE Capital after her first year of graduate work at the University of Wisconsin–Madison. After she got her MBA, in 1996, we recruited her to work on the GE audit staff, which is the proven training ground for GE finance leaders. She excelled, but after a four-year stint, she said she wanted to return to Asia. Before she was thirty, she became a Six Sigma quality leader for the Asia Pacific region of GE Plastics, based in Tokyo, and then, in 2006, became the first female CEO for greater China of GE Silicones. Just a few months after that promotion, though, we sold that unit, and Duan left GE to run it.

We might have lost her forever, but for the diligence of Susan Peters and our HR staff. They kept in regular touch with Duan and were impressed with what she was learning about running a stand-alone business in China (and then in the Asia Pacific region) without the safety net of GE to catch her. So in 2010, we rehired her to run GE Healthcare in China. That's when she and I really began spending time together. As a Chinese national, she understood the dynamics of the place we'd asked her to tackle. That was critical. Too many companies install managers in places where they have no credibility or understanding of cultural mores and local market needs. We shared an understanding that while it wouldn't always be easy to do business in China, it was imperative that we figure it out. We talked a lot about how avoiding risks there was not an option; the key was to mitigate risk.

Duan really proved her value. Not only could she speak English, Chinese, and passable Japanese, but she was also a hard-nosed negotiator and she understood how to build a strong team. Karaoke, which she loves to do, was a secret weapon, especially among Asians.

("When you're singing Shania Twain or Celine Dion in front of your people, it breaks down any hierarchical barriers," she says, adding that she also knows a few Japanese songs by heart. "You're all equal.") She also stood up for her employees, some of whom had been reticent to complain about leaders in the United States who scheduled meetings without regard to Asia's many time zones. Duan was not afraid to challenge the status quo. "Why don't we take turns having meetings in the middle of the night?" she suggested.

In early 2014, when I put Duan on the Corporate Executive Council, I wanted to send another message. Historically, GE's highest management committee had excluded regional leaders. Including her was the best way I could think of to show I was serious about walking our talk about our global expansion, which I'll talk about in the next chapter. Later that year, when we expanded Duan's responsibilities to include all of GE's China operations, it was a big deal within China. I remember on a visit to Beijing, a senior government official pulled me aside and told me how much he respected Duan. "The way you've promoted her proves that GE is about talent," he said.

Duan was the last appointment I made at the senior vice president level. I wish I could say she still works for GE. In 2020, after twenty-four years at GE, she left the company.

Numbers are only one measure of progress. As I learned back in 1999, during that chicken dinner with my African American colleagues at GE Healthcare, we have to care not just about head counts of diverse employees but also about what it's like for them when they come to work. That's an ongoing process, and there's always more to be done. But I'm still proud of the strides we made increasing representation. When I left GE, in 2017, just 41 percent of our officers were white men (down from 80 percent when I took over). Don't listen to those who say the goals of promoting diversity and valuing merit aren't in sync. They are, in my experience, and the best leaders work hard at both.

CHAPTER 7

Leaders Compete Around the World

My breakfast companions were youngsters—I think neither had yet hit thirty. Both born in West Africa, the two men were GE's only executives in Ghana. It was early 2010, and as we took our seats at a Formica four-top at GE's de facto headquarters at the one-star Holiday Inn at the Accra Airport, I could feel their enthusiasm before they started speaking.

What, they asked, if GE helped Ghana to build an integrated gas-to-power plant? At that time, the country had a population of about 25 million, but only about 2,000 megawatts of power (enough to fuel fewer than 2 million homes). Ghana had just discovered oil and gas reserves in its offshore waters, and it was rich with minerals and agricultural products. It wanted to industrialize, to become modern, but without a dependable power source—blackouts were all too common—there was no way it could. As my colleagues' words tumbled out with increasing speed, they wanted me to know: they had a plan!

It would be an ambitious project: first, liquefied natural gas (or LNG) would have to be brought onshore; we'd have to build a regasification plant (to turn liquid into gas), and then we'd have to construct the power plant, too, including transmission lines to deliver electricity to populated areas and industrial clusters. Not only would GE have to develop the project, but probably finance it as well. But the difference it would make, they said! All they needed was a little help.

"Look," they told me, "the government agrees we need a new plant, and they're willing to give us an off-take agreement"—basically a promise to buy power once the plant was up and running. Shell Oil was willing to invest, they continued. A global investment fund wanted to buy in. The project, they explained, would require an ecosystem of more than ten companies working together. "Both the gas turbines would be GE technology. Can you help make this dream a reality?"

I loved their dedication, and I said I'd do what I could. Before I left Ghana, we signed a memo of understanding with the government to begin something we called Ghana 1000, which would seek to expand the country's existing power supply by 50 percent. And yet I knew this was going to be an uphill climb. GE at that time was not organized to support this kind of complicated local project. Our people who had the required expertise to pull it off were 2,500 miles away, in the United States. I worried that, without intending to, our US-based bureaucracy would, at best, stymie Ghana 1000 and, at worst, kill it.

Not long after that, I was in Australia, where—thanks to China's building boom—investors were pouring big dollars into mining and oil and gas. Australia had iron ore, coal, and LNG in abundance. But the country was struggling to get it out of the ground fast enough and to move it where it needed to go. I'll never forget Steve Sargent, the Aussie who was running GE Capital Asia Pacific, showing me a photo on the front page of the *Daily Mercury* in Queensland. It showed a queue of a hundred empty tanker ships floating just off Australia's coastline, waiting to be loaded with coal bound for Asia. The problem: there wasn't enough coal being delivered to the port to fill the ships.

Australia was already bringing in $5 billion a year in revenues to GE—as big as a Fortune 500 company. The country had the kind of infrastructure and power needs that GE's products address. But Sargent, who I called "Sarge," told me he worried our lack of local man and woman power was about to cost us, big-time. "Frankly, we're not ready for the massive opportunity that's here. We don't have the resources in-country. We don't have the caliber of people we need to nurture the high-level relationships that will win us some of the biggest contracts. We need help."

Sarge gave me a concrete example. To sweeten our bid on a $7 billion contract from Qantas Airways, which leased some of the planes GE owned, our team in Australia had promised to lend the airline a quality-control person to help improve customer satisfaction. But the Aviation folks back in Cincinnati, nine thousand miles away, wouldn't pay for it. We won the contract, but only after our Sydney-based GE Capital people absorbed the cost of the added person. Sarge understood the value of helping other GE businesses, and he was happy to use GE Capital resources. Still, it was clear our system wasn't functioning as well as it could.

I don't think it was more than a few weeks later that the leader of our Healthcare business in China, a Brazilian named Marcelo Mosci, said something that made me feel like I was in an echo chamber. Mosci reported that in contrast to the US market, which was in a slump, his region was ripe with opportunity. The Chinese government was investing heavily in healthcare; there were new hospitals popping up everywhere. But when Mosci had approached his higher-ups in the United States, seeking to hire the army he felt he needed to capitalize on this investment, he was given authorization to add just ten people. "That's ridiculous," I said. "Hire a thousand." But I was beginning to see a pattern.

In the wake of the financial crisis, our business in the United States was growing very slowly. Some thought the domestic markets might never recover. But opportunities for high-tech infrastructure companies like ours were huge abroad. GE needed to expand its global reach and revenues—by my estimate, we needed to have as many as thirty countries in which we did at least $1 billion in business. And yet GE people around the world kept telling me that our centralized system of US-based decision making was impeding that goal.

At this point, GE called itself global simply because we had revenues outside the United States. But our attention was still focused on a pretty narrow swath of the planet, and to most GE executives, "international travel" still meant a visit to London, Paris, or Tokyo. In the early 2000s, GE split the globe into segments: the US, Europe, Japan, and Rest of World (in that order). This "ROW segment," as we called it, would eventually become a $50 billion business for us (or about a third of the company's revenues), but not before we made some big changes.

Globalizing a US-based company is hard. It is easier to let leaders back at headquarters make excuses for why deals in emerging markets can't get done. True globalization requires a transfer of power from headquarters to the field. It requires placing trust in people you can't see up close, in person. In the age of COVID, when going into work at headquarters is unsafe, companies realize the need to empower those closest to the action. Doing so requires cultural change, and today it is an ongoing trend. But back when we were tackling globalization at GE, headquarters still ruled.

To some, "globalization" had become almost a dirty word that meant only outsourcing—the sending of US jobs overseas. But in 2010, I was coming to believe it was time for a more nuanced approach to globalization, one that would create jobs both at home and abroad. I felt we had no choice. Without global markets, we'd shrink, not grow.

I had grown up with the notion that the United States would always take the lead on trade. But beginning in these years, the US's role in the world was being diminished and systems that had served for decades—global trade deals and 1940s institutions such as the World Trade Organization (previously known at GATT)—were failing. The Export-Import Bank, a tool the US government used to help exporters succeed around the world, was neutered. China was investing one hundred times more than the United States to sell its goods globally.

I could understand where politicians were coming from when they complained about the North American Free Trade Agreement, or NAFTA. Its main outcome had been accessing cheap Mexican labor (not selling our products in Mexico), and lots of American jobs were lost. In anticipation of NAFTA, in 1991 GE completed a joint venture with the leading Mexican appliances company, Mabe. The JV had two parts: to build gas ranges and refrigerators to sell in the US, a classic labor arbitrage; and to sell our products in Mexico and Latin America. These were thought to be roughly equal in value, but that was wrong. Over time, 100 percent of the JV's profits came from outsourcing the building of appliances for US markets.

The practice of wage arbitrage had really shaped my generation of business leaders. We lived in the world's biggest markets. If we could do things more productively by moving work offshore, why not? As capitalists, we thought this was our right; we didn't think much about the consequences. But I could see things changing as the US became more populist. In 2012, we decided to move GE's refrigerator production back to the US. My team thought I was crazy. But by then, the total cost in the US was comparable to Mexico. More important, I felt that American business leaders (even globalists) needed to give a shit about preserving American jobs. By 2020, if you relied on China as your sole source for products sold in the US, you needed to have your head examined.

People want to blame former President Trump for the anti-globalization movement, but he was not wrong about the impact that trade deals have had on American manufacturing. That's the reason protectionism predated him, not just in the United States but in every corner of the world. And business was losing the globalization debate by focusing on only the easy stuff (outsourcing, or seeking lower wages abroad) and skipping over the most important part: selling around the world. I was determined to change this.

Me, I didn't know what the WTO did anymore (and I no longer believed it could help GE). That meant we'd have to figure out for ourselves how to become more global. In order to break into new markets (and maximize existing ones), we needed to make our big, broad business more local, giving in-country executives more power to act, developing local leaders who grasped the complicated nuances of these markets, and being more responsive to customers' needs. We needed to put more senior leaders closer to the customers we were trying to attract. And we needed to allow them to make more decisions.

So in November 2010, with the support of GE's board, we launched what we called the Global Growth Organization, and I asked an old friend and one of our most canny executives, John Rice, to move to Hong Kong to head it. A plainspoken New Jersey boy who'd once been a formidable lacrosse goalie, Rice was a GE lifer, having started on the audit staff in 1978 right out of Hamilton College. He'd worked in half a dozen divisions—including Appliances, Plastics, and Power, which he'd run for six years—and was widely liked and respected. That was important. The GGO was bound to break glass and ruffle feathers, but no one who knew Rice doubted his commitment to GE. Rice always spoke his mind—he certainly pushed back on me more than once—but he didn't have a selfish bone in his body.

There was something else, too: because Rice and I are the same age, he was not seen to be campaigning to succeed me. When it came to his motivations, personal ambition was off the table. Rice's appointment sent a message: if a guy as accomplished as him was backing this initiative, it had to be taken seriously. When he began recruiting other senior leaders—tapping Jay Ireland, the head of GE's $120 billion asset management business, to run GE Africa, for example—that feeling only grew. A thirty-one-year GE veteran, Ireland was going to an emerging region with fewer than a thousand GE employees and revenues of just $800 million. Something was definitely up.

Over the next seven years, the GGO helped GE thrive by leveraging capital markets all over the world to solve local problems. We spent less time lobbying in Washington, DC, and more time selling in the 185 countries in which we had a stake. Our goal: to create company-to-country relationships that could withstand even the strongest surge of economic nationalism. And, of course, to make lots of money.

I wanted GE to be a company of competitors who could do business anywhere in the world, from Mexico to Iraq to Thailand. That's what the GGO was all about, and I committed to it with everything I had. I told Rice I'd give him ten weeks a year to put me to use, and boy, did he. I must've traveled 3 million miles to promote the GGO.

We were seeking a culture change at the same time. I wanted GE to have a dominant industrial sales force, one that could solve customer problems and close deals. We upgraded the sales force's financing capability, transferring teams from finance into sales. We streamlined deal reviews, making them faster, and reduced internal barriers that blocked success. You could really feel 300,000 people unifying behind an attitude of "win or go home—no excuses allowed."

We didn't conjure the GGO out of nothing. A year before, in 2009, we'd embarked on an experiment in India to test whether giving local leaders more autonomy would reap any rewards. At that point GE had been doing business in India for a century, but we still hadn't been able to get to $1 billion a year in revenues. The team we'd had stationed in New Delhi acted more as ambassadors than entrepreneurs.

So we changed it up, appointing John Flannery—a twenty-three-year GE veteran and a trusted member of my senior leadership team—as president and CEO of GE India. As such, he was responsible for all of GE's businesses there. Everybody in the country reported to him. He had his own profit-and-loss statement and had the authority to hire, fire, build factories, and launch products as needed, without any sign-off from me or the rest of the team in Connecticut. My only requirement: that he grow revenues.

Flannery delivered. By the time we created the GGO, which essentially expanded the India model around the globe, Flannery's team had increased both sales inside India and sourcing of GE products made in India to other regions of the world. And they were just getting started.

BECOMING THE JOBS CZAR

In January 2011, meanwhile, President Barack Obama asked if I would head his Council on Jobs and Competitiveness. Not since the

Great Depression had US unemployment been so bad for so long, and he wanted a group of top CEOs to come up with ideas for immediate long-term job growth. To some, this seemed at cross-purposes with what I was trying to do to expand GE's global footprint. Wasn't my commitment to growing GE overseas a threat to jobs in the United States? I didn't see it that way, but even some of my closest friends questioned why I would accept what was likely to be a thankless assignment. I told them that the federal government had helped GE during the financial crisis of 2008 and 2009, and this was the least I could do to pay some of that back. More fundamentally, I'm a patriot; although I am a Republican, I believed that when the president calls and asks you to do something, you say yes (even if the president is a Democrat).

As the so-called jobs czar, I took my lumps. In the fall of 2011, when the council met in Pittsburgh, I divided us into groups of three or four and sent each group out to have a town hall with the local business community to update them on progress and to hear their ideas. I'll never forget one town hall that I hosted with Intel CEO Paul Otellini and Rich Trumka, the president of the AFL-CIO. The three-hundred-person crowd included mostly local business owners, a few members of the International Brotherhood of Electrical Workers, and half a dozen followers of the Tea Party movement. That subset, in particular, took aim at Otellini and me and abused us for more than an hour.

"You guys are on the take!" they alleged. "You would never spend time on the Jobs Council if there weren't something in it for you. You're overpaid. You suck." The media was there that day, and the coverage reflected badly, some thought, on GE. I remember Obama called to thank me later, as did Vice President Joe Biden, Tim Geithner, and Valerie Jarrett. "We know this is hard," each of them said in their various ways, "but we appreciate you, because we're making progress."

I was impressed by Obama, though I often disagreed with him. And I got a better sense of how seemingly inept and unsympathetic "big business"—by which I mean groups like the Business Council and the Business Roundtable—had become. I remember at one point I organized a meeting with the president to try to convince him to let companies repatriate overseas cash reserves without paying high penalties. As four of us from the Jobs Council stood outside the Oval Office, waiting to be summoned, I tried to bestow a little strategic advice. "He's the president," I reminded my colleagues, "so let's not say, 'Here's what we want you to do.' Let's try to sound more like, 'Here's what we would do if any of us were you.'"

Minutes later, it was clear none of them had listened. Once the president was in front of us, my colleagues went in hard. "It's stupid to have this money stuck over there! We're being taxed twice!" Obama was like the best hockey goalie ever—he never let the puck get past him. He was so smart, he countered every one of our arguments with a better one of his own. We left empty-handed.

Observing Obama up close, I decided that he didn't empathize with the business community. But he was able to use it to accomplish his goals. For instance, he understood that business leaders had strong relationships abroad that he could use to further US interests. After the Arab Spring, the US government could do little to improve conditions for people on the ground in Egypt. But as blackouts loomed, GE could deliver what they needed: two gigawatts of emergency power. Obama saw how that helped him. So, despite trouncing us on the repatriation issue, he would sometimes help us out when we really needed something.

My primary contact was Valerie Jarrett, who was special counsel to the president. Valerie and I became friends. I respected her toughness and dedication to the president. Too often in presidents' administrations, people who should be there to serve others are more in it for themselves. Jarrett on the other hand supported the president faithfully every minute of every day, good or bad. I admired that.

Still, over time, chairing the Jobs Council left me feeling a bit like cartilage must feel inside a knee: caught between two hard surfaces. Later, I'd sum up my service to my country like this: "I asked for nothing and got less."

The best example of that was a segment that ran on *60 Minutes*, when Lesley Stahl grilled me. We went to Brazil together, and I showed her around a GE-built manufacturing-and-service hub in

Petrópolis, about ninety minutes outside of Rio. Back in the United States, when Stahl interviewed me in my office, I told her, "I think like a global CEO, but I'm an American. I run an American company. But in order for GE to be successful in the coming years, I've got to sell my products in every corner of the world."

Stahl looked skeptical. "You may personally think of yourself as an American, but your customers are over there, you put your plants over there, you even put research over—"

I cut her off: "If I wasn't out chasing orders in every corner of the world, we'd have tens of thousands fewer employees in Pennsylvania, Ohio, Massachusetts, Texas. I'm never going to apologize for that. Ever."

That wasn't the last of the fireworks. Stahl kept insisting that Americans see corporations as nothing but greedy, and I got tired of it. "I want you to root for me," I told her finally. "You know, everybody in Germany roots for Siemens. Everybody in Japan roots for Toshiba. Everybody in China roots for China South Rail. I want you to say, 'Win, GE!'"

"Do you not see any reason that maybe the public doesn't hold American corporations up here," she said, raising her hand to eye level.

I didn't flinch. "I think this notion that it's the population of the US against the big companies is just wrong," I said. "When I walk through a [GE] factory with you or anybody, you know, our employees basically like us. . . . They root for us. They want us to win. I don't know why you don't."

THERE'S ALWAYS A CRISIS SOMEWHERE

Because the GGO was built on the success of the GE India pilot, it made sense to inaugurate the new initiative there. So in March 2011, when our thirty-five-member Corporate Executive Council gathered for its quarterly meeting, we held it in New Delhi. The CEC was GE's highest management committee, but when it came to the GGO, I wasn't asking for permission. My message was: "We're going to double down on the markets around the world. If there's a problem we can solve in Kenya or Singapore or Bangladesh, we're going to solve it."

To bolster me, we'd invited a who's who of India's business leaders and entrepreneurs to come speak: the top execs from the conglomerate Reliance Group, the car manufacturer Mahindra & Mahindra, and the IT consultancies Wipro Limited and Infosys. One by one, they echoed my team's message, but from the customer's point of view. "We need your best minds here," they told the CEC. "Change is underway, and GE needs to show up to be part of it."

I was hoping that the leaders of GE's businesses would see the GGO, which was funded by the CEO's office, as a "free" resource that could drive their growth. But we knew that some of those US-based leaders worried the GGO would diminish their power. And indeed, in some instances, they would no longer have the last word. As I told those in attendance at the CEC meeting, "From now on, when you fight with our guy in Riyadh, sometimes he's going to win."

Luckily, John Rice understood that the GGO wouldn't succeed if he and his people stepped too often on the business leaders' toes or were perceived to be ruling by fiat. Rice knew how to use his influence without explicitly pulling rank. Even when talking to someone far lower on the organization chart, he knew he had to be convincing. Again and again, he stressed that the businesses would retain most of their powers, but the GGO would provide the benefit of local insight.

The week of that CEC meeting, meanwhile, will forever be colored in my memory by what was happening in Japan. On March 11, two days before the CEC landed in India, a magnitude 9.0 undersea earthquake struck off the Pacific coast of Tohoku, triggering a tsunami that sent ocean water surging as far as six miles inland. The tsunami moved at 435 miles per hour and killed nearly twenty thousand people. Fifty minutes after the quake hit, surge waters also swamped the six GE-designed reactors at the Fukushima Daiichi nuclear plant, knocking out all the plant's power. The reactors shut down, as they should have. But the flood disabled the emergency generators that were supposed to power the pumps to cool them. That meant meltdowns had become a serious risk. We monitored the crisis hour by hour. I barely slept.

In my nearly ten years as CEO, I had seldom thought about GE's nuclear business. It was relatively small—less than $1 billion in annual revenues—and it had been in a difficult thirty-year-stretch. Investors never asked about it. So when the Fukushima emergency came out of nowhere, it forced me to reeducate myself on the details of the industry. From New Delhi, I had my assistant send me GE's commercial agreement with the Tokyo Electric Power Company for the installation of the reactors—a 280-page document that had been written in the 1960s.

There was nothing to do but keep moving. At the conclusion of the CEC meeting, I flew to Perth, Australia, to visit customers and meet with a thousand GE employees who worked in our Oil & Gas division. Given the roll they were on—one that the GGO was only about to supercharge—the members of the Aussie team were expecting a congratulatory pep talk. But thanks to the tsunami, all I felt was dread.

I remember sitting in a conference room in Perth, trying to gather my thoughts. Above my head, a TV news channel displayed aerial photos of the Fukushima reactors, which analysts thought were ready to blow. Picking up the phone, I dialed into our morning briefing and heard shocking projections: the 12 million residents of Tokyo might have to be evacuated, and the nuclear fallout could end up as far away as Los Angeles.

Someone tapped at the door. They were ready for me. Moments later, I stood in front of a microphone in a large, packed ballroom and took a breath. "I'm sure you've all been watching TV," I began. "I want you to know we have our best people trying to address the crisis in Japan." Then, like a good juggler, I switched my attention to boosting employee morale. I thanked those assembled for their hard work and promised that the GGO would help them take even more advantage of Asia's building boom. When I opened the floor for questions, I was braced for anything. Still, I was surprised by what I heard from the first guy who raised his hand. "Big Macs cost fifteen dollars here," he said. "Is there any chance of getting pay raises in the near future?"

Here we were launching a company-wide global restructuring while a nuclear meltdown was underway, and this guy wanted to talk about the price of a fast-food burger. I wasn't sure whether to laugh or cry. But then I thought about it, and I realized it was an opportunity to learn. If a Big Mac cost fifteen dollars, there was a labor shortage. And that meant likely repercussions for our oil and gas projects in the region. A little later, I heard from a Chevron executive who said he was having trouble hiring enough people in the region. I took a mental note—even in the midst of crisis, you should pay attention to all the data that's coming in, even data you don't expect. Clues are everywhere.

In the end, three of Fukushima Daiichi's six reactors released significant amounts of radioactive contamination, but courageous emergency crews in Japan averted a more serious calamity. Cleanup continues there to this day. But as bad as the disaster was, it could've been much worse. Thankfully, most residents of Japan were allowed to stay put, and scientists concluded that any radiation caused no public health risk on California beaches.

INVESTING IN LOCAL CAPABILITY

When we first formed the GGO, GE had at best a tepid relationship with the Saudi Arabian Oil Company, or Saudi Aramco. While we'd been in the region for decades, our competition had won the majority of oil-and-gas contracts. We were selling lots of gas turbines to Saudi Electric, the state-run utility. (From 2000 to 2015, they'd purchase more than any other customer in the world.) But we needed to decide if we had the stomach for the fight.

John Rice flew to Riyadh in 2011 and got an earful. Khalid Al-Falih, the minister of energy and longtime chairman of Saudi Aramco, was the most vocal. "Where are you, GE? Why aren't you more interested in the kingdom?" he asked. The Saudis wanted GE to act more like a partner, helping them address their people's needs more broadly. Basically, Al-Falih told Rice, GE needed to put up or shut up.

Rice and Nabil Habayeb—the CEO of GE Middle East, North Africa & Turkey—agreed that GE needed to make a big investment in Saudi Arabia. It was four in the afternoon in Riyadh—9 a.m. in Connecticut—when they reached my assistant Sheila Neville.

"Is Jeff in?" Rice asked, his voice urgent. "We have a quick one."

When I picked up, Rice and Habayeb led with some context: The effects of the Arab Spring were rippling across the region. More and more, the Saudi government was realizing it had to be more responsive to the needs of its people. Our lack of investment, meanwhile, was beginning to hurt us. Some of our business leaders were having trouble getting meetings in the UAE.

Five minutes in, I was sold. The question was how much. "I think it has to be at least one billion dollars," Rice said. "With a capital *B*."

I had good reason to want to say yes. Saudi Arabia had a huge problem with its unemployed youth (it still does, to this day). At that time, more than 65 percent of Saudis were younger than thirty. Women, especially, were graduating from college with no prospects for jobs. Beyond that, I had an appreciation for the role that Saudi played in the region. To the extent GE made a big investment there, other Middle Eastern countries would take notice.

We'd soon launch Project Kingdom, whose organizing principle was to identify Saudi's most pressing needs, and then to meet them. We became excellent listeners. Habayeb and his team mapped out whom we had relationships with inside the kingdom, noting particular leaders' priorities. Then they created a master list of what those people said their communities lacked. Affordable healthcare was one of the key areas, and we committed to improving access to basic services.

Next we created a partnership with Aramco and India's Tata Consultancy Services to create an all-female back-office center with a thousand jobs. The women who worked there provided payment processing and other services for not just the Arab world but also fifty countries outside of Saudi Arabia. The venture was a huge success.

Today, particularly after the murder of Saudi journalist Jamal Ahmad Khashoggi, who the CIA determined was killed by agents of the Saudi government in 2018, there are those who believe US companies that do business in Saudi Arabia—and that list is long— should reexamine, and even curtail, their relationships there. But I take a broader view.

Whenever GE was criticized for doing business in countries with controversial civil-rights records (or worse), I'd explain that I thought it was far better for the people of these countries that GE be there than not. I can't think of a single country that cannot benefit from something that GE has to offer. Yes, some of the places where we were operating were autocracies. Others were corrupt. But I firmly believed that the only way they would ever improve was if GE and other good companies were on the ground there, promoting responsible development, transparency, and commercial integrity and diversity—all core GE values.

In the end, in the years after we formed the GGO, we invested about $2 billion in Saudi Arabia and did $30 billion in business—a good investment-reward ratio, I'd say. GE had sustained its engagement to achieve a shared outcome. We knew that judging another country from thousands of miles away didn't work. Change must happen from the ground up.

PERSISTING THROUGH VOLATILITY

India is the second most populated country in the world, with more than 1.2 billion people. It is a very noisy, bureaucratic democracy, and decision making is always slower than mud. For example, we worked on one locomotive deal in the remote eastern city of Bihar for twenty years. When I complained to the minister of railways about the delays, he told me he had written a three-hundred-page book called *The India Locomotive Tender Process*. If we wanted to secure the contract to make a thousand diesel locomotives, it seemed we needed to do it his way.

So we bid for the contract twice. Both times our bid was the most competitive, but the deal stalled. We were in a terrible position by that point because rival bidders now knew the terms we'd offered. By the time we submitted our third bid, we'd lost what leverage we'd ever had. And yet, because we hung in, we ultimately won the contract, beating out Caterpillar, who'd enjoyed the number one position there for more than thirty years.

While we were waiting for that locomotive deal to crystallize, we invested in manufacturing. We built GE's first-of-its-kind multi-modal plant in 2012 that could make aviation components, turbines, or PET scanners, depending on demand. Here was the thinking: it saved us money to build products in-country (instead of exporting them from the US), but we didn't have enough volume in India in each of our industries to merit building a specialized facility to make each one. We invested $200 million to build the flexible multimodal plant, and it paid for itself within three years.

We also localized our approach to the healthcare business with the help of Terri Bresenham, a great executive who had run GE's Women's Health, Ultrasound, and Cardiac X-ray divisions in France before transferring to India. In 2014, I'd sat down with Bresenham for one of my weekends with senior leaders. She told me she was so determined to improve our business in India that she'd taken it upon herself to move into a public hospital in Gujarat and live there for a week. When I asked why, she said, "Because if our products can't help people, then what are we in business for?"

Based in Bangalore, Bresenham worked to develop super-low-cost healthcare products that could be sold in Africa, Latin America, and Asia. This was a first for us: empowering leaders in emerging markets to champion products for one another, without US head-quarters approval. This improved speed and lowered cost. And it didn't hurt that GE's largest research facility was in Bangalore, too. It attracted the best technical talent in the country, which helped us build not just our healthcare arm but also our other businesses.

We had less success in our attempts to bring GE turbines to India. Whenever I visited the country, I remember frequent electricity outages in whatever hotel I was staying in. And yet India's bureaucracy blocked our attempts to bring a more stable power supply. Instead of getting exasperated, we pivoted to Bangladesh.

Before the GGO, we were pretty much absent in Bangladesh, and our revenues there reflected our lack of effort. I think we did about $150 million a year then. But within two years of the GGO's launch, we'd found good partners to work with locally, and business ramped up to $1 billion a year. Our patience was rewarded: about half of the country's power-generation capacity now relies on GE turbines.

Colleagues of mine who traveled with me to Bangladesh will laugh that I'm touting the virtues of patience. Because while I truly believe that a lengthy time horizon is essential when doing business in emerging markets, I was often anything but patient while actually visiting those markets. Ed Galanek, my trusted security guy who traveled everywhere with me, loves to tell the story of how, one morning in Dhaka, we found our driver and set off for a high-level meeting. Our destination was less than two miles away, but suddenly, our vehicle was at a standstill. I looked out the window to see five lanes of traffic squeezed into three lanes of road.

"Hey, Ed," I said from the back seat. "What's going on?"

To understand Galanek's and my dynamic, you have to know that Eddie is a former cop who could have easily been a stand-up comedian. The son of a hotel doorman from the Bronx, he talks with his hands, and he's impossible not to like. On 9/11, Galanek was among the first responders, but when I met him, he'd been manning the door at *Saturday Night Live* for years. If Eddie had a dollar, he'd give you fifty cents. But he also loved to give me a hard time. So when I asked why we weren't moving, he rolled down his window and craned his neck.

"Huh," he said, milking it. "It looks like we're in traffic."

I was itchy. I like moving forward. "You think we can walk from here?" I asked. Eddie turned around. It was his job to keep me safe. He'd seen this movie before.

"I want to advise you, Jeff, that we are currently in a safe and secure vehicle," he said, his voice dripping with condescension. "Outside of this vehicle is Dhaka. I will support you in your endeavor to walk. I'll point you in the right direction. I'll try to keep an eye on you, and you're taller than all these cars, so I'm pretty sure I'll see you. But here's where you and I go our separate ways."

"All right," I grumbled. "Enough already."

These trips to the region were well worth all my grumbling, though, because they paid off. When the GGO was born, I think we sourced less than $500 million of our products from India. Six years later, we were sourcing ten times that amount—$4 to $5 billion—from India for larger GE. Oh, and by the way, after five years we were on track to ship 1,500 locomotives, 50 percent more than planned. Something was working.

CEMENTING RELATIONSHIPS

It's a CEO's responsibility to develop personal connections with customers—what I called "doing the job retail, not wholesale." In 2010, on a trip to Aberdeen, Scotland, I'd stopped and had tea with Sir Ian Wood, the chairman of John Wood Group PLC, which had an oil-well business we were interested in. Less than a year later, that business came up for auction, and of the three bidders in the hunt, GE was in last place. So I picked up the phone and called Sir Ian. Soon we'd hashed out the details of a $2.8 billion sale. Our fledgling personal relationship "was pretty fundamental to getting the deal across the line," Wood told the *Wall Street Journal*.

Other relationships took years, even decades, to build. In 2004, I went to Russia and met with President Vladimir Putin to talk about making GE locomotive engines in his country. I offered to buy a majority share in the local locomotive company Transmec. He said he loved the idea and sent me to see Vladimir Yakunin, the president of Russian Railways. I thought we were in! But when I told Yakunin what Putin had told me, he was more than a little displeased. "Fuck off," he told me in English, though he'd spoken only Russian until that point. "You'll do that over my dead body."

Undeterred, we did a work-around, building a joint venture with Kazakhstan's national railway KTZ that continues to this day. But I didn't give up in Russia. In 2009, I flew fourteen hours to Sochi, the little town on the Black Sea where Putin has a summer home. I would be on the ground only four hours, before flying fourteen hours back. But in that time, I told Putin GE needed help getting traction in Russia, and for the first time, he seemed to hear me. (In 2013, GE and Rosneft, Russia's largest oil company, committed to a strategic partnership that would include gas turbines, oilfield equipment manufacturing, and locomotives.)

Putin wasn't the only strongman I sat across from as I tried to advance GE's agenda. I met several times, for example, with the president of Turkey, Recep Tayyip Erdoğan. Though now he is a dictator, Erdoğan was seen as a reformer then. He was friendly to American businesses and sought our guidance. I remember in 2007, when the price of oil was skyrocketing, I was in his office with his ministers of energy and industry when Erdoğan announced, "We're going to build a nuclear power plant."

I was surprised. As far as I knew, they had no expertise. "You know, those are hard to do, nuclear power plants," I said.

"Yeah, we're going to do it," he said. "But Mr. Immelt, how long do you think it will take?"

When I told him fifteen to twenty years, I could see the blood drain out of his minister of energy's face. Erdoğan nodded his head in the guy's direction. "He tells me he can do it in five years." The minister was glowering at me, but what could I do but tell the truth? I said, "Five years would be a world record by half. Considering it's your first one, I wouldn't count on it."

Whether I was meeting with Italy's Silvio Berlusconi or the new prime minister of Pakistan, I went into every meeting with a head of state with the same approach. Instead of saying what GE wanted, I'd ask what they needed. "What challenges are you facing? What's your biggest worry? What can we do to help you?"

Of all the leaders I met with, Angela Merkel was my favorite. The German chancellor was a great listener, and she was disarming. Of all the world leaders I've sat across from, she is the only one who I've ever seen wave assistants away so she could serve coffee to her guests. She'd stand up, offering cream and sugar, like a hostess. And then she'd sit down, look at me with those steely blue eyes, and say, "So, Mr. Immelt, what are you going to do for the German people?" She was formidable.

With Merkel and others, I figured out that the best way to sell GE products, and to get invited back, was to bring something to the table. Sometimes that "something" was a GE product we were trying to sell, but as often as not it was simply information or advice. Maintaining good relationships can sometimes be as simple as keeping your finger in the dike and holding it there until you can solve the problem. I strove to be worthy of people's time, even as I made clear I'd always have time for them.

Walking that talk could be exhausting. Consider this thirty-hour "day" from one of my itineraries: It began at a breakfast in Tokyo with representatives of Toshiba Corporation. We had a joint venture with Toshiba to repair the GE gas turbines that provided power to millions of Japanese consumers. From Japan, a few colleagues and I flew nearly thirty-five hundred miles east to Astana, Kazakhstan, to close a deal at a manufacturing facility that was making GE locomotives. We were chasing the sun, which still hadn't set when we got back on the plane and headed to the United Arab Emirates—two thousand miles to the southeast. We had a dinner date with the Abu Dhabi sovereign wealth fund. Mubadala, as it's known, was a key partner for GE's oil-and-gas business, and its members were among many crucial relationships I nurtured in the Middle East. It was midnight before we said our goodbyes and returned to the tarmac to board a GE jet. We'd sleep on the way home.

Since I retired, much has been made of the fact that when I flew overseas on GE business, there was often a "chase plane" deployed to follow me. The reason for the practice was to ensure I never got stranded in a remote location or missed an important meeting. In retrospect, I see that the chase planes made GE look terrible and made me look not just self-indulgent but imperial. I should have paid more attention to appearances. I can only stress that my global travel was all about hustling to help GE leaders be responsive to our customers. During this era, we rarely lost an important deal anywhere in the world.

I know some on my team—John Rice in particular—would try to protect me from hustling myself to death. Rice knew if I found out about a business opportunity, I'd be like a dog straining at the leash.

He'd tell the sales folks in the trenches, "You don't need Jeff to get on a ten-hour flight to Egypt for a twenty-minute meeting, just because the Siemens guy has been there the week before." And he used to warn me, "I don't want you to keel over from exhaustion." Rice also felt I needed to pay attention to the precedents I was setting. In Egypt, for example, President Abdel Fattah al-Sisi got so used to seeing me that he decreed he would only negotiate with me personally. Which would have been fine except that there were more than a hundred other countries whose leaders could, arguably, make the same request.

The son of an antiques dealer, Sisi, as he's known, loved to haggle. Usually, meetings with heads of state were more cerebral and could revolve entirely around high-level policy debates. But Sisi preferred to get into the minutiae of deals. And as a general who'd once been Egypt's minister of defense, he believed he deserved special treatment. He would rub his hands together happily as he said, "I insist on the general's discount!"

Sisi and I had a strong relationship because, as I've said, before the summer of 2014, GE had successfully installed two gigawatts of emergency power for him, averting blackouts. Still, I remember on one visit, we hadn't exchanged a minute of pleasantries before Sisi announced, "I've been told that you are charging too much for your turbines. What is your best price?" I had no idea what he was talking about. I hadn't been briefed on that particular deal, as we had many in the works in Egypt, and I'd thought I was there to talk strategy, not dollars and cents. I smiled as my colleagues scrambled to figure out what he was referring to. I don't remember the specifics, but if it was a $2 billion contract, Sisi cut it in half.

I was laughing as he demanded, "Stand up. Let's shake on it now." I didn't take offense. I admired the chutzpah. "Mr. President," I said, still smiling as I demurred, "I promise we'll give you a fair price."

I want to be clear that, while we didn't rely on the US government to pave the way for GE, we always communicated with top officials at the State Department. A typical call from me to Secretary of State John Kerry (or Hillary Clinton) started with me letting them know I was about to be in Russia (or Egypt or Turkey or Saudi). "Anything you need me not to do?" I'd ask. While I don't want to get into specifics, suffice it to say that when certain crises erupted in certain regions, GE responded. Sometimes we walked away from business in order to avoid the perception that we were endorsing the offending government's transgressions. First and foremost, my focus was on trying to see each country through the eyes of GE's people on the ground there. I trusted my colleagues who toiled at the local level, and I always aimed to make their jobs easier when I could.

HIRING LOCAL TEAMS

I've talked about the importance of making local investments, being persistent through cycles, and nurturing relationships with leaders. But when it comes to making your company truly global, there's one more job that is essential: recruiting talent to help you see the way. The story of GE in Nigeria is the perfect illustration of that.

Nigeria was a complicated place. When viewed from a distance—from London, say, or New York City—every deal there looked risky. Which was why we needed Lazarus Angbazo as our team leader. He'd grown up in a small village called Keffi, about one hour away from the capital, Abuja. His father—the paramount ruler, or chief, of the Eggon tribe—had raised his nine children to believe in the redeeming power of education. So after getting a bachelor's degree in math at Ahmadu Bello University in Zaria, Angbazo came to the United States to earn his master's in statistics at the University of Iowa and his PhD in finance at New York University.

Angbazo had taught at Purdue University and worked at Fannie Mae and at JPMorgan before joining GE Capital—an unconventional résumé for overseeing a team of industrial operators in a faraway place. But his affection for the parts of sub-Saharan Africa where we wanted to grow our businesses made him the perfect choice. He took great pride in facilitating GE projects there because he knew firsthand what a difference they would make.

The foundation of GE's strategy in Nigeria was a five-year country-to-company agreement (we called it a C2C) between GE and the government of Nigeria. The agreement, signed in 2009, stipulated that we would work collaboratively to develop solutions to Nigeria's infrastructure needs in myriad areas. For example, in 2013, GE started construction of a multimodal manufacturing, service, and assembly facility in the Calabar Free Trade Zone.

Like the one we'd built in India in 2012, the facility was designed to develop local service, repairs, and supply-chain capabilities to support GE's power-generation and oil-and-gas businesses, among others. The project was the only one of its kind in Africa, and it set GE apart. Not only did it assure we complied with local regulations, but it also strengthened GE's competitive position for major offshore projects and helped us execute on the long-term service agreements we had for the large installed base of gas turbines in Nigeria (about 80 percent of which were made by GE).

Our biggest projects in Nigeria were with the Dangote Group, a Nigerian conglomerate. We sold them turbines, locomotives, and healthcare equipment. There's no question that Dangote bought from GE because of our local team. The country's politicians liked the GE team, too. For example, in 2014, I came to Abuja for a meeting with Nigerian president Goodluck Jonathan and his cabinet. This was the fourth time I'd met Jonathan in person since his election in 2011, but this time I had something specific I needed: the renewal of the five-year C2C, which was about to expire. I arrived ready to talk about the progress we were making on a variety of fronts. But I would realize that the smartest thing I did was to bring a dozen GE leaders with me, all of them African and many of them Nigerian.

This wasn't hard for us to do. At the time, 95 percent of GE's leaders in Nigeria were local. But still, the impact of our arrival was palpable. As we walked into the meeting room—twelve black African men and women and one white American CEO—you could see the president's eyes twinkle. Once we found our places, Jonathan—who, despite being born into a poor family of canoe makers, always wore a snappy fedora hat—looked slowly around the room, appraising our team in a way that seemed to emphasize the point.

"I like your faces," he said finally, smiling wide. We got the C2C renewed that day, enabling several future service contracts, as well as equipment orders for oil and gas, power, healthcare, and aviation. Overall, orders for GE products in Nigeria totaled more than $1 billion that year.

CHINA MATTERS MOST

Of all the places where GE invested and sold its products, China was by far the most important. It offered the most potential for growth, and the market would soon be huge—bigger than that in the United States. Many of GE's peers—and even the Chinese government—wanted to position the company as the world's factory because of the cheap labor there. Not me. I valued our Chinese customers and the huge market opportunity. The factories we built in China were intended to serve markets throughout Asia, not the US market. I believed winning in China would make GE more competitive globally. I didn't want our team to be afraid of China, so I began calling it "GE's second home market."

I'd first visited in 1987, for GE Plastics. I flew to Hong Kong, then took a regional jet to the southern city of Shenzhen, in the Guangdong province. Then paramount leader Deng Xiaoping was driving economic reforms that opened the country to foreign trade and investment; he'd designated Shenzhen a "special economic zone" in which experiments with market capitalism were encouraged. But as I drove away from the airport, I was struck by how primitive the place was. People lived in small dwellings with outdoor bathrooms.

I was headed to the Nansha District, where we were about to build our first manufacturing plant in China. In just a few years, that plant would be able to produce twenty thousand tons per year of high-performance thermoplastics—those pellets I've told you about—for cars, computers, telephones, and other goods. After touring the site we'd chosen to build on, I went on sales calls. I remember meeting Terry Gou, the founder of Foxconn, the Taiwanese multinational electronics manufacturer that would eventually make motherboards for Intel. Foxconn's first plant in mainland China was about to open not far away, and they needed GE's plastic pellets as a main ingredient. (By the year 2000, Foxconn would be GE Plastics' biggest customer in the world.)

For the next three decades, I went to China two or three times a year. More than perhaps any other Western CEO, I had the opportunity to see the country evolve up close. While the popular take on China was that it was inhabited by IP thieves, I saw a people who were working tirelessly to better themselves. While articles about Chinese dissidents highlighted how personal freedoms were under attack, I witnessed how the migration of millions of Chinese from rural areas to cities had created a vast new middle class. A growing elite, meanwhile, was amassing private wealth. More and more, when I stepped outside my hotel, BMWs and Mercedes sedans sped by. China was transforming itself from the world's factory to an economic superpower.

| | | |

In the summer of 1997, when I was CEO of GE Healthcare, I decided to spend GE's traditional August break visiting twenty second-tier cities across China. I'd been to the first-tier—Beijing, Shanghai, Guangzhou, and Shenzhen are known as "the Big 4"— many times by that point, but I was interested in smaller places like Tianjin, Chengdu, Xiamen, and Wuhan, whose populations ranged from 4 to 6 million. I visited hundreds of hospitals and met with local leaders and customers. What I saw and heard during this trip made me realize: GE needed to be in China in a major way.

"No matter what happens," I told myself (and, later, anyone else who would listen), "we have to invest here. China equals growth." The facts were stark: enormous numbers of people needed healthcare and, notably, the government was committed to providing it. When I met with the mayor of Chengdu, he summed it up like this: "Of course we're going to do healthcare. It's the only way to liberate the people." It was clear China could be an enormous market for GE's MRI and CT machines.

On that trip I remember my GE leader in China, Chih Chen, told me, "If we can make CT scanners locally and hit the right price point, we'll sell five times what we sell in the US." We built a CT factory in Beijing in 1999, and Chen's prediction soon came true. If I hadn't already grasped how important the Chinese market was to GE, this would've convinced me.

I'd been to China thirty times when I became CEO, but I'll never forget my first visit after getting the job. It was right after 9/11, in September 2001, when I sat down in Beijing with twenty leaders who worked in the region. As we went around the room introducing ourselves, I was struck that only two of them actually lived in mainland China, and they were mid-level employees. (Of 185 GE officers, not a single one lived in China at that time.) I remember Steve Schneider, our GE executive based in Hong Kong, telling me that three hundred new airports were being built in China. My takeaway: as China grew, GE needed to better position itself to meet its needs.

In 2005, for example, the United States had one commercial aircraft for every forty-five thousand people, but China had only one per 1.6 million people. As their economy developed, I knew their demand for jet engines would be vast. As their cities grew bigger, they'd need electric-generating capacity and improved transportation corridors, which meant more locomotives. Their consumers and businesses would need financial services. China was going to buy all these things from someone. I wanted that someone to be GE.

So how did we make the inroads we needed in China? We'd long recognized the importance of relationships there, particularly with the government. During a trip in 1999, my predecessor had sat down with President Jiang Zemin and they'd created what we called the China CEO Program. The idea was simple: every year GE would host twenty to twenty-five Chinese CEOs for three weeks in the United States, at Crotonville. The attendees were chosen by China's Central Organization Department, a governmental arm that serves as China's de facto HR department in that it selects most senior leaders of state agencies and state-owned enterprises.

When the visiting CEOs arrived in New York, we'd send them to leadership classes to learn the GE way. All GE's top business leaders would come to talk to them, as would Jack Welch. The Chinese were eager to learn from insiders about the iconic American conglomerate. But we gained something, too: broad access to China's next generation of leaders.

There is a word in Chinese—*guanxi*—that refers to the system of social networks and influential relationships that facilitate business success. It's fair to say the China CEO Program was GE's silver bullet when it came to *guanxi*. By the time I became CEO, people who'd attended these Crotonville immersion sessions were in power all over China—several were among the country's top leaders. Every time I visited, I would meet with scores of them. Again and again, they steered business our way.

Early on, I saw that China was developing technical strength and talent. So I pushed to open a new research center in Shanghai. In short order, our team there was able to handle complex projects. But the GRC offshoot also helped us win business because we hosted the leaders of state-owned businesses there and got to understand, up close, what they lacked. We realized, for example, that Chinese companies were completely inept at selling outside of China. The government had done so much for them that they hadn't needed to develop the skills. That was yet another area in which I believed GE could prove its value.

In the early 2000s, GE landed the contract to make engines for a regional jet produced by the state-owned aerospace company Comac. The ARJ21 was the country's first step into commercial aviation. It was a fine plane and was backed and financed by the Chinese government. But they had no sales or service capability and no mechanisms to market the plane to increase its global footprint. Over the next decade, Comac sold some of them, but not many. Not even Chinese airlines would buy them.

To sell more GE jet engines, I concluded, GE Aviation needed to help the Chinese increase the demand for their planes. We built several joint ventures with Chinese partners who could help us penetrate the local market. There was always a risk that technology could be "borrowed"—giving ammunition to a global competitor—but I felt risk of that was lower than the risk of not competing in China at all.

Eventually in China, GE would have a 75 percent market share in aviation, higher than in the United States. China bought all their engines from the US or France. That would never have happened but for our willingness to invest in local capability. In 2012, we built Aviage Systems, a joint venture with the state-run avionics company Aviation Industry Corporation of China, or AVIC. When we launched Aviage, GE was number three in the world in avionics, behind Honeywell and Rockwell Collins. But we saw an opening in China's plan to expand Comac. We wanted their airplanes to feature GE's avionics suite as well as our aircraft engines. So we merged our existing avionics business with AVIC's, forming a fifty-fifty partnership. And we got our wish: when it came time to choose an avionics system for Comac's next airplane, the C919, we won the contract.

It's complicated to merge a bunch of Cincinnati-based engineers with their counterparts in Shanghai. There were culture clashes that required accommodation on both sides. It took leadership and the constant repetition—at least within GE—of a mantra that fit all of our businesses in China: "We're not going into China with the goal of extracting their last pint of blood. We have to strive to succeed together."

There were times when a local partner stole our technology to compete with GE. In 2007, for example, we'd taken our locomotive technology there, striking a $450 million deal to sell three hundred units. The first two were assembled in the United States and then shipped to China. The remaining 298 were shipped as kits. The idea was that, over time, more and more of the components of those locomotives would be locally sourced. Eventually, we hoped, 80 percent of the GE components would be China-made.

But that was not to be because China Railway, another state-owned company, soon began making its own locomotives. It seemed they'd opened ours up and replicated what they found inside. Later, we would be in the galling position of competing against China Railway for locomotive deals in Indonesia, South Africa, and Brazil. Our sales guys reported that our rivals pitched their locomotives as "just like GE's!" It sure seemed to us that they were selling our technology as their own. That wasn't fair, but I viewed it as part of the learning process.

Now, here's the really important part: we were still winning around the world. Global customers didn't want to buy Chinese products, even when they were based on American technology. GE had great sales and service people and we invested in local talent. The GE folks pitching locomotives in Brazil were Brazilians, not Americans. Our Chinese competitors did none of those things. As an American, I always felt that our government should have a single-minded focus on giving us access to the Chinese market. We could handle the rest.

Whenever we had any concerns in China, and aired those concerns privately with the Chinese government, I found officials appreciated our desire to find a solution, not stir up xenophobia. Besides, I knew the US government lacked the relationships (not to mention the will) to solve things on our behalf. Contrary to many popular conceptions about China's bureaucracy, it is not monolithic. Usually, when we flagged a problem, it was news to the person with whom we raised it. Because of the mutual respect we'd built over many years, the conversation would generally go something like this: "Look, we think there's an issue here." "Thank you very much, Mr. Immelt. It will go away."

Listening ruled in China, and I grew to respect it as a business strategy. At one point, in a bundled-energy deal, the Chinese government assigned local partners to GE and our rivals. Siemens was paired with Shanghai Electric, which GE had lobbied for (we got what we perceived to be the less attractive Harbin Electric). When I complained to the head of the National Development and Reform

Commission, the state's macroeconomic management agency, he said I was looking at it all wrong. "Jeff, this is a compliment to you," this gentleman, who was one of the seven most powerful men in the country at that time, told me. "You should feel good: we think so highly of GE that we're giving you the partner that needs you the most!" In China, you won't always get your way—far from it. But I learned not to obsess too much about each setback or triumph. Doing business there required a long-term view.

I always kept focused on the power of the Chinese market and the reach of the Chinese government. Let's face it: in some markets, China has replaced the United States on the economic development front. In the Middle East, Africa, and Latin America, Chinese construction companies built power projects with GE products and Chinese financing. That is the nature of globalization. But when you are "In China for China," as GE was during my tenure, you can succeed and work around trade wars.

When I retired, GE had twenty-one thousand employees in China—99 percent of them local and most focused on winning in China. This included seven GE officers. We were developing all of the capability required to win in the local market. We had an installed base of more than ten thousand jet engines. Our healthcare business was approaching $4 billion in revenue and was highly profitable. We were building life sciences parks with Chinese and American partners. We were positioned to capture a growing gas-turbine market. We were ramping up our exports from the United States to China. (GE always exported more from the US to China than vice versa—what I call being a "net exporter." That created a lot of jobs in the US.) We were respected by the Chinese government. That's what happens when you show up and treat people with respect.

The COVID-19 crisis has shone a harsh light on China. Even those of us who have long touted the potential of the China market and local partnerships are disappointed by the country's initial cover-up of the virus. Add to that the growing trade pressures and it is easy to envision a period of geopolitical volatility marked by anti-China sentiment.

I understand this sentiment, which exists at the grassroots level in America. And the voices of business leaders who could encourage a more constructive dialogue has gone silent. But does anyone think that a trade war between the world's two biggest economies is a good idea? Beyond that, I fear that the next generation of American business leaders will be afraid of China, or that they won't believe that it's their job to learn how to compete there. That is a mistake. Particularly when the United States and China are the only two countries that matter when it comes to solving the world's toughest problems.

China has transitioned from merely being a manufacturing powerhouse to commanding respect as an important intellectual hub. Today, "Made in China" no longer means cheaply produced goods. Instead, in industry after industry, it means: China has decided to stake out a position, and the world will likely follow. The only reason there is a solar industry, for example, is because the Chinese decided it would be so and set about making the solar panels and selling them below cost. I suspect they will outpace the United States in electric-vehicle deployment as well.

In a world of growing competition, we will never be protected from China. Every year for the past twenty-five years, China has graduated more engineers than the US and Europe combined. Moreover, on an increasing number of issues, China is "the decider." If climate change is your focus, look to China: they are leading not only in solar but in the next generation of batteries, nuclear power plants, and electric vehicles as well. China will be on par with the United States on next-generation AI and digital tools. Recently, when Boeing faltered, China was the first country to ground the 737 MAX narrow-body jet. Where China goes, increasingly, so goes the world.

Life has a way of bringing things full circle. In Jack Welch's last decade as CEO, GE Plastics had a chance to partner with China National Petroleum Corporation to build a $1 billion resin plant. Unlike the pellet manufacturing plant we'd built in Nansha, this would have required that GE bring its chemistry—the recipes for our polymers—into the country. Jack decided against it. "They're going to steal all our tech!" he said. But then the technology went off patent, and China built its own factories to make resins without us. Later, that was among the reasons we sold GE Plastics—because we'd lost that huge market. China had taught me a lesson, once again, that still holds true today: if you're not doing business in the biggest end-use market in the world, you're probably not going to survive.

A LITTLE BIT OF WE

From the start, I'd known that the GGO would be a bitter pill for some business leaders to swallow, but I trusted them to see how it served GE. In fact, most of GE's businesses—while agnostic, at first—slowly came around. One area on which the GGO shone a spotlight was how much we'd been duplicating or even triplicating certain functions, because each business had its own people in the regions. As we began to do more business abroad and operate more efficiently, many more GE people came to see the GGO as an ally.

One notable exception was John Krenicki, who was president and CEO of GE Energy. This guy was an incredible operator—self-disciplined and highly organized—and I respected him immensely. I'd known him for thirty years, and I'd promoted him three times, even making him a vice chairman in 2008 because I wanted his value to the company to be recognized. But there was one key area in which Krenicki fell short: when he dug in on something, it seemed to me he would refuse to collaborate with others unless he got his way.

I tended to think of the vice chairmen I'd promoted as big-picture thinkers. Running a company as big as GE, I needed a handful of advisers who could help me think horizontally across the company, even as they did their day jobs. These people took good ideas and made them better (while deconstructing and discouraging bad ideas). I'm thinking of John Rice, Keith Sherin, Mike Neal, Beth Comstock, and an executive I haven't introduced yet: aviation chief David Joyce. Coming out of the financial crisis, I was wounded; I needed these advisers more than ever. Krenicki never made that list.

I know sports metaphors are overused in business leadership books, but that's because they are often such a good fit. I spent a lot of my time as CEO thinking about how to get people to play well together, but when it came to the GGO, Krenicki simply refused to suit up. And he wasn't quiet about it. His feeling was that he knew his business best and he shouldn't have to suffer the input of anyone else.

It wasn't the first time I'd noticed Krenicki's refusal to collaborate. Every quarter, I'd do detailed reviews with each business. Joyce, the Aviation leader, would bring twenty people to these reviews, all of them immensely prepared, and we'd spend four hours together. Same with every other leader. Krenicki would usually just bring his CFO and himself to the table, and his relaxed body language—I remember him reclining lackadaisically in his chair—seemed to say, "When will this be over?" He seemed to radiate resentment.

A resentful leader can be tolerated when he is executing well. When Krenicki's performance started to suffer, though, I found his attitude hard to bear. We fought over everything. On his watch, we were falling behind in gas-turbine technology, but when I raised it with him, he made it clear I should butt out. I wanted Krenicki to help me develop a young executive named Lorenzo Simonelli. He refused, saying Simonelli wasn't experienced enough. But how was he supposed to gain experience if we didn't give it to him?

The situation made me sad. Krenicki had been one of GE's most accomplished leaders and he'd more than earned his promotion to vice chairman. But then he'd failed to take the next step—to see his new role as an opportunity to demonstrate his ability to lead change and collaborate with others. Years before, I'd considered him a great candidate to succeed me. But the way he behaved as he rose within the ranks, he took himself out of the running.

Then, at the end of 2011, in the midst of a tough market, he missed his numbers. My thinking was: Why do I put up with all the guff he gives me, when he doesn't hit his numbers either? In February 2012, I told him that I'd give him some time, but he needed to find another job. "Look," I told him, "you're duplicating everything that the GGO and GE corporate is doing. You have your own training classes, separate from Crotonville's. It's clumsy, it's slow, and we need to make a change." He looked shocked. I said, "John, I made you a vice chairman because I wanted to keep you in the company. But as part of that, it would've been great if you'd helped more broadly."

Unlike in Jack Welch's day, when all hangings were public hangings, during my tenure we tried to let people we'd fired maintain their dignity. When we announced the change, in July 2012, we made it sound structural. GE Energy would be broken up into three businesses—Power & Water, Oil & Gas, and Energy Management— each of which would report directly to me. It wasn't, we said, that I was promoting Krenicki's deputies—Steve Bolze in Power & Water, Dan Heintzelman in Oil & Gas, Dan Janki in Energy Management. We were just removing a layer, saving $1 billion in the process. What I didn't say publicly was that for years, this particular layer had made every problem inside the company harder.

There are many in the company who second-guessed my decision on Krenicki. His skills might have helped us over time, especially as we hit tougher energy markets. But I never looked back. I didn't expect our leaders necessarily to be loyal to me. I did, however, insist that they be loyal to our collective mission.

I have no regrets, however, about championing the GGO effort. While it was controversial within the company, there's no question that it paid off. When I became CEO in 2001, 70 percent of GE's customers were US-based. When I left in 2017, 70 percent of revenues came from outside the United States' borders and GE was doing business in 180 countries. Thanks to the GGO, between 2011 and 2017 annual revenues from GE's existing industrial businesses outside the US grew from $51 billion to $70 billion. When I retired, we had twenty-six countries where GE's annual revenue exceeded $1 billion. Increasingly, businesses must create their own future, without a road map. At GE, we created a new route to globalization.

CHAPTER 8

Leaders Manage Complexity

This was no ordinary party. The black-tie dinner to which I'd been invited in June 2009 was held at Clarence House, a London town house built in 1825. Stuffed with antique furniture, Chinese porcelain, and important artworks, the place feels more like a monument than a home. Following their marriage in 1947, Princess Elizabeth and the Duke of Edinburgh had lived in the four-story mansion. Now, Clarence House housed the Prince of Wales and the Duchess of Cornwall.

I was among about fifteen guests that night whom Prince Charles had assembled to discuss climate change. The UK, like the rest of world, was heating up (the country's ten hottest years on record have occurred since 2002), and the prince was alarmed. The guests included three or four other CEOs of industrial companies, several leaders of environmental nonprofits, and Connie Hedegaard, a Danish executive who was organizing the United Nations Climate Change Conference in Copenhagen, to be held five months later. As we mingled under gilded ceilings in the formal dining room, I was struck by the irony: there was no air-conditioning, and the temperature was hot as hell.

We were all dressed in stifling tuxedos and full-length gowns. This was the kind of tableau that you'd imagine preserving in a photograph to show your parents—look, Mom, I'm sitting next to Prince Charles! But I'll never forget looking across the table at Hedegaard, who was about to host the crucial global warming event that would pave the way for the Paris Agreement seven years later. She had perspiration dripping off her chin into her Brussels sprouts, just as I did.

Later that evening, on the way out, Andrew Gould, the CEO of Schlumberger Limited, the world's largest oil-field services company, took me aside. "You know, Jeff," he said, "when we look at potential competitors, the company we fear most isn't Halliburton or Baker Hughes. It's GE." In those days, GE didn't have a huge oil-and-gas business, but Gould was thinking about us anyway. "We've always feared that you would get serious about oil and gas, because your breadth—the scale of what you do, the relationships you have— would be really disruptive to us. Customers love broad capability."

Over the years, I would hear similar comments from customers. Breadth, they said, was a big part of our appeal. Matt Rose, the CEO of Burlington Northern, told me at one point that he'd much rather buy from GE than from Caterpillar. "Technically, you're pretty close," he said. "But GE brings new perspectives. The fact that you know healthcare, you're strong in China, it's helpful to us." Similarly, CEOs of major healthcare companies such as the Cleveland Clinic and the Ochsner and Northwell Health systems would send their leaders to GE for training. They told me they favored GE because of our ability to bring industrial practices to the healthcare setting. There was a reason why a conglomerate such as GE existed.

There has long been a debate about the role of vast conglomerates, but one of the main advantages is that your businesses can support one another through respective lean times. In the 1990s, GE benefited from loosening credit markets as we grew in financial services. When GE's Aviation division was in the tank after the terrorist attacks of September 11, 2001, GE Power pulled us through. In the 2000s, financial services were a disaster, but natural resources were a tailwind. From 2010 to 2020, Aviation grew, but natural resources struggled. In 2020, COVID-19 will negatively impact GE Aviation. Most successful conglomerates today have a digital foundation— Alphabet, Amazon, and the like. It is difficult to "time markets," by which I mean enter them only when they're growing and exit them right before they begin to shrink. The key is to run your businesses well, pick a few macro themes to pursue (like I did with globalization). You have to weather cycles.

There are other advantages of being a conglomerate. Conglomerates are more relevant in places such as China, where the government and the state-owned enterprises that drive growth place preeminent value on relationships that extend across industries. And, of course, conglomerates can share research and infrastructure. Nonetheless, conglomerates go in and out of favor with investors. In 2000, the stock market loved industrial conglomerates. By 2017, investors had shied from them. They wanted to put their money into companies that were easier to see and to understand.

The biggest disadvantage of a conglomerate is its complexity. At GE, we constantly looked for ways to make the place simpler. How do you get the best out of complexity without being complex? It almost sounds like an impossibility, but it's not.

CREATING INCREMENTAL VALUE

The ties that bind a conglomerate's components together are varied and change over time. Berkshire Hathaway's organizing principle centers on Warren Buffett and his ability to allocate capital and pick stocks. Its rationale is "Whatever Warren Thinks." Alphabet is still developing its conglomerate context, but my sense is that the application of artificial intelligence is its reason for being. Amazon is not really a retailer, though it dominates that space. It is a software company. It exists to use software to disrupt traditional industries (particularly retail).

Usually, GE's competitors were not conglomerates, which meant they were focused on fewer products than we were. Our main rival in locomotive sales was an Illinois company called Electro-Motive Diesel, or EMD, a formidable competitor that had once been a subsidiary of General Motors. They made high-quality diesel-electric trains, engines, and parts. But nevertheless, over twenty years, GE Rail's market share went from 25 percent to 70 percent. Why? Because when you're running your conglomerate right, you can do things that single-point companies can't do. For starters, the Global Research Center gave GE the scale and ability to lead in locomotive fuel efficiency. We offered financing through GE Capital. Then, because the CEOs of the seven big Class 1 railroad companies were eager to piggyback on GE's HR processes, we invited them often to Crotonville. The Global Growth Organization helped us win almost every international deal, and we could use the service technology we'd developed in our Aviation and Healthcare divisions to keep the customers who bought GE locomotives satisfied.

This idea—that GE's many divisions could share capability to find new solutions to customers' problems—was well understood within GE. At its core was technology for both products and services, delivered anywhere in the world and supported by financing and digital technology. This constellation of capabilities—innovation and services and financing and digital, all on a global scale—was unique to GE. I pushed to give the idea a name, so customers could reference it more easily. That's how we began referring to our horizontal platform as "the GE Store."

I'd developed a good sense for how to leverage the GE Store when I was CEO of GE Healthcare, which would grow from $3 billion in revenue in 1997 to more than $20 billion when I retired. Our Global Research Center developed the technology to create valuable products, from lightweight ultrasound probes to proprietary manufacturing tools for immunotherapy. Later, our Global Growth Organization would help expand GE Healthcare's global footprint ahead of our competition. Because GE was so comprehensive and present on the ground, we were able to form strategic partnerships with countries like India, Kenya, Saudi Arabia, and Turkey. About one-third of our US healthcare equipment sales were financed by GE Capital.

Through my experience in Plastics and Healthcare, I saw that our businesses should continuously expand into new growth segments as markets evolved. In Plastics, we'd let the business get stale. In Healthcare, we'd pivoted to growth. From a strong base in equipment (like MR scanners), we had moved into digital devices (like patient monitoring systems) and biology (like diagnostic testing). All were successful. I knew our business could expand through investments and acquisitions.

Beyond running a profitable business, GE was a dominant thought leader in the healthcare industry. This enhanced our reputation and our ability to influence policy. It was exactly because of our breadth that we enjoyed that leadership; we were uniquely suited to address the competing demands of needing to keep healthcare costs low while maintaining manufacturing competitiveness. Globally, being trusted in the healthcare industry created a sort of halo effect for GE in that it made others believe we could solve complex problems in other industries as well. That's why I believed so strongly that the GE Store was the foundation of GE's market leadership.

PATTERN RECOGNITION

In 2005, we made a big push to leverage the GE Store at a customer meeting held by GE Oil & Gas. This annual meeting's attendees hailed from more than seventy countries, and each year, we used it to take the pulse of the people who paid us to solve their problems. By this point, it was becoming clear to us that it wasn't enough to merely sell products and service them. More and more, our customers needed us to be their partner—to innovate with them. We told them to look at the GE Store as a one-stop shop for technical solutions.

We had first entered the Oil & Gas business way back in 1995, when we acquired a small Italian company called Nuovo Pignone that was known for its compression technology, which is an essential part of how turbines work.

Early on, GE Oil & Gas's success depended on its ability to package mechanical systems that were reliable and efficient in hazardous environments. This industry operates in the deepest seas, the hottest deserts, the coldest tundras, and the world's most remote locations. Given that, all our customers needed three things—safety, quality, and reliability—in the pumps and compressors that we sold them to deliver oil and gas from where it was sourced to where it would be used.

Even inside big companies, investments can depend on the vision of a single leader. At GE Oil & Gas that leader was Claudi Santiago. A Spaniard who'd worked his entire career at GE, Santiago recognized that the industry was in transition. Projects were becoming bigger and more technical, and they were often located in tough-to-access places such as Angola and Norway. Revolutionary technology, like horizontal drilling, was opening up shale gas in North America. Our customers—which included big oil companies (Exxon, Chevron, BP, Shell) and national oil companies (Russia's Rosneft, Mexico's Pemex, Brazil's Petrobras, Saudi Aramco)—needed new technical solutions. But a big oil company is filled with geologists, not mechanical engineers. There was an opening for us.

Oil & Gas is a cyclical industry. Demand goes up and down. But that didn't faze me because we weren't investing for a year or two. We were determined to build a technical leader over the long term. As the world grappled with climate change, we believed that natural gas would play a vital role in the transition to cleaner technologies. I believed GE could partner in that transition, and GE's board agreed.

I remember visiting John Watson, the CEO of Chevron, in 2007. Chevron was investing in a huge project off the coast of Australia, but it was struggling with its equipment suppliers, all of whom were delivering late or over cost. Watson said to me, "Jeff, we need GE to be bigger in this industry. GE already makes machines that function thirty thousand feet above the ground. We need you to build products that work at ten thousand feet below sea level." I began to think that GE could perform the R&D function for the entire industry.

So how did the GE Store work? Say one of our Oil & Gas customers wanted to put a turbine on an offshore platform in the middle of the ocean. Real estate was at a premium, so the turbine needed to be small. Weight was an issue—it needed to be light. And since the turbine would be difficult to access, customers needed it to be monitored remotely. Our engineers built the solution using existing expertise in aircraft engines, which are relatively small and made of strong, lightweight materials. X-ray and directional drilling technology we'd developed in our Healthcare business came in handy, too—we could use it to calibrate the weight and resistance of the materials we were using. Under the umbrella of the GE Store, we marshaled all our know-how to serve our customers' needs.

GE Oil & Gas, which grew to a $25 billion business, added to our global footprint, and it gave us geographical leverage. Governments around the world valued our breadth and that meant we had an easier time securing a toehold in emerging markets. When we went on the road to developing countries, we could get a meeting with anyone. Why? Because we had the products that met their most basic needs: healthcare, rail, airplanes, power, and financing. We often received better treatment than a freestanding industrial company would.

AN ASPIRATION TO LEAD

From the earliest days, we benchmarked GE Oil & Gas against the gold standard: Schlumberger. So we needed great GE people to lead it. In 2013, we tapped Lorenzo Simonelli. He was the best young talent at GE, and I thought this job would test him.

Simonelli worked as hard as anyone I knew. His family had run an estate and vineyard in Tuscany for a time (he was born in Rome). But when Simonelli was nine, his banker father had moved the family to London. Simonelli had completed college at Cardiff University in

South Wales, majoring in business and economics. He'd joined GE in 1994 and did stints in Corporate Audit and Consumer Products, living all over the world. In 2008, I'd tapped him to become CEO of GE Transportation (at just thirty-seven, he was GE's youngest-ever division head). Five years later, he'd transformed that division from a North American rail business to a global equipment and solutions provider.

Now that Simonelli was running Oil & Gas, it had a great year in 2014 before heading into a down cycle the next year. During this period, as oil prices fell from over one hundred dollars a barrel to less than thirty dollars, I told Simonelli to keep an eye out for good deals.

Though we'd grown significantly, our customers still viewed GE Oil & Gas as a second-tier player. Perhaps this down cycle was a chance to change that. Simonelli had been tracking an attempt by Halliburton, the number two oil-field service provider after Schlumberger, to force a hostile merger with Baker Hughes, the number three company. For two years they'd worked on the deal, even as some predicted the Department of Justice would prohibit it. Simonelli kept me informed because we presumed that, if the deal closed, Halliburton could be forced to dispose of some assets, and we were the logical buyer.

Then, in March 2016, the DOJ blocked the merger. Simonelli reached out to Martin Craighead, CEO of Baker Hughes. One of Baker Hughes's key businesses was something called artificial lift, a technology that forces oil out of older wells as they run dry. As low oil prices led to reduced new drilling activity, artificial lift became even more lucrative. Maybe Baker Hughes and GE could help each other.

By this point we were deep into GE Digital's attempt to create its successful industrial analytical platform, Predix. Simonelli and I both saw the Oil & Gas business as one that could really benefit from what Predix had to offer. Why? Because so many parts of the oil-and-gas universe are in hard-to-reach places—a city of pipes far underwater, say, or out in a desert. No wonder the industry was clamoring for a system that could provide diagnostics from far away. Moreover, in this business, downtime caused by equipment malfunctions could be precisely measured (if you knew how many gallons of oil could be pumped when the system was working, you knew how much you weren't pumping when it broke). Services with a quantifiable value are easy to sell.

All that informed Simonelli's thinking as he considered Baker Hughes. In August 2016, he was at the Olympics in Rio de Janeiro when he sent me an email. He wrote: "Why don't we put GE Oil & Gas and Baker Hughes together and create a new company?" The next day, I told Simonelli he should come to the September 2016 board meeting and brief our directors.

Just as with Amersham in 2004, I knew that transformational deals rarely presented themselves at the most convenient time. We didn't have the cash to buy Baker Hughes outright, so we needed a creative solution. This could be our one-and-only chance to compete with Schlumberger. (There were only four companies that competed in this space, and the other three weren't for sale and didn't seem likely to be in the future.) We needed to act.

I was also interested in different models of what a conglomerate of the future could look like. Here was an opportunity to create a public company within a conglomerate—a separate, publicly traded business that remained GE's partner. I was always looking for smarter ways to run GE. Over the years, I had gotten to know Joe Tucci, the CEO of the tech equipment company EMC. He had acquired the software company VMware but kept it as a stand-alone public company. I'd watched as VMware created substantial value, and I viewed it as a great capital-markets experiment.

On October 30, 2016, with the support of GE's board, we announced the merger of Baker Hughes and GE Oil & Gas. The new entity would be called "Baker Hughes, a GE Company," and it would be 62.5 percent owned by GE and 37.5 percent public. It would be led by our Oil & Gas CEO Lorenzo Simonelli and would list on the New York Stock Exchange in July 2017 with a market capitalization of more than $40 billion.

Later that year, at our annual customer conference on oil and gas, I was onstage interviewing Bob Dudley, the CEO of BP and a good friend. At one point, we were talking about the price fluctuations that dogged his industry, and I asked him how he thought oil-and-gas companies would survive such volatility. He didn't hesitate. "Through digital transformation," he said. "We've got to get more productivity out of our oil fields by making them digital." It was another confirmation of my belief that GE's many businesses could raise one another up.

Incidentally, the GE Baker Hughes experiment wouldn't last long. After I left GE, my successor backed away from it. Finally, in July 2020, GE announced it would sell its entire stake within three years. More important, Simonelli realized that it is impossible to run an energy service company without a robust digital capability. This is necessary to deliver on customer productivity and environmental requirements. So as GE de-emphasized its digital platform, he decided to partner with Tom Siebel's C3.ai, taking a 10 percent stake in the company. Together, Baker Hughes and C3.ai are recognized as the energy industry's leader in the Internet of Things (and Baker Hughes's stake in Siebel's company is worth more than $1 billion). And Simonelli is building new technical platforms in carbon sequestration and hydrogen as the world transitions from oil.

Today, Baker Hughes is the industry's most successful competitor as measured by growth, earnings, and cash flow. They have the global position we had envisioned leading in the Middle East, Russia, and North America—the markets that matter most. The business is in a tough cycle, but investors are bullish on the company; they like its diversified portfolio, global position, and digital position. They rave about the leadership team. Of the company's top ten leaders, five are GE veterans.

PRIVATE EQUITY: A MODERN CONGLOMERATE?

On a Saturday morning in March 2015, I attended the memorial for G. G. Michelson, the trailblazing Macy's executive (and former GE board member) on whom I'd so often relied before her death at the age of eighty-nine. I'd flown into New York City at 2 a.m. that morning, having been in Colombia, Argentina, and Brazil to review our businesses and meet with customers. So as I walked into the Society of Friends Meetinghouse on Rutherford Place, I was a bit bleary-eyed. Then I saw Jack Welch. We shook hands and sat down next to each other.

Maybe it was the setting, but Jack and I found it easy to talk. I told him about my trip to South America, adding that he'd been right, as he left me in charge in 2001, to warn that the job would be grueling. For ninety minutes, we listened as people shared their memories (for his part, Jack said G. G. was one of the few who'd been able to tell him when he got "too big for his britches"). Afterward, as we walked out of the building, Jack returned to the subject of how a GE CEO's work was never done. "You'll love private equity someday," he said. "You don't have to work as hard and you make more money."

I'd already been a keen observer of the private-equity world. The firms were customers of GE Capital, where we bought and sold businesses together. In 2005, while serving as chairman of the Business Council, an august group of the world's top CEOs that was founded when FDR was president, there had been a move to add new members. I suggested we expand to include the leaders of private-equity firms. I nominated Steve Schwarzman from the Blackstone Group, Henry Kravis from KKR & Co., David Bonderman from TPG Capital, and Don Gogel from Clayton, Dubilier & Rice (CD&R).

My colleagues were surprised. "Those are investors, not CEOs!" they said derisively. But when I pointed out that each one of them could buy and sell the rest of us—"These guys run entities that are bigger than almost all our companies," I said—I prevailed.

Private-equity firms, which invest directly in private companies or buy out public companies and take them private, have been around for forty or so years, but in the last twenty, they've become dominant. While the number of public companies has dropped significantly in recent years, private equity has flourished. Today, private equity has nearly $2 trillion under management. Legacy companies must compete with these private funds for capital and talent.

There are several reasons for their success. First: sustained low interest rates have made it easy to use debt to buy companies. Second:

big companies often overlook smaller divisions and run them poorly—or, at least, without a commitment to winning. And third: when a private-equity firm takes a public company private, it gives the companies they invest in the space (and time) to solve problems. In contrast to publicly traded companies, those backed by private equity can be run out of the public eye. And sometimes that's what a company needs.

There are two kinds of conglomerates: operating companies and holding companies. CEOs of operating companies, such as GE, actively engage with each of their businesses to help set priorities and hold leaders accountable. CEOs of holding companies, by contrast, are more hands-off; they typically manage by allocating resources to each business, then standing back and seeing what happens.

Private-equity firms are a pretty good blend of these two—part operating company, part holding company. They are professional capital allocators. They know their way around a balance sheet, they know how to use the debt markets, they know how to structure financing. And they don't have the public pressure to make their quarterly earnings. At the same time, they can hire an experienced operator. They bring a clarity of thought—what some in the industry call "the rule of 40." In other words, you have forty months to hit cash and operational targets. Nothing else matters. Teams can relate to this simple message.

If GE had a business that was not being run well or that had suffered from lack of attention, I found it was sometimes better to sell it to a private-equity firm than to try to fix it in-house. A private-equity firm could take it off the radar as they made improvements. They could hire a retired Fortune 500 CEO and tell him or her, "We'll give you fifty million dollars if you turn this around." (Within GE, had you gone to the comp committee with such a proposal, you'd get fired.)

I have to admit that I understand some of the appeal. In 2006, the world was shocked when GE vice chairman Dave Calhoun left the company to run Nielsen, a small market-research firm owned by private equity. But when I thought about it, I wasn't so shocked. Calhoun was immensely talented and could do anything he wanted. Private equity gave him the freedom to control his schedule. In private equity, his overseers were investment bankers with spreadsheets. With them, Calhoun was usually the most knowledgeable guy in the room, and that gave him immense power. Nielsen was a great success for private equity, despite the fact that it never became a very competitive company. That is one of the secrets of private equity. Investors often generate great returns even when their businesses don't become winners.

Here's another GE experience with private equity: GE had been in the industrial supply business for decades. We used it to sell lighting and electrical products, but it was never one of our core businesses and we weren't a distribution company. So in 2006, we sold GE Supply to Rexel, the world's largest distributor, which renamed it Gexpro. Rexel's majority shareholders were an investor group led by CD&R, Eurazeo, and Merrill Lynch Global Private Equity. Their main contribution was financial, not operational. CD&R was able to make several acquisitions of other distributors, adding product lines and repairs. Today, Gexpro is a bigger player, and its investors have made a lot of money.

Occasionally, we also bought businesses from private-equity shops. In 2012, we paid about $4 billion to CVC, a major European PE firm, to acquire an aviation supplier called Avio. The company, which made gears and engine components, had once been a division of Fiat. Back in 2002, Fiat—concerned about the fate of commercial aviation in the wake of 9/11—had sold the division for a song. For the next decade, the asset was owned by a series of PE firms. When we bought it, we were motivated by our need to control our supply chain. But we knew Avio's quality had suffered from years of under-investment, so we had to make changes.

This was typical, I found. Private equity was masterful at timing and financial restructuring. But if you were developing technology that flies at thirty thousand feet, private equity's penchant for trading assets every four years didn't work so well. I remember having lunch in 2011 with Jim McNerney, who was then Boeing's CEO. At that point, the Boeing 787 was more than two years behind schedule, and McNerney told me part of the reason was that his company had outsourced too much of the plane to suppliers that were owned by private equity. Too often, he said, private equity underinvested in its businesses. I tended to agree with him.

I guess my point is that private equity gives CEOs of public companies an alternative to continuing to run a troubled business. But that option also comes at a price. There will be times when you think you know how to fix a floundering venture, but you get pushback because an activist investor is lobbying, "Just sell it to private equity!" In that way, private equity creates more noise and makes managing harder.

DEVELOPING TRUSTWORTHY LEADERS

If you're running a conglomerate, you need the kind of business leaders on your team who private-equity firms covet, but you need them to stay with you. These people know they could be making more money somewhere else, but they don't leave because they love their markets, they're loyal to their teams, and they want to be long-term builders.

As a CEO of a conglomerate, then, you can't be a micromanager, because it will drive these people away. You have to relax control, empowering each business leader to succeed in his or her market. This requires that you trust them. For me, the key to trusting any executive is believing that they are masters of their domain. But there are only a handful of leaders in any company who are true systems leaders. These are people who see what is next, without losing sight of what is most important today; they see the long term while still delivering short-term results.

There were several great systems leaders inside GE. I've mentioned Simonelli, who had what I would call a typical GE background, having served in many different capacities in several businesses. No matter where he worked, he immersed himself deeply to create expertise.

The best leader I knew, however—the person who understood most how to harness GE capabilities to win in the market—was a man who'd devoted himself to just one business: David Joyce, the CEO of GE Aviation. Smart, driven, and ethical, he joined GE in 1980 as a product engineer and spent fifteen years designing and developing GE's commercial and military engines, so he could go toe to toe with any technologist in his division. But he also understood the market he was selling into. He had huge connectivity with customers; they respected his command of the ecosystem in which he worked. They believed, as did I, that his mastery of all aspects of the business, from the supply chain to the service contracts, enabled him to make better decisions.

Joyce was strategic. He created a $4 billion avionics business, which meant we had more technology to sell to our existing customers. Similarly, he recognized the benefits of GE owning more of our supply chain to grow profit and improve quality. People talk about leaders' intuition, but this is developed, not inherited. Joyce had conviction, which allowed him not just to see what was coming next, but to act on it. Joyce was stubborn in a good way.

In 2014, Airbus was launching a new wide-body aircraft, the A330x. I wanted to pursue the contract to make the engine because, if we won it, it would take another application from Rolls-Royce and bring us closer to Airbus. But Joyce argued against it. He felt like it would be a distraction, given we were already launching six engines during that period. Plus, it would complicate our relationship with Boeing, Airbus's chief competitor. I knew that Joyce knew more than I did about all of those variables. I trusted him. So we didn't pursue the contract.

This incident wasn't unique. Joyce consistently pushed back on me, especially when it came to bureaucracy. He kept monthly tallies, for example, of how often GE corporate made demands on his time. We all agreed that Joyce's waking hours were best spent running his business, but his tallies proved how, too often, those hours were eaten up by corporate busywork. Joyce didn't point this out to harass me; his goal, always, was to make GE better.

To that end, Joyce was transparent on good days and bad. The first iteration of the GEnx engine resulted in a major design flaw in the low-pressure turbine. This caused significant delays and cost GE hundreds of millions of dollars to fix. Joyce was open, honest, and focused throughout this period. Upon reflection, those three qualities top my list when it comes to evaluating leaders. And at a conglomerate, in some ways, those qualities matter even more.

Under Joyce's leadership, GE Aviation never missed. Customers received our engines on time, we won every campaign that mattered, we grew around the world, we delivered for investors. GE Aviation disproved the notion that focused, single-business companies perform better than conglomerates. Even before Boeing's troubles with the 737 MAX, GE Aviation was better run than Boeing. Within a strong conglomerate, good leaders can win every time.

A BIAS FOR INNOVATION

The best leaders are able to see new systems and build businesses around them. This is what Amazon does with Amazon Web Services, its on-demand cloud computing platform, and what Google has done with Alphabet. The idea is to take a unit that you've created to make your conglomerate run better and then ask the question: "Could you sell it as a service?"

At GE, we tried to do this with additive manufacturing, or 3D printing. We'd developed the technology especially for use by GE Aviation, which needed to mass-produce lightweight metal parts called fuel nozzle injectors for its LEAP engine. Later, we designed the next generation of turboprop engines, reducing parts count and weight. For a high-tech industrial like GE, additive manufacturing—which allows you to make complicated parts (that previously were assembled from dozens of other parts) in a single piece, saving money and time—could revolutionize our product design and productivity.

I remember asking Joyce, who'd taken on GE Additive as well as his GE Aviation role, to assign a team to see how many parts we could make using additive techniques across GE. The answer? Five hundred. They estimated that we could potentially save almost $5 billion. So we decided to evaluate the market for additive manufacturing equipment. Since we were the technology's biggest customer and we held more than five hundred patents, we felt like we had an advantage. This was a $25 billion market that was growing 20 percent a year. Moreover, it fit our skill sets in design, services, materials, and financing. Could we build a better additive printing machine? The question reminded me of GE's race to design a better CT scanner; both required precise assembly of valuable components.

In September 2016, we announced plans to acquire two suppliers of additive manufacturing equipment. We hoped to grow the business to $1 billion in revenues by 2020. This became a new division inside GE, and we immediately became the industry leader. Plus, having this division gave us access to a new group of customers. Steris Corporation, the global leader in medical implants, built their company using GE additive technology.

I'd long thought it was important for GE to retain what I called a bias for innovation. So in 2012, we'd established a Ventures group based in Silicon Valley, led by Sue Siegel. I'd met Siegel several times over the years, and I was impressed by her thirty years of experience as a corporate executive and venture capitalist, with a particular focus on innovation at scale. When I approached her with this GE Ventures idea, I told her I wanted it to help GE innovate by creating a nimble vehicle that could partner with start-ups. Why are start-ups getting all the credit, I asked her, when GE has more scale?

Siegel didn't waste time. As she introduced herself to the GE businesses, she asserted a new methodology that included ring-fencing of risk and the deployment of very little capital—if you didn't meet clearly set milestones, you didn't get funded. GE Ventures' job was to link GE to the external world. Over a five-year period, we'd invest in 120 start-ups that we believed could empower our existing businesses. I liked to say that the members of Siegel's team were like Sherpas who helped those start-ups navigate the mountain that was Big GE. The idea was that if we could connect them to the company's many constituencies, we would up our chances of forming successful partnerships.

In addition, GE Ventures created several new companies from scratch. Our Oil & Gas customers sparked one idea when they asked for our help making inspections of oil rigs safer. Sending men to climb an oil stack in the middle of Texas's Permian Basin was time-consuming and dangerous. Wasn't there a better way? So we founded

Avitas, which uses unmanned drones in the air, robotic surface crawlers on land, and autonomous underwater vehicles to remotely monitor hard-to-access equipment.

Avitas, in turn, sparked another idea. Everyone wants same-day delivery of their packages—a reality that is expected to lead to more and more businesses employing commercial drones in highly populated areas. Our Aviation folks believed that whoever could design a system to manage all that traffic would make a lot of money. That led to AiRXOS—an interactive registry of routes for drones (much like what regulates commercial and military airspace). Its technology would enable many new applications, including the speedier transport of organs for transplant in traffic-clogged cities. It remains within GE Aviation today and is an important part of its future.

Of the nine start-ups we built from the ground up, eight are still flourishing. And of the 120 companies we invested in, 56 percent eventually formed some type of partnership with GE. Our bias for innovation was keeping us connected to new ideas, new innovators, and new markets.

CONSTANTLY SIMPLIFYING

Despite our best efforts, sometimes we couldn't get out of our own way. In 2012, I was in GE's large motor plant in Peterborough, Canada, which was losing money. I remember asking a dozen managers who each of them reported to. Every one had a different boss, and none of the bosses were on-site. The manufacturing guy worked under someone based in Atlanta. The service guy reported to a supervisor somewhere else. Ditto for the engineering leader. They'd created a matrix within a matrix, and no convening force existed to connect the leaders together.

I took that to heart. Over time, I tried to watch how GE people worked and to root out bureaucracy with a few simple questions. First I'd ask: Who do you work for? If the answer was more than one person, it was a bad sign. You should have only one boss. Next I'd ask: How are you measured? If workers didn't understand the metrics they were expected to live up to, it would be hard for them to succeed. People should have no more than three or four measures they are trying to meet, and those metrics must be clear and simple to understand. Finally, I wanted to know: Where do you live? If the person I was talking to was responsible for Africa but lived in London or Dubai, there was trouble in paradise. It's important to live close to where you work (I'll come back to this in chapter 10, with a cautionary tale).

I decided to pick one operating process and track it for a while. For eighteen months, I followed GE's commercial operations (known as comm ops), delving deeply into how orders got booked within the company. I had people come in and teach me how contracts were written and how they got approved (and by whom). Going behind the curtain to observe the nitty-gritty of working in comm ops, I learned that roughly half of the people who our system had empowered to sign off on key decisions were, in actuality, "stateless stakeholders." These were people who had neither special expertise nor accountability, but they felt they needed to opine. And that was our fault because we had charged them with doing so.

From these exchanges, I saw that we had overcompensated as we came out of the financial crisis. When going through a rough patch, there is a tendency to grip the steering wheel more tightly. But instead of solving problems, sometimes you merely review them more frequently. By 2012, that was where we were: bloated. We had allowed complexity to morph into dysfunction. Here were some clues: One common information system inside GE is customer relationship management, or CRM. The supplier is Salesforce.com. We had thirty-nine applications of CRM, with no synergy between them. As a result, a large GE customer, like Exxon, could receive a dozen different invoices from different GE businesses. When we compared our administration costs to those of Honeywell (a similarly complex company that we admired), ours were $1 billion higher. Our engagement scores, which measured things like whether our employees would recommend GE as a good place to work, had slipped below 60 percent. Bureaucracy was killing us.

High costs, low engagement, and slow movement tend to go together. We set a goal to cut $2 billion in administrative costs over four years. We called the initiative "simplification," but we were really aiming to improve organizational speed and flexibility. Complexity shows up in two ways: employees with overlapping responsibilities and a pervasive "Check with me!" attitude. We set out to clarify responsibility, empower frontline decision makers, break down organizational boundaries, and delegate capability throughout the company. For employees, we wanted simplification to mean more engagement; for customers, higher satisfaction.

My team and I did an analysis, counting how many layers there were between me and a worker on the factory floor. The number was thirteen—way too many! Then we went outside GE for help. Late one night, I'd stumbled upon a TED Talk on YouTube by Yves Morieux, a senior partner at Boston Consulting Group. He had just developed a simplification framework and I felt he was speaking directly to me.

BCG's Morieux is not the only one to contend that as the world has gotten more complex—with more regulation, more technology, more globalization, shorter product cycles, faster information sharing—organizations have responded with increased bureaucracy. But he and his colleagues have quantified the matter, estimating that since 1955, the world has become about six times more complex, while organizational complicatedness has increased by a factor of thirty-five.

What does that mean inside a conglomerate? It means more meetings, more committees, more processes, more task forces, more scorecards, and more oversight and reporting structures. Any time there is a problem or an opportunity, it seems, another layer of bureaucracy is born, and once it exists, it's difficult to remove. Why should we care? Because all that slows down decision making, suffocates innovation, and creates a discontented workforce. It isn't that the bureaucrats are bad people. But even good people can be detrimental to your company if they are aimed in the wrong direction. As we began to say after working with Morieux: "A good manager of a bad layer is equally problematic to a bad manager at any layer."

As Morieux and his cowriter Peter Tollman lay out in their 2014 book, *Six Simple Rules*, employees of overly complicated organizations feel like they are stuck in a labyrinth. They lose meaning and satisfaction as they become burned-out and stressed by the overwhelming requirements of servicing the bureaucracy.

So what to do? Of their six rules, the first three are about making it easier for people to use their judgment and take ownership: (1) understand what your people do; (2) reinforce integrators—the people who get tasks done cross-functionally—and empower them with resources and authority; and (3) increase the total quantity of power available—when creating new roles, empower people without taking power from others.

The second three rules were about making sure that this enhanced autonomy was used to face complexity and improve performance: (4) increase reciprocity by setting clear objectives that stimulate mutual interest to cooperate; (5) extend the shadow of the future, by which they meant: expose people to the consequences of their actions; and (6) reward those who cooperate and blame those who don't.

We asked Morieux's team to help us put those ideas to work in a pilot program at GE Healthcare. BCG stressed that the key was to enable our people to find their own solutions, not hand them down from on high. So the BCG folks asked our team to identify areas that seemed bogged down by inefficiency. They came up with several, including their desire, when a defect was found in a product, to recall it as fast as possible. What BCG helped us do was to form small teams to cut through the fossilized processes that were impeding the goal. They helped those teams ask a series of simple questions: What are the critical roles involved in product recalls? What are the key interfaces by which different managers pass the baton from one to the other, or where collaboration is key? What, in an ideal world, would be the behaviors for these critical roles and at these interfaces? What are the behaviors we observe today? And what are the root causes for the gap between the ideal behaviors and the current behaviors? Within a few years, we had dramatically improved our speed and engagement.

We also had help from a firm called The Ready, led by Aaron Dignan. The Ready is an organizational design firm that believes that battling bureaucracy is essential but won't be successful unless more attention is paid to enhancing humanity at work. In 2012 and 2013, we spent a lot of time with The Ready team talking about how we could become more adaptive and human-centric.

Here's a concrete problem that The Ready helped us solve: In 2008, the Environmental Protection Agency had finalized new regulations that would create both complexity and opportunity for GE Transportation, which made about two-thirds of new locomotives in the United States. The regulations sought to drastically cut emissions (particle, nitric oxide, and nitrogen dioxide) from the diesel-electric engines that pull the trains that haul 40 percent of US freight over 140,000 miles of track each year. The most stringent set of regulations, called Tier 4, were due to take effect in 2015. We knew that if we could meet them, there would be money to be made. And if we didn't, we wouldn't be allowed to sell locomotives in the United States.

Given this looming deadline, we changed the way we worked, establishing a "team of teams" that would try new ways to solve problems. That team was accountable to the mission at hand, not to the bureaucracy. In the past, we'd been stymied sometimes by the contradictory demands of our functional siloed metrics—there were six or seven engineering metrics, say, and an equal number being measured by the folks in supply chain, or finance, or marketing. It wasn't integrated. This time, with The Ready's help, we simplified the proposition, asking essentially, "Okay, what are the two or three key metrics from a shareholder and a customer perspective?"

In 2010, GE's engineers began working in earnest to develop cleaner-running engines. They looked at how to manipulate the fuel, how to control the combustion process, and generally how to improve efficiency. Older diesel engines used a urea-based after treatment to scrub engine exhaust from the air. It worked, but our customers found the process—which required a bulky add-on to the engine—difficult. Was there a way, they asked, to avoid the after-treatment process? It turned out the answer was yes.

Reducing complexity had upped our employees' level of satisfaction. By freeing them from bureaucracy, we'd made it easier for them to be creative and solve problems. In the end, GE would be the only locomotive manufacturer who met the Tier 4 deadline; in 2015, we had the U.S. market to ourselves.

OPERATIONAL TRANSPARENCY

To combat complexity, it helps to have a few operating mechanisms common across your company. At GE, I wanted a way to compare business performance quarter over quarter and to address macro themes.

We'd always had regular meetings with each business to discuss important issues. For a long time, though, we'd had separate meetings on purpose and strategy, resource and workforce issues, risk and compensation, on an annual or semiannual basis. Financial reviews, meanwhile, would happen constantly. This created a mismatch in the time horizons for our concurrent goals. In one meeting, the renewable energy team would cut spending to achieve a quarterly goal; in the next meeting, we would yell at them for falling behind in the area where they'd made cuts.

When we introduced the Blueprint Review system, we collapsed the number of meetings. Now each business had a single, formal Blueprint with clear goals in each of the four key areas: financial, strategic, people, and risk. Whether or not those goals were met had a predetermined impact on how the team was paid, and that incentive compensation was clearly defined. Four times a year, in the Blueprint Review meetings, we would focus on exceptions, meaning if something was on track, we'd touch on it only briefly or skip over it altogether. Also, the Blueprint Review was the only place where business decisions were made, so there was no chance of getting our wires crossed.

In 2015, the folks at GE Renewable Energy used a Blueprint Review to bring up the implications of a new public policy decision: a five-year extension on tax breaks for renewable energy. It was clear to everyone that this policy shift would lead to a dramatic increase in demand for some of our products—wind turbines, in particular. So before the review ended, we decided that, to control our supply chain, we would acquire the company that made our wind turbine blades. Particularly in rapidly changing markets, the Blueprint Reviews allowed us to make smarter operating and strategic decisions.

Beyond that, the Blueprint Reviews created a sense of informality. When there was a problem, we would circumvent the regular meeting structure and just work on the most pressing issues. We had multiple meetings, for example, on the LEAP engine scale-up or on Oil & Gas economic cycles or on digital transformation. We were analyzing the businesses in real time, based on what was most important—not just going through the motions.

Blueprint Reviews revealed how well—or how poorly—team members were working together. Frequently, the corporate team would sit around after a review, sharing our gut reactions to what we'd just observed. Sometimes we felt the team we'd just met with was in sync, but other times we were left with the impression that they weren't grinding hard enough or worse: "Those two people hate each other!" It was up to me to fix the organizational dynamics that would improve our results.

PEER LEARNING & PEER PRESSURE

Twice each year, we would bring horizontal groups of GE leaders together to share results and best practices. Whether we were discussing "Using Data Tools on the Factory Floor" or "Improving Coaching with Your Team," we wanted our leaders to align with the goals of Big GE. Every quarter, meanwhile, all the CEOs of GE's many businesses would get together as a group to review their Blueprint progress. This was a chance to instill mutual accountability. Without my prompting, the CEOs who were making their numbers turned up the heat on those who were missing them.

In a conglomerate, peer pressure is especially effective. In a mono-line company, the manufacturing guy might compete with the sales guy, but they are doing different jobs. It's apples and oranges. At a conglomerate with, say, eight separate businesses, you have eight of every type of top executive. They can learn from one another by competing against one another more directly on productivity, employee effectiveness, and everything else. That's a definite advantage.

Another way to judge your top leaders' capability is to observe them as they talk about their businesses in front of their peers. I was always impressed by those who could explain their missions simply and those who had new ideas that we could benefit from. Could they retain their confidence during hard times? Did they solve problems or pass them on to others? I had my opinions, but I'd also watch the other faces in the room, looking for how many of a leader's peers trusted him or her to deliver for them.

Ultimately, not everyone can succeed. Of the 185 GE officers in place when I became CEO, just three remained sixteen years later. Some retired, some left GE, and some we fired. Creating transparency around performance, with clear metrics and open debate, is essential in a conglomerate.

At GE, we found that when we adopted a few simple operating mechanisms that drove accountability, it motivated our people to focus. From 2012 to 2018, we reduced the number of leadership layers between me and the factory floor from thirteen to eight. We did away with approximately one-third of our processes and shared services, which eliminated overlap. We cut our IT systems in half. And our engagement scores improved to more than 70 percent, reflecting a happier workforce.

But we also were responsible for making the company easier for investors to understand, and that was an ongoing challenge. Coming out of the financial crisis, we were making progress. Our stock was trading at a premium to the sum of GE's parts. However, some actively managed portfolios could not hold financial stocks, or shares of GE, given the volatility from the financial crisis. At this point, it was clear to us that investors would give GE no credit for financial services earnings. Only industrial EPS growth would move the stock. For decades, GE Capital had been the magic that fueled the GE conglomerate model. Now our investors hated our finance arm. It was time to address the Blob once and for all.

CHAPTER 9

Leaders Solve Problems

I 've always been an avid reader. I devour mystery novels, bio-graphies, leadership books, everything. Once, when George W. Bush was president, Andy and I were invited to a White House din-ner for the prime minister of India. Andy was seated next to Karl Rove, which she was dreading. (Bush's deputy chief of staff had a Rasputin-like reputation; he turned out to be spectacularly nice to her.) I had no such reservations about my seatmate, the historian David McCullough. I was a superfan. When I got to the table, I was excited to meet him. "I've read all your books," I said.

McCullough looked at me skeptically. (He's written thirteen lengthy books, though at this point, I think he'd written only eight.) So I started ticking them off. I'd loved the early histories of the Brooklyn Bridge and the Panama Canal (all 1,334 pages of them). I'd learned so much from his book about the Wright brothers. Of all the presidential biographies—he'd written three—I liked *Truman* the best. "Here was a guy that was an abject failure at age fifty," I gushed.

"He'd declared bankruptcy twice. And then he turned out to be a two-term president. He was a complete nobody and then became this hugely consequential figure. Only in America." And I couldn't overlook *1776*, about the start of the American Revolution. I love military history, I said, and that one was terrific.

"Wow!" McCullough said when I paused. "You really *have* read all my books!"

Whenever anyone asks me to recommend a book on business leadership, I always point them toward military histories, because everything goes wrong in those books. Read *Gettysburg*, by Stephen W. Sears, and you learn that the battle wasn't won; it was lost. Confederate general Robert E. Lee was too aggressive. Before the infantry assault at Pickett's Charge, Lee said, in essence, "This is our shot, and we need to go for it because we don't have enough troops to win this war." The charge's commander, Lieutenant General James Longstreet, predicted the result: Lee's troops got slaughtered.

Read about D-Day or Waterloo, and it seems like 80 percent of what happens is a mistake. In World War II, many criticized General Dwight D. Eisenhower for how he led the Allied forces in North Africa, but by 1945, his troops had become the world's best fighting machine. There is chaos in battle. Even good ideas rarely seem to work right the first time. But that's how you learn: facing failure, absorbing fear, making and owning your decisions, and keeping your cool as the story plays out.

MANAGING RISK

On July 21, 2010, President Barack Obama signed the bill known as the Dodd-Frank Act into federal law. Spearheaded by Senator Chris Dodd and Congressman Barney Frank, it was aimed to remedy flaws in the regulatory system that had contributed to the global financial crisis. One way it did that was by creating the Financial Stability Oversight Council, which had broad authority to monitor, investigate, and assess risks to the financial stability of the United States. The council published a list of systemically important financial institutions, or SIFIs, that were deemed too big to fail and thus would be subject to increased oversight. Then it began putting the SIFI label on insurance companies and other nonbanks. In July 2011, the Federal Reserve began overseeing GE Capital, and two years later, regulators slapped GE Capital with the SIFI label.

The enhanced regulation was in some ways ironic because while GE Capital was big in 2013, it was a lot smaller than it had been. At the end of 2008, GE Capital's assets had swollen to more than $660 billion. Five years later, encouraged by a new GE motto that I admit sounds ripped from a *30 Rock* script—"Shrink to Grow"—we had worked hard to get down to about $400 billion. But we were still the nation's largest nonbank financial institution, and that was enough to earn us a SIFI designation.

Initially, we were naive about what being a SIFI meant. We knew we had to appease our new Federal Reserve supervisors and that we were required to hold more equity capital than we had in the past. Still, GE Capital had never been regulated this comprehensively and we didn't know how much we didn't know. We needed help.

I reached out to Dave Nason, an assistant secretary at the US Treasury, and asked him to fill a newly created role: chief regulatory officer and compliance leader. I'd gotten to know Nason a bit during the financial crisis. The son of a UPS driver, he was wicked smart but unpretentious, with immense common sense. When I described the job at GE, I told him: nobody likes regulation, but if we were going to do this, I want to do it right.

Nason joined GE as an outsider, and it was immediately clear to him how unprepared GE people were. For example, early on, the New York Fed got in touch to set up a first meeting with the senior management of GE Capital. Nason knew that was a rare step for them—getting to know us before beginning formal regulation—so when they threw out a few proposed dates for the meeting, he was quick to pass them on to the GE team. Soon, his assistant was standing in his doorway with bad news. The GE Capital folks said none of the dates worked for them.

Nason was incredulous. "Are people out of the country?" he asked. "Did someone die?" It turned out the dates the Fed had suggested conflicted with some internal meetings; no one seemed to grasp that this was a command performance. Nason had to explain that when the government says, "This is when we can be there," there is only one correct response: "Works great for us!"

The Fed's demand that we hold more equity—no less than 14 percent of our financial-services assets, a threshold presumably suggested by their financial models—limited how much debt GE Capital could use to fund its operations. We could still fund new assets, but the higher ratio of equity to assets meant that returns on the business went down dramatically. Previously, GE Capital had generated a 25 percent (or higher) return on investment. But now, as our leverage dropped, that figure fell to 6 or 7 percent. You want to have a ROI that's above your cost of capital. Given the Fed's restrictions, GE Capital's fifty thousand employees in twenty countries were having trouble maintaining that ratio.

But that wasn't the hardest part of being a SIFI. The most difficult part was that GE suddenly had a new stakeholder that was more powerful than any other: the Federal Reserve. And the Fed had different motivations than our shareholders, our employees, and our board. The resulting culture clash was inevitable, but that didn't make it any more pleasant.

The supervisors from the Fed seemed perplexed by GE Capital, and we were the first to admit that our decentralized systems were not a good fit for their regulatory model. The finance arm's computer systems in its various businesses weren't connected to one another. That limited our ability to provide analytics as quickly as the Fed expected.

The Fed asked us for huge amounts of data. All of us chafed under the weight of their processes. For so many years, GE Capital had been the goose that laid the golden egg. We'd operated under less regulation and enjoyed low funding costs, and our GE Capital underwriters were terrific at identifying opportunities to lend money at a favorable spread. We'd earned a lot of money, throwing off annual cash dividends of between $5 billion and $10 billion. Now regulators were telling us that our business had to follow new rules. Overnight, we went from having structured advantages to having huge disadvantages.

GE Capital had survived the financial crisis, and for that we were grateful. While I'd hoped we could continue to shrink GE Capital gradually, now it was clear we needed to do it quickly. Instead of throwing off cash, GE Capital now required infusions of it. That not only drove our stock price down; it would change the company forever.

If you'd asked me in 2013, I would have said GE's regulators were overly worried about rainy days. What the regulators wanted was for us to run GE Capital like pessimists. The Fed always believed that GE people were too optimistic. I remember one of our earliest meetings with Caroline Frawley, the Fed regulator who'd been assigned to GE. She gave a withering presentation to our board, listing GE's flaws one after another, and I wigged out, ticking off all the pressures GE was facing. "You're just trashing us for no reason," I huffed at her. But moments after she exited the room, GE board member Geoff Beattie gave me what for. "You are out of line because GE Capital is out of line," he said. "This is not going to work the way you seem to think it will. We need to work with Frawley, not against her."

I was chastened, and I shaped up. Because while GE Capital's people knew their businesses well, there was no denying that we were not so good at assessing all the other kinds of risks that existed outside GE—those that were tied to being big and complicated. We weren't organized in a way that asked macro questions. When you have $400 billion in assets, you need to think about more than whether or not your debtors are going to pay you back. You need to assess what the Fed calls "enterprise risk"—to ask what-if questions about how your company's complexity might leave it open to harm. Now, with regulators involved, and with our cost of funds shooting dramatically up, I knew we had to pivot.

WELCOME TO THE HOTEL CALIFORNIA

To comply with the Fed's oversight, we spent heavily. We hired thousands of people—at its largest, GE Capital had more than five thousand full-time employees dedicated to working with regulators at an annual cost of nearly $1 billion. The mandates regulators placed on us were hard to argue with. But they were burdensome—not just to the frontline audit employees but also to GE managers.

At one point, Tom Gentile, whose regulatory expertise had made us recruit him from GE Healthcare to be the COO of GE Capital, made what's called a Gantt chart that listed all the ways that GE Capital had to change to become Fed compliant. The resulting bar chart showed not just the required tasks but also their dependency on one another. I swear it was twenty feet long.

For both my leadership team and the GE board, being a SIFI was claiming 80 percent of our mindshare. While the Fed's remit was technically limited to GE Capital—they approved GE Capital's balance sheet and reserves—they soon began to ask questions about Big GE, too. In that way, when it came to making capital allocation decisions, being a SIFI was like wearing a straitjacket. We couldn't imagine having to ask the Fed for permission to fund the next generation of aircraft engine technology, say, or some other business line. We couldn't let it get to that.

Like the other nonbank SIFI designates (insurers American International Group, or AIG; Prudential Financial; and MetLife), GE was frustrated that regulators hadn't laid out a clear path for us to ever shed the designation. Senator Mark Warner of Virginia referenced this at a Senate banking hearing in March 2015, when he alluded to the Eagles song lyric, "You can check out any time you like, but you can never leave." As Warner told Treasury Secretary Jacob "Jack" Lew, it seemed that SIFIs had become stuck in a virtual Hotel California. And just like in the song, it wasn't such a lovely place.

For all these reasons, we began to start thinking seriously about getting out of the lending and financing business. It wasn't the first time we'd considered this, but now it felt more urgent. The bottom line was that we weren't being sufficiently compensated for the risk we were taking. Investors had long complained that finance was too precarious an undertaking for an industrial company and that GE Capital was keeping our stock price below thirty dollars. All of GE's top twenty-five investors wanted the lending arm gone.

But there were reasons we hadn't tackled this problem before. The structure of GE Capital, decades in the making, was extremely complex. We had large international operations—basically an intertwined set of twenty-seven or so business lines around the world, each overseen by different regulators. These many component businesses contributed to our low tax rate (we were a big leasing company, for example, and leasing companies can deduct depreciation). Whenever we'd looked at dismantling GE Capital in the past, the tax implications alone—$20 billion or more—had appeared prohibitive. Could we figure it out? We had to try.

SHOOTING FOR THE MOON

Back in June 2013, as the SIFI designation put more pressure on GE Capital's leadership, its CEO Mike Neal had decided to step down after thirty-four years at the company. Neal had been a terrific leader, hugely respected by all (he'd even been considered to run Citigroup at one point). He'd helped us steer GE Capital through the most difficult time.

Now Keith Sherin—who'd been GE's CFO—replaced Neal (and Jeff Bornstein, who'd been CFO at GE Capital, stepped into Sherin's old job). Sherin quickly dispatched a group of analysts to quietly look at the idea of spinning off most of GE Capital to GE shareholders. To ensure secrecy, this group called itself Project Beacon and delivered its report to Sherin in September 2014.

Then, just after Thanksgiving 2014, Sherin tapped another Skunk Works team to attempt something far more difficult: breaking up and selling GE Capital. Past approaches had failed because they relied on first selling GE Capital's overseas assets, then repatriating the proceeds to pay down debt in the United States, creating an enormous tax bill. So when Sherin approached three top GE Capital leaders—Mike Gosk, head of tax; Daniel Colao, head of financial planning; and Aris Kekedjian, head of mergers and acquisitions—he asked them to find another way. The trio commandeered a conference room in one of the glass office buildings in Norwalk, Connecticut, that comprised the nerve center of GE's financial operations. Throughout December, they were there at all hours, scribbling on whiteboards and flip charts, filling up yellow legal pads with equations and simulations. They also recruited other experts within GE to help them.

Mike Schlessinger, a brilliant lawyer and twenty-year veteran of the company, had touched every major deal we did during my tenure as CEO. Now he proved his mettle. In what would come to be regarded as the first of two "Eureka!" moments, Schlessinger had a new idea: focus on selling our US assets first and, while we were completing that process, continue to operate the international assets (mostly our GE Capital aircraft leasing unit). The goal: to de-SIFI ASAP while incurring a substantially lower tax charge. People who were there remember that when Schlessinger first explained his plan, the room was stunned into a rare silence. This was a significant change in strategy.

The second "Eureka!" moment came as the group talked about the nitty-gritty of finding actual buyers for GE Capital's assets. They needed to sell those assets at book value, which effectively eliminated the chance that GE Capital could be sold to a single buyer (because nobody in the world had the scale to fund what was basically a $400 billion bank). GE Capital was just too big, and besides, at this point, the Fed was not allowing any banks to do any significant M&A. The team realized that before they could put a price tag on GE Capital's assets, they needed to know how much GE's investors were factoring those assets into GE's stock price. An analysis was done, and its conclusion was promising: investors valued the bulk of GE Capital at only about 70 percent of book. That meant there was some wiggle room. If GE Capital's many assets could be sold at 100 percent book value, we would exceed expectations and come out ahead.

As it began to look as if this team might be getting somewhere, there was pressure to find a name for their top-secret initiative. That's when the youngest member of the team spoke up: a British economic analyst named Matthew Vaughan, who was just seven years out of college. What about Project Hubble? he asked—a reference to the Hubble Space Telescope. Everyone loved the shoot-the-moon audacity of Project Hubble. The name stuck.

In the fall of 2014, the Hubble team took their ideas to Sherin, who was impressed. Then, in January 2015, they visited Bornstein, GE's CFO. They cautioned that the only way the deal would work was if Big GE guaranteed GE Capital's debt. They feared Bornstein would say no, but he was supportive. The proposal was hugely intricate, but it appeared it could be done in a way that didn't violate the covenants of GE's debt. This was the closest anyone had come to an achievable way forward.

Around this time, Bornstein sat down with me to talk about where we were with the Fed. The short answer: a bad place. It wasn't that GE's people were refusing to comply. We were trying. But it seemed we were always falling short. There was always another twenty-thousand-page report being requested. It was killing us.

In mid-February, Bornstein, Sherin, and I agreed that, while myriad issues still needed to be vetted, selling GE Capital piece by piece looked doable for the first time ever. It helped that at that time, our industrial businesses were doing well. When they were underperforming, we knew we couldn't catch a break. Even when we cut costs by more than $1 billion in a single year, we still wouldn't get credit on Wall Street, where the focus remained on GE Capital. But now industrial profit growth was 11 percent. If we could divest ourselves of the GE Capital businesses, this could be a great time to try to move the needle on the stock price.

We got an unexpected affirmation of this view in February when Kekedjian had dinner at Rebeccas, an upscale spot in Greenwich, Connecticut, with Steven Hudson, CEO of Element Financial

Corp., the Toronto-based financial-services company. Outside, snow was beginning to fall. Inside, Kekedjian noticed that Hudson seemed fidgety. He kept reaching into his jacket pocket. Finally, Kekedjian asked: "Is there something you want to give me?"

"Yeah," Hudson replied. "And it's not a marriage proposal." With that, he pulled from his pocket a detailed offer for the US portion of GE Capital's multibillion-dollar vehicle-fleet management unit. Kekedjian played it cool, not letting on that we were already considering selling nearly all GE Capital's assets. The timing wasn't right, he told Hudson—they should keep in touch. But this was a good omen. If unsolicited offers were already coming in, maybe the assets wouldn't be as hard to unload as some had worried.

As we pondered the Hubble plan, however, we were all mindful that secrecy was paramount. GE Capital's prime assets were its excellent employees. If word of a possible divestiture leaked, the value of the businesses would erode as people fled for the exits. At this point, only eight or so people outside the Project Hubble group knew what was being proposed.

In early March, I convened my leadership team in the third-floor boardroom of GE's Connecticut headquarters. The room was old-school opulent, with big sturdy chairs, wood paneling, antique rugs. Just a few days later, on March 6, our board of directors would be gathering in that same room. In anticipation of that, I wanted to poll my top lieutenants: Was it time to bring Project Hubble to the board?

Unequivocally, Sherin and the Hubble team said yes. They made a presentation, and at the end, Sherin said, "It's our recommendation that we try to unwind GE Capital. And we think we've found the way." The room buzzed as we asked one another questions about the mechanics of the plan. Would we have to pay breakage costs on the debt? If we wrote off a bunch of the value of the assets, would that hurt our balance sheet? Could we maintain our debt rating? What would happen with the remaining runoff assets? What would the rating agencies say? There was no way to know. I waited a beat and then addressed the room.

"What do each of you think?" I said. "Should we explore this?

And if so, are we ready to fill the board in about what we're considering?" I turned to my right, locking eyes with GE's CFO.

"Where are you on this, Jeff?" I asked.

Bornstein looked grave. He loved the people in GE Capital, where he'd worked for ten years. He knew how seriously they took their responsibilities and how much they'd contributed to GE's bottom line. But times had changed, he said. "We've got to do it."

I went around the table, putting the question to Robert Green, GE Capital's CFO; Brackett Denniston and Alex Dimitrief, the general counsels of GE and GE Capital; our chief risk officer Ryan Zanin; our treasurer Dan Janki; our VP of investor relations Matt Cribbins; our chief marketing and commercial officer Beth Comstock; and Puneet Mahajan, our VP of corporate financial planning and analysis. One by one, each person echoed Bornstein's words. "We have to." "It's time." The room was unanimous. When it got back around to me, I stood up, said, "All right, let's do this!" and walked out of the room.

It's hard to capture the mixed emotions that came with this decision. There was so much competence within GE Capital—really talented people who we would surely lose if we succeeded in selling most of its various divisions. Moreover, for all the negativity that critics of our financial-services arm had been stoking for months, I wasn't sure how investors would react to divestment.

But in the end, we all felt we were fighting the tide. Every day, we were getting pummeled in the press and by sell-side analysts who thought our complicated conglomerate model—basically a holding company made up of two independent companies, one industrial, one financial—was dragging our stock down. GE Capital's earnings were being discounted. We had to act.

KEEPING THE LID ON TIGHT

The March 6 board meeting was on a Friday, and the entire agenda was Hubble. Keith Sherin and the Hubble team walked us through the plan. I remember Aris Kekedjian told the board, "If you're ever going to do this, this is the moment. You've got markets that are in your favor, and people are looking for yield and quality businesses. The window is open. We need to move before it closes."

Then I addressed our directors. "In order to determine whether any of this can work, we're going to have to float this idea with the Fed and with some of our bondholders," I said. "Rumors may spread. I would never want you to hear something this important from anyone other than me. Do we have your blessing to go have those conversations?" The board gave us a green light.

We wasted no time. Just minutes after the March board meeting ended, Bornstein, Sherin, and I met with Jamie Dimon, the chairman and CEO of JPMorgan Chase, and his vice chairman and top deal maker, Jimmy Lee. I knew Lee well and Dimon, my Harvard Business School classmate, even better. "What do you guys think?" I asked them. "Can you sell these many pieces? Are we going to have buyers?" They told us they could and that we would.

For the next month, we worked day and night to make Project Hubble a reality. Early on, we set a tentative date to reveal the divestment plan to investors—April 10. But what happened in the weeks leading up to that announcement is nothing short of heroic. The timing of this coincided with spring break, and many GE Capital people who had kids had scheduled vacations. Everybody canceled them (or their spouses and kids went without them). And that was just the beginning.

Across the board, our people told their families to pretend they were on a thirty-day assignment in China: unavailable and hard to reach. The Hubble team was tireless. Since we were still running the business (Fed regulators and all), many working on Hubble still had to attend normal operations meetings during the day, so a lot of the restructuring work happened at night.

During this period, every person within GE corporate had a role to play. But what GE Capital's HR people accomplished stood out. Remember, up until the moment we green-lighted Hubble, they'd been hiring auditors and other finance folks at a rapid clip to meet our regulators' demands. Now, suddenly, we told them to hit the pause button. And because we feared that GE Capital's employees might leave if word got out, they couldn't tell even their most senior people the reason why.

Jack Ryan, GE Capital's senior vice president of HR, remembers coming to work on the Monday after that decisive March 6 board meeting and telling his team, "Everybody take a deep breath. We've hired a lot of people. Let's take a beat and absorb them." But it was such an about-face that many of his colleagues were confused. They'd made job offers to people. Were those still valid? What was going on?

One high-ranking colleague came to Ryan seeking guidance. "I don't want to seem dense," she said. "But for the last six months we've hired compliance people as fast as we could. And now you don't want us to? What gives?" Ryan understood her exasperation. It wasn't that he didn't trust the woman, a second-generation GE leader who he knew would do anything for the company. He just couldn't elaborate. Finally he said, "Have you ever been in a situation where you knew something but you couldn't tell?" He could see the light go on in his colleague's eyes. "Please," he said. "Don't push me about this right now. Just do what I ask."

Other than secrecy, another priority during this period was that we wanted to have at least one deal in the bag, to signal our momentum, before we revealed Project Hubble to the world. We decided our real estate holdings were the best deal to tee up first. The reasoning: it was an asset class that both our investors and our regulators had come to hate more than anything. If we could sell those assets first, it would send a strong message that this was for real. The most obvious buyer was one of the largest real estate investment managers in the world: the Blackstone Group. Sherin approached the head of Blackstone's team, Jonathan D. Gray, and offered him an exclusive opportunity to buy—provided he moved fast and paid us well.

"If you can hit this bid on an exclusive basis, it's yours," Sherin told Gray. If not, GE would open up the bidding. Gray said he would try.

The third week of March, Sherin and Alex Dimitrief flew to Europe. They needed to begin the process of persuading more than twenty regulators around the world to approve what we were getting ready to do. Sherin and Dimitrief explained that we were exiting financial services in two phases. First, we were divesting our lending and leasing businesses in the United States (so that we could, we hoped, de-SIFI). Then we'd launch phase two: exiting our lending and leasing businesses in Europe and Asia. As a result, for the first time in GE's history, the center of gravity of GE Capital would shift from the United States to Europe. If we could shed our SIFI designation in the US, we expected that the Prudential Regulation Authority (PRA) in the UK or the Autorité des marchés financiers (AMF) in France would replace the Federal Reserve as GE Capital's consolidated supervisory.

Securing the required European approvals for GE Capital's reorganization was no small feat. These regulators did not share the American perspective on the SIFI process and, with the exception of the PRA in the UK, were not accustomed to hurrying to meet deadlines that had been set elsewhere. So our team had to find tactful ways to push regulators in Germany, Italy, Brussels, Japan, Korea, India, Australia, and several other countries to review and approve our regulatory applications.

At the end of March, meanwhile, I headed to Washington, DC, with Sherin and Denniston, our general counsel. There were people we needed to brief, confidentially, about what was coming. I started with Valerie Jarrett, President Obama's senior adviser. I felt an announcement this big shouldn't catch the president by surprise. She thanked me for the heads-up and wished us well.

Next we went to see Jack Lew, the secretary of the Treasury. Lew had been chief operating officer at Citigroup before entering public service, and I knew he understood how hard it had been for GE to be regulated alongside the banks. After I told him what we were getting ready to announce, I put him on notice: "You've indicated there was going to be an off-ramp for SIFI designates. Well, GE wants to be the first car on the off-ramp." He was encouraging, but of course it wasn't solely his call. He could make me no promises.

Finally, on April 1, we went to see Janet Yellen, the chair of the Federal Reserve, and her team. We had a mixed reputation with them. The New York Fed, who we dealt with the most, didn't really like us that much, and we'd earned some of that ire, for sure. So this was a very important meeting. We told the assembled group some of the complexities of what we were trying to accomplish. Bit by bit I painted the picture of what we wanted to do.

Yellen sat stone-faced for much of our thirty-minute presentation—listening, but not giving anything away. When we finished, thanking them for their time, Sherin and Denniston headed for the door, with me right behind them. That's when a member of the Fed's board of governors, a guy named Daniel Tarullo, pulled me aside. Tarullo was known—and feared—for his attention to detail. If Yellen was hard to read, Tarullo was blunt in the extreme. While she was never exactly the good cop, he definitely played the bad cop, so I wasn't sure what to expect.

"I approve of what you're doing here, and we're going to reward you for it," Tarullo said. "We know you don't want to be a SIFI. And we don't want you as a SIFI. While all these other people won't give you the nod, I will. I'm going to help you get out of jail."

I tried to keep my cool, but on the inside I was rejoicing. Tarullo had the power to do what he said he would do. We talked for a few minutes, and when we said goodbye, I practically sprinted to the car to share the good news. "That," I told Sherin and Denniston, "was a great meeting."

On April 2, GE's board met one last time about Hubble, and this is a day I will always remember. In addition to our board—which had grown to eighteen directors because we felt we needed additional regulatory expertise—we had the entire GE Capital leadership team. Also in attendance were the finest group of legal, accounting, and investment advisers in the world—folks from Davis Polk, Weil, and JPMorgan. Each of those outside advisers made presentations. Sherin, Bornstein, and I talked about the mechanics of the deal. Sherin and Jack Ryan, his HR leader, described how our retention strategies would seek to hold GE Capital together as we tried to sell its businesses. There were briefings on the Blackstone deal (while not closed, it looked likely) and on the Fed, which looked to be casting a favorable eye on our plans.

We told our board that if anyone had reservations about our scheduled investors call eight days later, there was still time to pull the plug. But if we went forward, I warned, there was no way of knowing how the stock market would react. While we thought the impact would be positive, I was braced for as much as a 20 percent hit. "This could be a really bad day in GE land," I warned them. "Not that we haven't had a few." But our board didn't waver.

Easter Sunday was April 5. With Hubble on the launchpad, holidays were on hold. Everyone came to work.

On Thursday, April 9, the day before our planned investor call, I did what I could to try to ensure April 10 would be a good day in GE land. I had lunch with Larry Fink, the chairman and CEO of the investment management company BlackRock, in his office. After I laid out the broad strokes of what would be announced the next morning, he looked stunned. If I hadn't already known how unprecedented this restructuring would be, Fink's facial expression would have confirmed it.

Before I left, I asked for a favor. "You're a guy that everybody trusts and respects," I said. "So if you get a chance in the coming weeks to talk this up—even if you say, 'This wasn't completely stupid'—I'd appreciate it." He said he would.

Then, after the market closed on April 9, someone (almost surely a banker) leaked details about the pending Blackstone deal to the *Wall Street Journal*. From what we could glean from the reporter's request for comment, the story treated the possible sale of our commercial real estate holdings as a one-off—no one had revealed the broad scope of what was about to happen. Still, everyone at GE freaked out. By this point, about sixty people at the company were in the loop. We'd spent so long keeping this secret, it was bracing to have it revealed, even if only partially, in the waning hours.

But then we realized: the leak was actually a gift. It set the table perfectly for our much bigger news. We said "no comment" to the *Journal*, and minutes later, their story, headlined "GE Close to Selling Real-Estate Holdings," posted online. Then, at 5 p.m., we sent out a blast email invite—"Please join us for an investor update on GE Capital tomorrow at 8:30 a.m."—and provided a link to the webcast. Given the *Journal*'s story, no one was going to miss this call.

There was just one problem: the *Journal* was correct when it reported that the Blackstone deal still wasn't closed. Alec Burger, the CEO of GE Capital Real Estate, had been trying his best—at this point, he and Aris Kekedjian had been up for forty-eight hours straight, going back and forth with the buyers' representatives. With just hours to go before our investor call, we wrote up two press releases—one that had the real estate deal in it; one that didn't.

In the wee hours of the morning on April 10, Burger and Kekedjian, Blackstone's Jonathan Gray, and a phalanx of lawyers and advisers were still locked in a conference room. Timothy Sloan, who ran wholesale banking at Wells Fargo, a partner on the deal, listened on speakerphone from California. Discussions were tense as the buyers began trying to omit certain less desirable assets from the deal. Our guys pushed back, but they were worried the arguments would continue indefinitely. Not only might the deal not close in time for the investor call; it might not close at all.

During a break, Kekedjian turned to Burger. "We need something to cut through the bureaucracy and force the issue—like a buzzer," he said, pulling out his cell phone and searching the App Store. Quickly, he found one that simulated the sound of the bell you hit when you want to summon a hotel porter. Perfect, he thought.

When Kekedjian went back into the meeting, he didn't reveal his new toy right away. But the next time the opposing lawyers agreed on a point, he rang it: *Ding!* "Perfect," he said. "Next!" Later, when discussions began to lag, he used the bell—*Ding! Ding!*—to prod people to keep moving. The sound was irritating, and the lawyers were testy, but the bell did what Kekedjian and Burger had hoped: it kept the negotiations on track.

The pressure was on. "Look," our guys said at one point, as the first glimmers of dawn began to streak through the sky, "the deal has to be done right now if you want to keep your advantage." They were dogged. "We really don't care, guys," they told the Blackstone and Wells Fargo reps, "but if you don't nail this right now, we're going to take it to all the other people who want to make a name for themselves in the real estate space."

Finally, at 6:30 a.m., everyone signed off on what we felt was a fair price. Blackstone Group, Wells Fargo & Company, and other buyers agreed to buy $26.5 billion worth of our office buildings and commercial real estate debt. Kekedjian called Sherin, stoked. "You can send out the press release," he said. "We're good to go."

SECRETIVE NO MORE

Just two hours after the Blackstone deal closed, Sherin, Bornstein, Denniston, and I took our seats in Fairfield and began the investor call. We'd been rehearsing our roles for days. I went first, revealing the general outlines of the divestiture plan. Then we took turns describing how the assets would be bundled and how we would pull this off. We explained we'd be hanging on to our aircraft leasing operation, as well as financing for the energy and healthcare businesses—all lending lines that supported our industrial base. But the bulk of the GE Capital businesses would be sold over the next two years.

In the end, we said we'd bring back some $36 billion in cash from overseas subsidiaries, a move that would cost us $6 billion in taxes. That was just a 17 percent rate, but when added to foreign taxes already paid on those earnings, it worked out to about 35 percent, the US corporate rate. In all, we expected to record about $16 billion in after-tax charges. It was a price worth paying to simplify the company.

We'd already won approval, we said, from several overseas regulators and were in talks with the rest (that very morning, Dimitrief had been in Warsaw securing a sign-off from the Polish Financial Supervision Authority, or KNF). We also announced that the GE board had authorized us to distribute the proceeds of the divestiture to our shareholders through a buyback of up to $50 billion in common stock, which would reduce our share count to about 8.5 billion by 2018. By 2018, we hoped financial services would contribute less than 10 percent of our income, down from 25 percent at the time of the announcement and 50 percent when I became CEO in 2001.

In those days, few analysts had been as hard on GE as Barclays's Scott Davis. In the fall of 2014, Davis had even proposed a "full AT&T-style breakup" of GE. But at the end of our investor call, Davis addressed me directly: "I know we've all given you a lot of crap over the years, but this is pretty good stuff for redemption," he said. "That's the best apology I can make. You can keep your job a little longer." Sherin, Bornstein, and I all laughed, out of exhaustion more than amusement.

There's no way the call could have gone better. The fact that we had already sold one of our biggest portfolios—real estate—for above-book value had the desired effect: people were impressed. Shares jumped nearly 11 percent that day, closing at $28.51. It was the stock's largest one-day percentage gain in five years.

LEVELING WITH OUR PEOPLE

We'd revealed our secret. Now we had to make good on our promises. Gratifyingly, on the day of the announcement, we fielded more than 450 inquiries from prospective buyers, and several bankers came in person to GE Capital's Norwalk offices, where they could be seen waiting in the lobby for in-person meetings.

But in addition to greeting our potential suitors, we had a pressing need to reassure our people within GE Capital. It was essential that we communicated clearly how much we wanted (in fact, needed) them to stay in their jobs as we sought buyers for their businesses, and that we would make it worth their while to do so.

In the run-up to the April unveiling of Project Hubble, one of our newer senior compliance leaders had asked GE Capital's HR leader Jack Ryan if they should prepare a security plan—basically protocols to keep employees who decided to leave from stealing proprietary information as they walked out the door. "Employees are going to be angry," the GE newcomer had said. "If this happened at one of the big banks, many people would be so pissed that they'd get up and walk out. Should we take some precautions?" Ryan said no. This isn't a big bank, he'd explained. While GE Capital's people would feel profound sadness and a sense of loss, they would remain loyal to the end. "We need to help them grieve," Ryan said. "And if we do that well, they'll execute the new game plan with dignity and grace."

So Sherin and Ryan hosted a series of meetings and conference calls. On one call, there were seventeen thousand people listening, and employees had sent in written queries. Some of them were wrenching. "I was talking with my HR manager 48 hours ago, and she said one thing. And now you're saying something different," one person had written. "Why are your HR people lying to us?" When Sherin read that question aloud on the call, Ryan remembers wincing. But his stomach clenched tighter when Sherin said, "I'm going to flip this over to Jack."

Ryan took a breath, then nailed the answer. "Listen," he said, "your HR manager didn't know this was coming. I promise you: she didn't lie to you. Anything that was going to have this kind of material impact on the markets and on GE was something we had to keep very close. The few people who knew had nondisclosure agreements. She told you what she knew when she knew it, and that situation's now changed."

People can sense when you're telling them the truth. In that moment and in many others to come, Ryan and his team defused the tension by leveling with GE Capital's employees, who were understandably worried about their futures. The HR team, led by Executive Compensation Manager John Hinshaw, developed a retention plan aimed at three distinct groups. Senior leaders were offered incentives; the higher the price of assets sold and the faster they sold them, the more money they'd make. Employees of businesses that were about to have new owners were offered bonuses if they helped manage the transition. And the infrastructure employees, who we'd rely on to manage GE Capital through the transition period, were rewarded for serving until they were no longer needed.

The HR folks put together generous packages that included bonuses for those who stayed at the company past a certain time. They accelerated vesting in stock options. They promised employees that if they for some reason were not offered jobs after a sale, GE would help them find work. And it succeeded: GE Capital lost just one of the 101 employees on its "Tier 1 Retention" list.

"We're not sentimentalists," I'd told the *New York Times* on April 10, putting on a brave face. But make no mistake: asking the GE Capital team to retreat was emotionally brutal. They had won in their markets for decades and, after our SIFI designation, had built a new regulatory structure. The fact that we were now asking them, in essence, to work themselves out of their jobs was difficult for all of us.

Before he'd become GE's CFO, Bornstein had helped build a huge GE Capital team in Chicago that did lending and leasing and inventory financing. Some of these people had joined the company through acquisitions we'd made, and most had been GE employees for only five to seven years. So six weeks after our April announcement, Bornstein traveled to Illinois to do a question-and-answer session with what he expected to be about a hundred employees.

Instead, the main venue was packed with several hundred people, and four times that number were gathered in rooms all over the building and around the region, watching on closed-circuit TV. Bornstein usually had a tough exterior, but when he took the stage that day, he was overcome. It was heartbreaking for him, after spending more than a decade building up GE Capital's businesses, to face so many scared employees and tell them goodbye.

It helped, he told me later, that he had enormous confidence that their particular business—like the others we were selling—would soon be owned, intact, by someone else. "You will have jobs," he promised the group. Still, he struggled to keep from crying. Everyone in the room believed in what they were doing. They'd prided themselves on excelling in ways that banks didn't. They saw themselves as feisty underdogs.

"Trust me," he said. "We did not make this decision because we don't love the businesses we've built together. We do. But given the regulatory climate, we believe this will be the best answer for you long-term." The meeting lasted forty-five minutes, and when Bornstein answered his last question, the room went silent. Turning to leave the stage, he hadn't taken five steps before the place exploded in applause.

ACTIVISTS ABOUND

I need to rewind a bit to describe something else the April divestment announcement had set in motion: a swarm of activist investors. In mid-May, I got a call from a respected Wall Street guy I'd known for years: a banker named Joe Perella. "Okay, Jeff," Perella said. "You thought you were out of the deep end, but you're not."

Perella was connected. After years at First Boston Corporation, he and two of his colleagues had started a boutique investment bank—Wasserstein Perella & Co.—back in the late 1980s, then sold it for $1.4 billion. He'd started another financial-services firm, Perella Weinberg, and had been a member of Morgan Stanley's Management Committee. I was eager to hear what he knew.

He was happy to share. "Now that you've cleaned up GE Capital, there are four or five activists that are underwriting GE. None of them would touch you with a ten-foot pole when you were a SIFI. But now that you're on your way off that list, here they come." I remember he mentioned two firms in particular: ValueAct Capital, a San Francisco–based hedge fund, and Trian Fund Management, a Park Avenue firm whose website's home page features the phrase "HIGHLY ENGAGED SHAREOWNER" in all capital letters.

"Look," Perella continued, "your stock has underperformed. You're a conglomerate. You've cleaned up, in theory, what they saw as a toxic mess. Now these guys are going to come in and say, 'Fire the CEO, break up the company, blah, blah, blah.' I just wanted you to be aware."

I thanked him for the call and told him I wasn't entirely surprised. I'd first met Nelson Peltz, Trian's CEO, in 2006, after reading an article in *Fortune* about the H. J. Heinz Company. Known as a take-over titan, Peltz had won two seats on Heinz's board in a proxy fight, but the CEO of Heinz told *Fortune* that had been a good move—he appreciated Peltz's input. I liked the sound of that, so I reached out to take his temperature about possibly joining GE's board.

That will come as a shock to many, given what's happened since, but back then I was always looking for good director candidates. I knew Peltz's hard-nosed reputation, but I figured if I invited him onto the board (instead of having him force me to accede at the end of a bayonet) he might be in my corner. We met a few times and got to know each other a bit, but then the financial crisis hit, and I decided not to move forward.

So now it was 2015. Not long after Perella called me, I got another call—from Peltz. He congratulated me on our breakup of GE Capital. I thanked him. Then, somewhat casually, I said, "We'd love to have you in the stock."

Of course, I knew Trian was already in the stock—Perella had tipped me off to that. But by this point, we'd done an analysis. Of the twelve or so big activist investors, about half were radical bomb throwers—the kind who'd push leaders of companies in which they invested to make drastic changes to drive up stock prices. The other half were more reasonable. I counted Trian in the latter group.

Peltz called himself a constructivist, and I took him at his word that his intention was to improve the companies in which he invested. I wasn't naive—as a rule, I knew, activist investors complicated the jobs of CEOs. In truth, in the wake of our GE Capital divestment, what I really wanted to do was just run the company for a while—to execute Hubble, get out of the headlines, and just manage the place. But if we were going to have an activist in the stock, I wanted it to be one I knew. I hoped Trian would be patient and focused on the long term, provided that GE was delivering good results.

Some of my closest advisers and I had debated this seriously. I remember one day Blair Effron, one of the bankers who'd helped us with Hubble, played devil's advocate, arguing against me inviting Trian in. "This could get ugly," he said.

I knew he was right. But I also felt that, theoretically, activists could add value. "Let me be very clear to you," I told Effron. "If we do well, will it get ugly? No. And if we don't do well, will it get ugly? Yes. But why shouldn't it? If I'm fucking up, why shouldn't somebody beat me up?" I believed my team and I should be held accountable.

SELL, SELL, SELL!

We had essentially told the world we were going to get rid of $300 billion of loans, leases, and other assets and that we were going to do it quickly, at 1.1 times book value. That's not the usual strategy when approaching a sale. But we felt so good about the quality of these businesses, and interest rates at the time were virtually zero, so the timing couldn't have been better.

After the April 10 announcement, we knew who our first call had to be. Kekedjian reached out to Steven Hudson, the Element CEO whose unexpected February offer had buoyed our spirits as we considered whether Project Hubble was even a possibility. Hudson was still interested, and soon, Element agreed to buy most of GE Capital's vehicle-fleet management unit for $6.9 billion.

Next the team turned its attention to one of GE Capital's crown jewels: GE Antares, our leveraged lending business. We had to get a good price for it to set the benchmark for the rest of the assets. There were quite a few private-equity firms circling GE Capital, hoping for a fire sale. We looked at this deal as an opportunity to prove that we weren't desperate and that we were in a position to drive a hard bargain. Our message was: "We have something everyone wants, so don't even think about lowballing us."

Our lead bidder was the Canada Pension Plan, which at the time was run by an Ontario native named Mark Wiseman. Apollo was in the second position, but we wanted the CPP to get it, in part because we sensed they were willing to pay a premium. We pulled out all the stops, asking our Canadian board member, Geoff Beattie, to coax the deal along. It was a classic bidding war, with Apollo and CPP battling until the end. Ultimately, we closed the deal with CPP for $12 billion—a great price for us. This proved that our Blackstone real estate deal wasn't a fluke.

The GE Antares deal was also the last we'd do with Jimmy Lee, the influential Wall Street investment banker. In June 2015, after a workout in his Connecticut home, he died suddenly at the age of sixty-two.

CEOs rarely talk about how solitary the job is. I was always on the lookout for people I could speak to "out of sequence," as I put it, by which I meant: without either of us needing anything from each other. Lee had been one of those people. I loved him and I felt he wanted the best for GE and for me. Another trying part of a CEO's job is that you have to absorb a lot of bad news every day. Good stuff rarely reaches your desk. Lee was the guy who would call you when you were down. His passing was a huge loss.

At this point, the pace and complexity of our sell-off was breathtaking, even for our hard-charging M&A team. We cut a $9 billion deal with Capital One Financial Corporation to sell a unit that lent to hospitals and nursing homes. We sold an online bank to Goldman Sachs, and our rail-car finance unit to the Bank of Montreal. We offloaded our 43 percent stake in Hyundai's credit business and sold the bulk of our US commercial lending and leasing business—a three-thousand-person operation that included about $32 billion of assets—to Wells Fargo & Company.

Each of these platforms had hundreds if not thousands of people who worked in the trenches. There were people who serviced the loans, collected money, and managed the assets. We assigned Sharon Garavel and Maria DiPietro—two experienced operating leaders— the task of holding the team together as we sold each business.

I have to say that it was key during this period that we didn't know what we didn't know. Before we launched Project Hubble, we went to the board knowing about 60 percent of the full picture—at least I see that now. If we had known the extent of what we were about to attempt, we might never have done it. Sometimes you must act instead of dithering. If you wait for the perfect moment, when everything is crystal clear, you will often wait forever.

MISSION ACCOMPLISHED

In September 2015, Trian revealed publicly that it had been buying up GE stock—$2.5 billion worth, or roughly 1 percent of our market capitalization. That made them one of GE's ten largest shareholders, and right away, they were outspoken. In early October, Peltz told the *Wall Street Journal* that he was unhappy that we'd retained the credit operations that helped us sell airplane engines, medical equipment, and power plants. "At Trian," he said, "we don't like industrial businesses who get into a business where the raw material is money."

But not even a month later, Trian sounded downright bullish on GE, issuing an eighty-page position paper that predicted we'd hit a $2.20 earnings-per-share target by 2018. They were particularly thrilled about our plans to do a stock buyback, which in the end we did to the tune of about $35 billion. The goal was to make our GE Capital divestment an EPS-neutral proposition—to reduce the denominator (the number of outstanding shares) in proportion to how much the numerator had been shrunk by the GE Capital sell-off.

Some of the most unfair criticism that's been directed at my team during the past three years is the allegation that we used stock buy-backs to prop up our stock price, when we knew full well we weren't going to make our $2-a-share earnings target. This is revisionist history at its worst. We were transparent and forthright about what motivated the buyback. Anybody who says I knowingly bought back shares at $22, even as I suspected the price would go down to $6 in 2017, is dead wrong. Back then, even people who predicted we weren't going to make $2 a share still thought we'd come in at $1.90. People who say we wasted billions of dollars on the buyback are, frankly, full of it.

The board and management had openly debated the options for capital allocation as we disbanded GE Capital. Also, during this time period, we were selling GE Appliances and GE Water, so we felt we had a lot of cash. Instead of a share repurchase, we could have left the cash on the balance sheet. But when we made the stock buyback decision in 2015, we expected GE Power's pending acquisition of the energy assets of the French multinational company Alstom to generate even more cash. Further, having been a SIFI for six years, we believed that our GE Capital balance sheet was very strong. Both of these assumptions would later prove to be wrong.

Trian had been studying the company for six months. Apparently, they thought we were doing something right. So, it seemed, did a lot of our investors. In December 2015, when we held our annual outlook meeting—our version of a State of the Union for investors—Trian seemed happy, and so did everyone else. We welcomed a large group of investors on a Thursday afternoon to the set of *Saturday Night Live* (which we still rented, as needed, from Comcast), and then hosted a dinner that night with our biggest investors.

The next morning, we met with our sell-side analysts and another group of investors and did an informal breakfast Q&A at 30 Rock. It was at that meeting that one of our most hard-core hedge fund investors buttonholed Matt Cribbins, our VP of investor relations. This hedge fund guy had covered GE for thirty-plus years and he was known not to mince words. Now he told Cribbins: "You know, a year ago, only twenty-five percent of the people in this room would have supported Jeff. Today he is a god. How quickly things change."

If you'd asked me then, I would have told you I felt all too mortal. We'd been lauded for our "bold decision" to exit financial services, but I never felt good about it. While we got out of GE Capital whole, I feared we'd left money on the table that we could have captured had we had the option of waiting. But we didn't. Restructuring was the right decision for GE. But I saw it for what it was: capitulation. The hardest decisions are the ones that don't maximize upside, but merely avoid a greater loss. I accept that learning how to retreat is a leadership skill. I just wish I hadn't been required to learn it.

In April 2015, we'd said we were going to complete the sell-off within three years. We essentially finished it in two years—more than one hundred transactions in sixty-two countries—and we came in, as predicted, at 1.1 book value, maybe a little bit higher. On June 29, 2016, just fourteen months after we'd announced the unwinding of GE Capital, GE became the first big financial institution to shed the SIFI label. We had accomplished what many said was impossible. We could focus once again on running the company.

CHAPTER 10

Leaders Are Transparent

One Saturday in 2005, I was at the office in Fairfield, Connecticut, catching up on work. Once my desk was clean enough, I considered my options. I knew Andy and our daughter, Sarah, who was then a senior in high school, had gone shopping, so I had no urgent need to get home. As I headed to the car, I decided it was finally time. Time to get a tattoo.

The possibility of getting inked had been something my daughter and I had been teasing each other about for months. She would threaten to get a tattoo, I would tell her I was going to beat her to it, and she would roll her eyes. "You're all talk," she'd say. But this kind of self-expression fascinated me.

I set off for the town of Danbury, where I'd noticed a few tattoo parlors. I chose the least sketchy-looking place, walked in, and told the proprietor what I wanted. I kept it simple, requesting the cursive GE logo, known as the GE meatball, in blue. The tattoo artist said that was a first. I didn't want to tell her I was CEO, so I made up a story.

"I work at GE," I said. "I made a bet that our bowling league would win, but we lost. So here I am." The woman laughed. "So you *have* to get a GE tattoo?" she asked. "That's so funny!" Then she got to work on my left hip, just below the beltline. Before she finished, I asked her to make two additions in red: the letters "A.I." and "S.I."— the initials of my two favorite people, my wife and my daughter.

Over the years, I've been at a few dinner parties where guests are asked to write down something interesting about themselves on scraps of paper. After everyone puts their paper scraps into a hat, the snippets are read aloud, and people have to guess whose secret belongs to whom. My go-to submission: "I have a tattoo." No one ever guesses I wrote that. I almost always win the game.

But my tattoo has way more significance than a party trick. For me, organizing my life narrowly around work and family (or what I used to refer to in my CEO days as "one company, one wife") helps reduce stress. Memorializing those primary loves in ink was a gift to myself, a reminder of my own priorities. Hardly anyone at GE knew about my tattoo. I didn't show it off. I'd gotten it as a private testament to my dedication to GE.

Since I left GE, some have questioned that dedication, particularly when it comes to what went on inside GE Power. The popular narrative about what went wrong is that GE made a terrible acquisition—our 2015 purchase of the energy assets of the French multinational company Alstom—and that I championed it all by myself. But that's not accurate. GE Power was a good business in an essential industry, so buying Alstom made sense. The Alstom deal was completed just before the power industry entered a tough cycle, but that alone doesn't explain what happened next. GE had led every one of our businesses through tough cycles before, and our leaders had performed well on complicated deals. (For example, back in 2004, shortly after we acquired Amersham, we discovered a quality issue that threatened the entire deal, but our Healthcare team fixed it.) No, the lessons I learned from the Alstom deal are not only about capital allocation but also about leadership. My board and I disagreed about the capabilities of GE Power's leaders. As a result, we ended up with the wrong team in place. That was my fault.

The story I'm about to tell is a difficult departure for me. For forty years, when something's gone wrong or when someone's cast aspersions on my character or my judgment, I've always kept my mouth shut and worked through it. But I'm making an exception to that long-time practice. I'm telling this story now, for the first time, because what happened at GE Power has done so much damage to so many people. The story has been reported incompletely and, at times, untruthfully. I take no pleasure in the telling, but people deserve to know what really happened.

A SIMPLE DEAL (IN A MARKET WE KNEW)

Of all the deals we did while I was CEO of GE, Alstom gets the most criticism.

The transaction has taken on an almost mythical quality. The deal was initiated by GE Power's leadership and supported by our board, our investors, analysts, and other stakeholders, including me. The transaction was transparent. We knew what we were buying was largely a power-services business, one that complemented our own. We knew what shape the company was in and we were aware of the challenges it was facing. We liked the deal for two reasons. First, it took a competitor off the field. Second, we knew how to integrate and run the business, and we believed it would boost our earnings and generate a lot of cash in a short period of time.

It's not a bad idea to be in the power market, especially when you're General Electric and you've been the most trusted name in the business for a hundred years. GE had a leading share and a reputation for innovation and reliability. But that didn't mean the power market was easy. Then and now, it was an intense confluence of technology, economics, and public policy. Governments' use of subsidies and regulation also have an outsized role.

Underlying these complicated dynamics was the promise of long-term growth. The global market for electricity is huge and getting huger. By one estimate, demand will grow by 60 percent by the year 2030. Even today, one-third of the world's population still lacks access to electricity. We knew that places such as Indonesia and Vietnam could eclipse Europe for new demand.

At the time the Alstom opportunity arose, we were in a strong position to consider it. In 2014, GE had had a solid year. On an industrial revenue base of $110 billion, our organic growth—we were up 7 percent—was noteworthy, ahead of all our competitors. Our earnings, meanwhile, had grown 10 percent, as had our cash.

The power business was a strong contributor to that performance. In my estimation, GE Power was the most successful competitor in the sector by almost any measure: earnings, cash flow, market share, global footprint, and social impact. With a big position in gas turbines and wind turbines, we owned about a third of the world's installed base of power generators. We had smaller positions in nuclear power, steam, and electricity distribution. Through GE Capital, we were a leader in financing power projects, particularly in renewables. We had even created a business platform, called GE Current, to finance solar projects for commercial buildings and hospitals.

I really felt that we had our competitors, Mitsubishi Heavy Industries (MHI) and Siemens, on the run. We had launched the H-turbine, which was the industry's largest and most energy efficient turbine. Our Global Growth Organization was working: we were winning all the big global deals that had previously gone to our rivals. More important, we had broad access to low-cost financing, which we could use to build power plants all over the world. And the bigger we got, the huger our service profit stream. Power was benefiting from Predix, which helped our service business grow more quickly at higher margins. I knew the equipment market was volatile. But I felt confident in our ability to execute.

Experts predicted, and we believed, that natural gas consumption would grow at least 5 percent annually for decades. It was clean, cheap, and available, and the demand for it would boost demand for turbines and services. We knew that the only renewable equipment market with profit potential was wind. We had written off $300 million in investments in solar and battery technology—industries that had lost billions. Nonetheless, we were committed to developing technologies that would reduce carbon emissions; we felt the cash generated by Alstom would help us do so.

It is important to keep climate change in mind as you make an investment in the power industry. Today, 93 percent of electricity is still generated using traditional technologies (coal, gas, nuclear, and hydro); renewables make up only 7 percent. Changing this mix will take decades, even with the best of intentions and strong, unified political leadership across the globe. In the meantime, billions of dollars will have been invested in services to reduce pollution in the traditional installed base.

We ran GE's power business with a set of clearly stated goals: to keep our 50 percent market share around the world; to grow the wind business onshore and offshore; to maintain the superiority of our gas turbines; to lower cost; to be positioned to do business everywhere in the world, using financing if necessary; and above all else, to capture profitable services, which required maintaining, fixing, and updating existing turbines. We had made investments to grow this last part of our business. The more turbines we sold and installed, the more units we had to repair, and the more revenues we'd bring in. The Alstom deal would give us more turbines to service and, we thought, boost our bottom line.

A POSITION OF STRENGTH

Over the years, we had analyzed Alstom several times. In fact, in 1999 we had acquired a portion of its turbine manufacturing capacity. The French company was big not only in energy but also in high-speed rail transport and signaling technology. But its power and grid divisions were the only ones that GE wanted to acquire, and in the past, Alstom had never been willing to sell them. Then, in 2013 to 2014, Alstom's stock price dropped from 80 euros to 30 euros. In 2014, Alstom CEO Patrick Kron called GE Power CEO Steve Bolze to suggest a meeting.

I'd never met Kron, but Bolze was enthusiastic in a way that caught my attention. I'd known Bolze for years—he'd been at GE since 1993, based in our Energy and Healthcare divisions. Until 2012, Bolze had worked under a hands-on boss, John Krenicki, who'd helped steer his decisions. That meant I'd had only two years at that point to appraise Bolze's solo leadership abilities, but so far, I was satisfied. In meetings with me, he seemed to know the ins and outs of his business. When he suggested we meet Kron together, I said yes.

In February 2014, we met for dinner in Paris. In addition to Bolze and me, GE's CFO Jeff Bornstein and John Flannery—then the head of GE's business development—were there, and we all came away intrigued. Alstom had a profitable service business, and their renewables business—in particular, large offshore wind turbines, where we lacked a presence—was complementary to our own. (About this, we were dead-on: in 2020, offshore wind is a $2 billion business for GE.) Kron, meanwhile, brought some urgency to the table. He implied that he was determined to sell Alstom's energy assets quickly, so if we weren't interested, we should be prepared for one of our rivals to acquire it.

For me, the expansion of services was appealing, both financially and strategically. Services were less volatile in a cyclical industry. I felt that acquiring Alstom would give us a substantial leg up on our competition and enhance our existing plan to reduce carbon. More important, GE Power's customers wanted digital service solutions, and adding Alstom would allow us to leverage our investments in that area across a larger installed base. Buying Alstom would give us a dominant position.

In March 2014, we briefed the GE board, saying we viewed the Alstom acquisition as a simple transaction that would grow our share of the world's existing turbines by 50 percent—a huge long-term advantage. Alstom would help us to improve our large gas-turbine technology, which at that time trailed Siemens and MHI. On the downside, Alstom had a business that built power plants that we didn't understand. And there was what we called "French country risk": there would likely be geopolitical turbulence around the deal.

I asked Bolze and Flannery to lead the due diligence on the deal. I thought it was a good test for both of them. As I've said, Bolze had only recently stepped out from under Krenicki's shadow; asking him to evaluate the Alstom deal would be a good way of gauging his capabilities. Similarly, Flannery had just been promoted, so I was eager to see him in action.

While succession wasn't yet top of mind, I knew both Bolze and Flannery could be contenders to replace me, and this was one way to prepare them.

The more due diligence Bolze and Flannery did, the more we became convinced that the deal would likely boost earnings. We had acquired Alstom's gas-turbine capability in 1999, so we were comfortable doing business in France. When Bolze and Flannery gave the final Alstom presentation to the GE board, the major concern among our directors was Alstom's construction business, where we had limited experience. But overall, the board reaction was positive.

By the April 2014 shareholder meeting in Chicago, we'd hashed out the economics of the deal. The trickiest issue was what would happen if GE ultimately decided not to move forward. Kron and his team met us secretly in Illinois, holing up in a hotel near the venue where our shareholders had gathered. There we negotiated a breakup fee, agreeing that if, as we went through the approval process, regulators forced GE to sell more than 10 percent of the business, we could walk away by paying Alstom $700 million. But if that threshold wasn't reached, we had to close.

We shook hands in Chicago on a Wednesday. Unfortunately, the next day, April 24, our agreement was leaked to the media. The French government, which saw Alstom as a national jewel, felt blindsided by the news and disrespected by GE. Valued at $13.5 billion plus working capital, the deal would be GE's largest acquisition ever. But the media leak set it off on a weak footing.

The French would soon punish us, fighting the deal on the grounds that France needed to maintain its technological sovereignty. In the meantime, at the invitation of the French government, Siemens and MHI were assembling their own joint counterbid.

Our first day in France, a Sunday, President François Hollande refused to meet with us. He sent an emissary instead—a backbencher named Emmanuel Macron, whose title at that point was deputy secretary general of the Élysée. Macron asked us not to sign the deal for a few days. Initially, I wanted to tell him to jump in the Seine. Luckily, our CEO and president of GE France, a well-connected executive named Clara Gaymard, told me to give them some time. I agreed.

I finally met with Hollande on Tuesday. His manner was formal, and it was clear he was under a lot of pressure from his opponents on the left. On Wednesday, we signed a definitive agreement. Or so we thought. Though we had agreed to create a thousand jobs in France (not a big reach for us; we had a hundred thousand people in Europe at this time), many there preferred a European solution to the Alstom deal—a bid now led by Siemens, which had matched our economics dollar for dollar. In early May our deal was blocked by France's economy minister Arnaud Montebourg, in a move that was counter to everything the EU stood for. A Socialist, Montebourg saw foreign takeovers of French businesses as contrary to the national interest. So he stopped our deal in its tracks.

Thus began sixty days of limbo. We were stuck at the starting gate. Europe always gave more lip service to globalization than it ever acted upon. They favor their companies by using regulations as weapons. In this case, Montebourg was violating EU rules to keep an American company from acquiring a French company. In so doing, they favored a German company. It wasn't likely that the EU would help us. We were left to figure it out on our own. This is why when I hear people today lamenting that former President Donald Trump was a protectionist, I have to laugh. He didn't invent protectionism.

Finally, in June 2014, our deal received approval from the French government. But this was just a preliminary step. The main event would take place in Brussels, the home of the Directorate-General for Competition—the EU's ruling body on competition policy. Given the Power team's enthusiasm for the deal, I felt comfortable using GE's clout to get it approved.

A LEADER STOPS LEADING

Bolze had initiated the Alstom acquisition, and seemingly relished the early negotiations. The ball was firmly in his hands. I wish I could say he ran with it. It wasn't that Bolze failed to communicate the details of the deal to our board and executive team. It simply seemed he wasn't committed to executing on those details.

That hadn't always been my feeling. In the two years that he'd been reporting directly to me, I'd seen that Bolze was strong on the commercial side. Previously, when Krenicki was in charge, if one of our people in Argentina needed help selling a turbine, they knew better than to ask headquarters. Bolze was changing that by exerting his own energy to drive business around the world. Moreover, he was a great morale builder on the front lines; he knew how to walk a factory floor and connect to GE workers. Bolze always seemed extremely well prepared in meetings. Those who worked for him knew that he expected detailed briefings before major presentations, so he could appear knowledgeable.

Increasingly, however, as the Alstom deal moved forward, I had the feeling Bolze was more maître d' than chef: terrific at social graces, but less comfortable when asked about ingredients that went into the main course. In my opinion, Bolze lacked what I can only describe as a CEO's intuition. We hired him a coach, and all of us spent time with him on strategy. But it wasn't enough.

We would soon learn that Bolze also lacked what might be called "succession etiquette." In the summer of 2014, he went to my HR leader Susan Peters. "When Jeff steps down, I want to be CEO," he said. "Unless I get a clear indication that I am getting his job, I'm going to leave."

Peters was surprised less by the bluntness of his ambition than by how little he understood the process. Peters took Bolze to dinner and explained that the entire board would choose GE's next CEO, that such a decision was not imminent, and that it could not be rushed. Peters urged him to be patient—not because she thought he was the right person for the job (she didn't), but because she knew some on the GE board thought highly of Bolze, and she wanted him in the running so they could consider him. As for me, I thought Bolze was just naive and that he would grow out of it.

INTEGRATING ALSTOM

From the start, we'd known that time was our enemy. The longer the Alstom deal took to close, the worse it would be for our customers and our team. We had warned our directors of this risk and continued to discuss it in twice-a-week conference calls with the board while we were negotiating in Paris.

We approached integrating Alstom into GE Power with great intensity. I tapped three senior leaders to lead the four-hundred-person effort. I moved Mark Hutchinson from China because I thought he had the political savvy we'd need in Brussels. Sharon Daley was an unemotional HR leader who had spent her career in Power, so I was confident she knew all the players and would give me the straight scoop. And Jose Ignacio Garcia, who'd been the CFO of GE Latin America and spent much of his career in Power, was our hard-nosed finance lead.

Integration plans were updated monthly with me and my leadership team, who in turn updated the board nearly every meeting. Throughout this period, I insisted that when GE Power's leaders made updates or registered concerns, I wasn't the only one in the loop. Problems and setbacks were discussed openly. These meetings included more than fifty people from throughout the company and around the world. Frequently, the meetings included Alstom managers as well. I wanted to hear their views. It is not unusual after an acquisition for the acquiring company's people to look upon the acquired company's employees as losers. But I valued the scrappiness of the Alstom team. I didn't want to lose that spirit. There were always a variety of opinions and everyone had a chance to speak.

It took only six months for the Alstom deal to win approval from the US government. But in Brussels, we would encounter the most powerful regulator in the world, known as the DG COMP. This group, which establishes and enforces competition policy for the EU, had a new leader, Margrethe Vestager, and she seemed to be out to make a mark on this, her first big deal.

By the time I met Vestager, I'd been walking the halls in Brussels for fifteen years, and I can definitively say that she was the most purposeful and effective minister I'd ever encountered. She and I got along—we chuckled, for example, over our shared admiration for the Danish TV series *Borgen*, a political drama about the rise to power of a prime minister (whose writer has said was based on Vestager herself). But Vestager's plodding approach was exactly what GE didn't need on this deal.

We tried everything we could think of to accelerate Vestager's review of our deal. Brackett Denniston, our general counsel, took the lead. Alstom's CEO and the French government (which by this point was on our side) tried to help. But it would soon become clear that the bureaucrats in Brussels weren't buying our claim that they were hurting a French enterprise by slow-playing this deal. And the US Department of Justice declined to engage with their European counterparts on our behalf.

While I've been working on this book, Vestager has been given expanded responsibility over digital policy in Europe; she is now being called Silicon Valley's biggest foe. But back then, she had GE in her crosshairs. It wasn't long before I became convinced that she would push us right to the limit. We would spend another twelve months haggling with the European Union. This delay harmed Alstom. Customers were unwilling to buy products from a company in limbo, so sales declined dramatically. And we lost some key people within Alstom because they questioned whether they had a future there.

At the same time, however, our integration planning was gaining momentum as we discovered more redundancies and cost savings than we'd seen at the start. We'd agreed to assume all of Alstom's liabilities, but we now succeeded in getting what's called a carve out: Alstom, not GE, would pay about $800 million in legal fees to address a bribery charge that had predated our bid. As we became more comfortable running the business, meanwhile, we developed a way to save $2 billion in taxes by moving the headquarters of GE Power Services to Switzerland. That, too, improved the deal profile.

OVERT TRANSPARENCY

I don't think I've ever done a deal that went exactly according to plan. That's why with Alstom, I insisted on transparency: many board reviews and regular internal meetings. We had walked away from deals before. In 2005, we were about to bid on the Westinghouse Electric Company, which makes and services nuclear power plants, when GE board member Roger Penske spoke up. "I hate this business," he said. "It's all risk, no reward." So we stepped back. More or less the same thing happened when GE looked at Dow Jones in 2006, and Abbott Diagnostics in 2007. With Alstom, though, we decided to go forward.

I was relying on GE's system of internal checks and balances. Our board reviewed this deal twelve times. The GE Power team made all deal-related presentations to the board, so there were plenty of chances to ask questions. For years, I had insisted that, in addition to attending eight board meetings, each director had to visit two businesses each year without me present. These visits gave the board exposure to the team, enhanced transparency, and promoted the board's knowledge of complicated businesses. The itineraries of those trips were designed by the business leaders, not by me. There were no fewer than four board visits to GE Power during the Alstom deal process.

Moreover, we had a 450-person audit staff that reported to the board's audit committee; many of them worked on the deal. We paid the accounting firm KPMG $110 million each year. They, too, reported to the audit committee and reviewed the deal.

Bolze, Hutchinson, and Denniston, GE's general counsel, led our final negotiations with Alstom. Over the summer of 2015 we negotiated price reductions from Alstom and concessions to the EU. Vestager and her competition commission were aware of our negotiated breakup fee (the one that said if concessions destroyed 10 percent or more of value, we could exit the deal). They meticulously kept just under that threshold.

Meanwhile, our investors seemed to like the deal, including Nelson Peltz at Trian. But as we kept moving forward, I wasn't seeing the leadership I was hoping for from Bolze. At one point, he came to me, worried about Alstom's diminishing unit sales, which as I've said were no surprise to any of us. I was dumbfounded. We had been proceeding to close a deal that Bolze had sold to our board based on numbers and projections that he and his team had calculated. "Steve," I said at one point, "do you believe in this deal or not?" Yes, he said, absolutely. He just felt like we should get it for a lower price.

I told him what I believe today: that the difference between the final price tag and what he was hoping for was negligible for GE, a company with a $300 billion market cap. "Look," I told the team, "at this point, the best thing we can do is close the deal and start executing. Let me take the blame for how much we paid." Based on numbers Bolze had provided, I felt we were better off moving forward and starting to realize the gains we'd predicted in our integration plan.

I thought the Alstom deal made all kinds of sense. I still do. But at this point, I was beginning to understand just how serious a problem we had at the top of GE Power. I was hearing rumblings that, although Bolze could parrot data convincingly, he had to memorize it. His grasp was not innate. Those detailed briefings that I'd heard he required his staff to give him? They began to look less like diligence to me, and more like cramming, last minute, for an exam. It seemed to me that he didn't have command of the most basic material. Not only was Bolze indecisive, but his CFO Lynn Calpeter seemed to have checked out. She only visited France once over the two years we were planning the Alstom deal. Many days, it felt as if the integration team was more engaged with the Alstom deal than our leaders in GE Power. Three integration leaders told me that if, when I retired, Bolze was named CEO, they would sell all their GE stock. That wasn't a good sign.

More than once, I told Bolze, "This was your idea. Own it." As the CEO of Power, he was responsible for assessing the strategic impacts of the transaction. Instead, he kept complaining about how the numbers weren't as good as they'd once been. "Based on the projections you've given me and the board, the deal still has a fifteen percent return," I told him. "Yes, fifteen isn't as good as twenty, which you'd originally projected. But we have a financial buffer, and for an acquisition of this size, a fifteen percent return is pretty great. Do you still want to go through with it?" He always said yes.

As Bolze's wishy-washiness made me lose confidence in him, what bothered me wasn't that he was reporting bad news to me. Passing along bad news was fine, as far as it went. During this same time period, I was hearing bad news every day from Lorenzo Simonelli, the president and CEO of GE Oil & Gas. But Simonelli was taking action. I wanted Bolze to do the same: to tell me how he planned to execute the deal in what had become a tougher environment. He seemed incapable of making the difficult decisions that required. Instead, it seemed he merely wanted to cover his ass by sharing how certain numbers were going up or down.

In late July 2015, one year after making his first run at the CEO job, Bolze again approached Peters. Now, he said, he was *really* going to leave GE. "I have decided," he said. "Because if the company doesn't see me as the right person to succeed Jeff, then that says something."

Peters again counseled patience, although hers was beginning to wear thin. "Steve," she said, "as I told you a year ago, nobody is going to declare you the CEO-in-waiting when succession could still be a couple years out. And again, it's the board that makes this decision." Bolze countered that in 2012, eighteen months before the Ford Motor Company named Mark Fields its CEO, it had given him the chief operating officer job. "You could make me GE's COO," he suggested.

Instead of excoriating Bolze for overstepping, Peters appealed to his common sense. "Here's what I recommend you do," she said, noting that as per GE tradition, most everyone within the company was about to take time off in August. "I want you to think about this over vacation. Really think about this. And if you feel the same way when you come back after the August break, then you should talk to Jeff."

| | | |

In September 2015, when everyone returned from the summer break, Bolze beelined for my office and asked to be made COO. Everyone knew by this point that there were four internal candidates in the running to replace me: Bolze, Flannery, Bornstein, and Simonelli. Bolze's entitled self-assurance astonished me, as it had aston-ished Peters.

I had some big decisions to make. I still believed there was a sound rationale for buying Alstom, though I knew it would take superb execution to realize the potential. At the same time, I felt Bolze had to go. He was not operationally sharp and he didn't seem to be thinking ahead. And I was disappointed that at this critical time, he appeared to be putting his own interests ahead of the team's. I knew that we could be putting the business at risk.

I went to Jack Brennan, the lead director of the GE board, and discussed the situation with him. I knew some directors liked Bolze, who'd had more face time with them than other candidates because of the Alstom deal. I also knew that the board wanted to manage the succession process. But I didn't think it was fair, let alone merited, to move Bolze to the front of the line. To keep the succession process intact, but also to be responsive to Bolze, Brennan decided to have him meet with the members of the Management Development and Compensation Committee—basically the board's HR department—so they could assess him.

If this had happened five or ten years earlier, I wouldn't have hes-itated to fire Bolze. However, at this point, I was striking a delicate balance: being a hands-on CEO, but a nonregal chairman (for my entire tenure, I'd occupied both roles). In essence, I was saying to the board: "I know my days are numbered. I defer to you." I had prob-lems with Bolze, but I wanted the compensation committee to get its chance to weigh in. Like Peters, they told Bolze that the process could not be accelerated. He'd have to wait.

Then a curveball: At the September 2015 board meeting, after Bolze gave an enthusiastic presentation on the Alstom deal, Sandy Warner, a longtime GE director, turned to me and smiled. "I think we have our next chairman," he said.

Warner's words made me panic. In my opinion, Bolze was the wrong guy for the job in a thousand ways; his unyielding politick-ing was something I knew the GE leadership team would abhor.

Warner, the former chairman of the board of J.P. Morgan & Co., was a forceful guy, and I worried he would try to strong-arm the board into naming Bolze the next CEO. I also suspected that Warner, who we'd passed over for lead director in favor of Brennan, was anxious to see me leave. I would always be grateful for Warner's many contributions to GE, but I felt he had become a corrosive influence in this and other ways.

So in early October, at the direction of the board's governance committee, I asked Warner not to stand for reelection to our board the following April. He was angry and wrote a letter to the board questioning how long I should be allowed to remain as CEO.

CLOSE THE DEAL, LOSE THE LEADER?

To provide downside protection for the Alstom deal, GE CFO Jeff Bornstein put in place a conservative underwriting case. We built in $3 billion of extra value—tax savings, cost controls, and more corporate synergy—that would protect us, we thought, if the market softened. To be conservative, we wrote down most of the power plant construction projects (meaning we reduced their book value on our balance sheet).

Analysts continued to support the deal. So did Trian. In the eighty-slide white paper that the activist fund released in October 2015, Trian declared, "We believe the Alstom transaction creates value." The economics of the deal appeared able to generate solid earnings and a 15 percent return. Now we had to execute on that.

At long last, on November 2, 2015, the deal closed. GE combined Alstom's energy business with its power-and-water unit. Headquartered in Schenectady, New York, this expanded GE Power would be led by Bolze, would employ more than sixty-five thousand people around the world, and would have an estimated annual revenue of about $30 billion.

That day, GE stock increased 5 percent. Reviews from analysts, brokers, and commentators alike continued to be excellent.

TheStreet's Jim Cramer was just one pundit who called the acquisition "brilliant . . . because the world is going to switch to cleaner power plants, and now GE has a hammerlock on the business."

A week after the Alstom deal closed, on November 9, 2015, Peters and I were in Greenville, South Carolina, for a meeting at the big GE Power production facility there. After the meeting wrapped up, Bolze asked to see me. He was resigning, he said.

"You obviously don't see my worth," he told me. "You don't see that I should be your guy, and, therefore, I'm going to go." I didn't argue. Honestly, I was exhausted by Bolze at this point; to me, his behavior had become self-serving to the point of outrageous. Given all his previous threats, Peters and I took him at his word. That night, a Monday, on the plane back to Connecticut, we strategized about who could run Power. It didn't take us long to realize there was only one person with the experience and skills to step in: John Rice, my trusted Global Growth Organization president and CEO. From 2000 to 2005, he'd run GE's energy business, which had included the power business.

We called Rice and asked him if he'd be willing to take the job. I don't think he wanted to say yes, given the circumstances, but he knew we were in a pinch and said he'd do it. That's Rice: always willing to serve. Then we called Jack Brennan, the board chair, to let him know: Bolze was out; Rice was in.

Unbeknownst to us, though, Bolze wasn't done lobbying. On Tuesday, without telling Peters or me, he called several members of the board to discuss his resignation. Among others, he rang up Robert Lane, the former CEO of Deere & Company; and Jim Cash, a Harvard academic. In conversation after conversation, he pled his case—he was underappreciated! Clearly, Bolze was still angling for the CEO job; now he was taking his case directly to the board.

Tuesday night at 9 p.m., Bolze called Brennan and said he'd changed his mind: he wanted to stay at GE after all.

The next day, November 11, was Veterans Day. Brennan called me and said he wanted to grant Bolze's request to stay. Brennan worried Bolze's departure would focus undue attention on the succession horse race. I told him I'd sleep on it.

In the years since my departure from GE, I've had to laugh sometimes at claims that I stifled debate about Alstom and within GE Power. Nothing could be further from the truth. Moreover, during a span of six months, the leader of GE Power had had private sessions with several members of GE's board. Had Bolze felt uncomfortable with the Alstom acquisition, or the results he was being asked to achieve, he could easily have confided in them. No board member has ever told me he did anything of the kind. Instead, his main concern seemed to be self-promotion.

I empathized with our board. We had been through a lot together. As I've said, I didn't want to be the imperial CEO. The board wanted to run the succession process, and I agreed that they should. Beyond that, axing the Power CEO just weeks after closing the Alstom deal would confuse the markets and our customers. So I made what I now see as a terrible mistake, maybe the worst I ever made: I listened to them and acquiesced. In doing so, I violated one of the essential rules that I lived by: the company always comes first, ahead of the individual. Leaving Bolze in his job is something I'll always regret.

THE BUSINESS SUFFERED

The power business was dealing with a lot in 2016 and 2017. The markets were tougher. As we continued integrating Alstom, the team was focused on another layer of complexity: new revenue-recognition accounting rules that, beginning in 2018, would change how we reported on our long-term service agreements.

Our business and corporate teams (including GE's audit staff and the outside consultant KPMG) had been getting ready for these rule changes for several years. The audit staff had independently reviewed every single long-term service contract in every GE business to understand the impact of the new standard, which our team embraced. We'd advocated with the SEC's Office of the Chief Accountant for a more conservative framework than the ones that other companies with similar business models were lobbying for. These accounting changes—combined with a challenging market, an unfocussed team, and the Alstom deal—would shine a bright light on GE Power's strengths and weaknesses.

At GE's August 2016 corporate officers meeting, Power CFO Lynn Calpeter was scheduled to give a presentation on Power operations. Usually I'd get a look at these reports ahead of time, and this was no exception. When I read what Calpeter was planning to say, I was shocked. She'd laid out what GE Power would do to generate better working capital, but she didn't say what it was currently doing. It seemed half-assed to me. The entire company was depending on her. In my opinion, she just wasn't taking her job seriously enough.

I called her on the Sunday morning before she was due to present it and said, "Lynn, in all my time at GE, this is the crappiest presentation I've ever seen. It's lazy. Get your shit together."

In their Blueprint Reviews, each business set goals that we approved, and their compensation was determined by how well they made those goals. At this point, that system was working everywhere but at GE Power. As I've said, when GE Oil & Gas had missed its numbers, they reacted—and rallied—as a team to get through it. The leadership of Power, by contrast, wasn't a team. They lacked strong guidance from their CEO and CFO; they were incapable of making rapid decisions necessary for good execution.

One of the many ways people have tried to rewrite the history of GE Power since I left GE is by alleging that the Power leadership team regularly raised concerns with me, and I dismissed those concerns. This is the crux of the *Wall Street Journal*'s charge that I created an atmosphere of so-called success theater and turned a deaf ear to anything negative. This is simply untrue. I'd intentionally surrounded myself with top executives who insisted I hear when we were off course or when we couldn't achieve certain goals. We had teams of people crunching the numbers on whether various concessions we'd made had reached 10 percent of the Alstom deal's value—meaning we could, and should, walk away. But we never reached that point, and the people who were best informed about the deal always told me they believed in it. The teams on the ground in France and the product-line leaders who were responsible for delivering results all supported the deal.

In one journalistic account, an anonymous GE Power source has claimed that a corporate officer who was overseeing the deal told him not to speak up because this was "Jeff's deal." But that's bunk. This was the company's deal. We all needed to own it. It was originated by the GE Power team. They did the planning. We needed them to take responsibility for the results. Between board meetings and internal reviews we held more than twenty-five public sessions; people were encouraged to speak their minds.

As GE's former general counsel Alex Dimitrief has written on his LinkedIn page, we "tried to cultivate a culture of open reporting that made it safe and valued for employees to raise their concerns about accounting and other integrity issues without fear of retaliation, including via anonymous reporting channels. We fielded thousands of concerns on a wide variety of topics each year. We investigated the merits of all of them and, when warranted, took disciplinary and remedial actions." Everyone knew that I supported this system.

At this point my corporate finance team—Jeff Bornstein, Puneet Mahajan, and investor relations pro Matt Cribbins—were now telling me they believed that Power's leadership team had checked out. They were begging me to replace Bolze. I had put Bornstein, in particular, in an impossible position. He had to intervene, in effect coming over the top of Bolze and Calpeter, to reduce costs in the Power business.

Twice in 2016—in May and in November—I pleaded with the board to remove Bolze. I said we were putting a huge GE business at risk leaving him at the helm. It was still the board's view, however, that it would look bad to remove a CEO candidate in the midst of the succession process, which was now fully underway. I backed down.

GE Power results in 2015 and 2016 had been okay but not on plan. Revenue and earnings were about flat. We were gaining market share. The wind business was going strong. Alstom made its expected numbers in 2016. Despite all the external noise, the coal business was steady and profitable.

At the end of October 2016, meanwhile, we'd announced we would merge our oil-and-gas business with Baker Hughes and put Lorenzo Simonelli in charge. After the announcement, some on the board worried that this decision effectively removed Simonelli from the list of contenders to replace me. I reassured them that, if needed, we could still tap him for the job (though I knew that some worried Simonelli was, at forty-two, too young). But Simonelli's new job only made some board members more reluctant to remove Bolze. They worried it would appear that only two people, Bornstein and Flannery, were still in the running to be GE's next CEO.

In November 2016, I was beginning to fear that none of our CEO candidates were ready. So I suggested splitting the chairman and CEO roles. The chairman sets the board's agenda; the CEO runs the company. One person can do both, as I had, but now I thought it might be a good idea to put a strong operator in the chairman's job to bolster whomever the board chose to be the next CEO. John Rice was the ultimate GE elder statesman, with deep knowledge of the company. But Rice soon discovered he was sick with multiple myeloma. His treatment plan was being developed and would eventually involve a stem cell transplant. His health and family had to come first; the idea of splitting the chairman and CEO roles evaporated.

In December 2016, Cribbins, our investor relations guy, and I helicoptered down to New York to have lunch with some investors. There was much to talk about. In contrast to 2015, when GE had way outperformed the market, we were now lagging behind. Our biggest problem was in our Oil & Gas unit, which had been hammered by a more-than-two-year slump in the price of crude, which prompted customers to rein in their spending on equipment for petroleum exploration and production. Our pending merger with Baker Hughes would set us up well, we hoped, when the sector recovered.

Later that day, I flew to White Plains to meet with Peltz and

Trian's chief investment officer Ed Garden. Our relationship had been amicable, and when we sat down in a conference room at the tiny private airport there, that veneer of friendliness was still evident. President Donald Trump had just been elected, and Peltz—a Trump confidante—said he'd been on the phone with the president-elect several times that week, to discuss cabinet appointments.

Suddenly, Peltz's tone shifted. "Jeff, I want you to know I love you like a son in a lot of ways, and I would never do anything to harm you, but we're at a point where we need to make a change," he said. "I want you to announce that you're going to take out $1 billion of costs. If you don't announce that, we're not going to get into a public fight with you. But we will make it known that we're selling out of GE."

As it happened, in response to the challenges in GE Power and Oil & Gas, Bornstein and I had already been working on a cost-cutting plan, and I shared our thinking with the Trian guys. But Peltz's threat unsettled me. For a major GE investor to walk away could have serious implications in the market.

Peltz made a request: he wanted Garden to join the GE board. I wasn't totally surprised, but the request made me aware, more than ever before, that my time as CEO was growing short.

To the extent Trian was kicking our ass, we deserved it. We hadn't adjusted costs as quickly as we should have. But still, I wanted our directors to be able to execute on succession without Trian's help. I didn't want Garden on our board yet.

Then GE Power missed its profit goals. On January 18, two days before we would make that miss public, Bolze was at GE head-quarters in Boston, walking down the hallway, when he ran into Cribbins. Bolze raised his palm in the air as they passed each other, to give Cribbins a high five. Why was Bolze celebrating? "Look at our operating income and our earnings," Bolze boasted. "It's even better than we thought!"

No celebration was in order, however. GE Power's earnings were less than Bolze had committed to in his operating plan and less than what we'd told Wall Street to expect. Moments later, Cribbins walked into Bornstein's office with a frown on his face. "I don't think Bolze has a clue," he said.

I'd had enough. In January 2017, I told the board for a third time, "This is embarrassing. We must remove Bolze." But again, the looming topic of succession made the board say no. The world perceived Bolze to be something we believed he was not: a strong candidate to replace me. Even Susan Peters worried that firing him would push the succession story onto the front pages earlier than desired, making me, effectively, a lame duck. Other top advisers agreed.

We knew at this point that the board would not make Bolze CEO, and that when he didn't get my job, he would likely exit on his own. The reasoning behind leaving Bolze in place was: within a year, my successor would be named, and Bolze would depart without any bad press. So why ignite a media firestorm by firing him now?

So I acknowledge that the Alstom deal didn't work as we'd envisioned. Despite all the support for Alstom inside and outside the company, I wonder if I should have just broken the contract. Mind you, this would have prompted a major lawsuit, probably in France. But look: it was a complicated transaction and we had a team in disarray and a pending CEO transition—it was just too much. When in doubt, don't.

Beyond that, our execution around the deal was not what anybody should expect from GE. In that regard, the way the Alstom story has been distorted over the past three years has not served GE well. I regret not at least attempting to debunk it sooner. I felt I should hold my tongue and let the company's new leaders lead. Instead, they created a culture defined more by victimhood than by a sense of purpose. Leaders who were bullish on Alstom and thought GE could win in the market were silenced. People who'd failed were given too loud a voice. The result: with Alstom, GE Power was stopped at the starting line.

CHAPTER 11

Leaders Are Accountable

In March 2017, I learned how unhappy Nelson Peltz was from a Fox Business headline: "General Electric CEO Immelt in the Hot Seat with Trian's Peltz." The article said I'd missed key performance benchmarks such as increasing earnings growth and cutting expenses. If GE continued to miss those targets, according to "people close to Immelt and Peltz," Trian might formally seek my ouster.

The article's most telling sentence read: "When asked . . . whether Peltz and his company might seek a change at the top, Trian said in a statement: 'Trian and GE continue to work constructively together to optimize shareholder value.'" Rarely has a nonanswer said so much. By not denying that my head was on the chopping block, Trian was sending me a clear message: it was.

The next day, I flew to Shanghai for a three-day meeting with the GE board. In contrast to what Fox's nameless sources had just implied, this was a moment of triumph for GE. We took our directors to a Comac hangar, where we celebrated the launch of the Chinese airline's new narrow-body aircraft, which had more GE content than any other plane on earth. Then we ticked off our other local initiatives. GE Healthcare was building a bioprocess manufacturing plant in Guangzhou that would partner with drug companies around the world. GE Power had another joint venture with Harbin Electric, one of the country's three largest manufacturers of power-plant equipment. GE Aviation had grown the engine installed base in China to about ten thousand—a number that would soon be bigger than that in the United States.

GE was also one of the few Western companies that could leverage the Chinese government's One Belt One Road financing initiative, which was seeking to build a twenty-first-century Silk Road connecting Southeast Asia, Eastern Europe, and Africa. While OBOR got its name from the need for new "belts," or overland corridors, and new maritime "roads," or shipping lanes, it also necessitated new infrastructure projects like power generation. That's why GE could now access China's capital markets and share global funds, which helped offset the US shutdown, in 2015, of the Export-Import Bank, known as EXIM.

My favorite night of this trip was a dinner we hosted for our board and fifty Chinese customers. Many of the guests were alumni of GE's China CEO program, and our eyes lit up when we saw one another again. GE had taken chances in China at a time when most other American CEOs were steering clear, and they were grateful.

Such conviviality would have been impossible but for the hard work of so many GE people, and it buoyed my spirits. But this trip also included many awkward moments. At one point our directors met in an executive session without me for nearly two hours—a rare occurrence. I was pacing outside in the hallway, fielding questions from my team about what was going on (and having only the vaguest idea how to answer). It was clear that the pressure being applied by Trian and the pending issue of succession were causing rifts between the board and me. I didn't need a headline to tell me my time as CEO was almost up.

GROOMING THE CANDIDATES

I've described how in the late 1990s, when I was a candidate to become CEO, I sometimes chafed at the pageantry of Jack Welch's succession process. It was just too public, and I felt it skewed decision making by encouraging candidates to take short-term actions to impress Jack and the board that weren't best for GE. So I'd vowed to run my succession planning differently.

When I thought about the qualities that were essential in GE's leader, I valued a track record of hard work and commitment to the company. To that end, in 2012, when my team and I first began talking in earnest about my succession planning, the goal was to identify potential candidates and to broaden and test their competence by placing them in new roles. Jack had done much the same thing with me, Bob Nardelli, and Jim McNerney. But unlike Jack, who had stoked what *Fortune* called "the most closely watched, highly anticipated, and frequently second-guessed corporate succession drama ever," I wanted no drama. I wanted discretion.

Like I often had, I turned to Susan Peters. Peters and her team got to work honing a job description for the next CEO. In writing (and rewriting) it, they factored in everything they knew about the changing business environment and GE's culture. They polled experts and scholars to create a list of what they called essential "enterprise leadership capabilities." They believed that the next CEO's success depended less on what they knew going in and more on how fast they could learn and how resilient they would be.

In 2013, in consultation with the board, we decided we'd name my successor sometime in 2017. The precise date wasn't etched in stone, but choosing the year was important because it set in motion all that needed to happen next. It takes time for a board to establish criteria to select a new CEO for a new era, and then to identify and evaluate candidates. We had our eyes on a dozen people and were already moving them into roles within the company that would challenge them.

During this period, I extended my thought process to a few GE alumni. I had long admired Greg Lucier, an executive who'd left GE in 2003. Lucier had created a new medical-device business for us, and then had gone on to run a series of life sciences companies. He was strategically sharp, and at one point, I thought he might be a good candidate to run GE Healthcare (and, potentially, to replace me as CEO). We met for dinner and I liked him. He struck me as a savvy guy who could see around corners. But I wasn't sure he was ready to give up being a CEO in exchange for merely a chance of being CEO of GE, and I worried about the message that tapping him would send to internal candidates.

Also on my mind was Marijn Dekkers, then the CEO of Bayer AG. He'd worked for GE in various research capacities from 1985 to 1995, then left to get his management chops at AlliedSignal. Dekkers was a world-class executive, and I'd asked him to join the GE board in 2012 in part because I wanted him in the succession mix. He'd proven to be a great addition; as a member of the compensation committee and as chair of the risk committee, he knew both GE's top people and its biggest challenges. Today, with the benefit of hindsight, I wish I'd pushed his candidacy for CEO more forcefully. But at the time, our lead director, Jack Brennan, felt strongly that, given the complexity of our conglomerate, it was important to choose an inside candidate. I'd agreed.

In 2015, I'd told the board, "My job is to prepare the candidates, your job is to select them." In a fast-moving world, the lame duck CEO becomes irrelevant pretty quickly. The board needed to own and support its choice. In retrospect, I may have been naive about how difficult that process would be. When I had gone through it as a candidate in the late 1990s, the company had been cruising at top speed, so it was easy to make succession a primary focus. In 2015, by contrast, we had the GE Capital unwind underway; we had begun the Alstom acquisition and would soon move to buy Baker Hughes; and we had a new activist investor, Trian. It is rare to find a leader who is simultaneously working his ass off to accomplish positive change while also fully preparing to hand over the reins to someone else. The two thought processes are in opposition, in a sense—kind of like putting your foot on the gas and the brake at the same time. But I loved GE and never wanted to leave it in the lurch, so despite all the demands of my "day job," I took succession planning seriously.

By the end of 2015, the board had narrowed the field to Steve Bolze, Jeff Bornstein, John Flannery, and Lorenzo Simonelli and had begun making time to watch them work. As I've said, we'd always required our directors to visit two businesses a year, in groups of three to five, to see our executives in action. But now those visits became completely succession-related. One group dropped in on Flannery in Uppsala, Sweden, where GE Healthcare had a life sciences unit. Board members also met with Simonelli in Florence, London, and Houston; with Bornstein in Boston; and with Bolze in Schenectady and Greenville, South Carolina, where GE has a gas-turbine factory. Directors weren't just learning about the businesses at this point—they were evaluating the business leaders.

I had worked closely with Bornstein for twenty years, and he'd played a key role during the financial crisis, when he was GE Capital's CFO. Since then he'd been a true partner to me as GE's CFO. Operationally solid and widely admired within the company, he had a deep understanding of both the industrial and finance businesses and the ability to communicate clearly. While notoriously gruff on the outside, Bornstein was kind on the inside. I worried that the immense criticism one inevitably gets as a CEO would kill him. And the fact that he had never run a business was a limitation.

I had worked with Flannery, too, for almost twenty years. He had broad experience—having started in GE Capital, then running our business development—and was doing well at GE Healthcare. I loved his global background—he'd worked in South America, in Asia, and in India. And yet: I worried that Flannery couldn't make a decision. He was ponderous and always needed reams of data before choosing a course of action. I remembered that he had been the biggest laggard in our digital effort—another sign of his inability to move with force.

I'd mentored Simonelli as he tackled some of the most difficult operational jobs within GE—among them, globalizing GE Transportation's customer base and moving its manufacturing headquarters from

Pennsylvania to Texas. He was a tireless worker—something I really valued. The only thing that gave me pause was his formal style. He was the product of British boarding schools, and I sometimes worried that might hinder his ability to connect with GE people. (Such worries, I think now, were unfounded.) Meanwhile, I thought because he was in his early forties, Simonelli would get another chance to run GE if he wasn't chosen this time. In an era when CEOs were being scrutinized so relentlessly, I had begun to believe that GE's top job would never again be occupied by one person for twenty years straight.

Significantly, my opinions of the four finalists made up only a sliver of the data that the board was considering. Board members had settled on a list of qualities they sought, and to focus their thinking, they'd had those attributes printed on laminated cards they kept in their wallets, for easy access. On one side were intrinsic leadership skills, such as being self-aware or adaptive. On the other side were learned skills, such as having past experience allocating capital or making complex deals. Peters's team had painstakingly assembled 360-degree leadership assessment profiles of each finalist—some written by GE's vice chairs (John Rice, Beth Comstock, David Joyce) and others written by outside consultants.

I admit that some days I'd wake up and think, "NFW to any of the finalists," and in retrospect, we may not have had a strong enough pool. John Rice and Marijn Dekkers were first-rate, but they weren't being considered. I now think that of the agreed-upon candidates, Simonelli would have been the best choice. But I acknowledge that over the years, we'd let some top-notch leaders get away: in addition to Greg Lucier, who I've mentioned, there were at least two others who could have been great GE CEOs. After I passed over Omar Ishrak, a true superstar, for CEO of GE Healthcare, he left GE to be CEO of Medtronic. And Scott Donnelly, the former CEO of GE Aviation, went to the Rhode Island–based conglomerate Textron. Both these departures were huge losses. But back in 2016 and 2017, whenever my doubts about the candidates would flare, I would say to myself, "Maybe that's the way I looked in 1999." Being CEO of

GE is such a disproportionately big job that it can be hard to imagine anyone doing it—until he or she does.

I believed that whomever the board chose, it was imperative that the next CEO be surrounded by a strong team. Keith Sherin wouldn't be part of that team—at the end of August 2016 we'd announced his retirement. But Rice would be there, not to mention Comstock, Joyce, Peters, and our general counsel Alex Dimitrief. I was reassured that this layer would bolster my successor as he found his footing.

THE HOME STRETCH

On May 13, 2017, the board interviewed the four finalists at the Beekman hotel, a trendy spot in Lower Manhattan that we chose in part because our board members wouldn't be recognized there. I did not attend. We all wanted candidates to feel free to sketch out their visions for the company, even if they differed from mine.

It was a marathon session that began at 7:30 a.m. and went until 4 p.m. Each contender spoke for ninety minutes or so about what Brennan called "the road forward for GE," and then they answered questions. Peters's team had assembled a list. Among them:

- *What would your current leadership team say they most appreciate about how you lead them?*
- *What strategic changes would you drive, including capital allocation or portfolio management?*
- *What do you see as the most beneficial aspect of GE's culture that would be important for you to maintain? What would you plan to change?*
- *What is some of the toughest personal feedback you have received?*
- *How do you learn?*

That night, I was curious to hear how everyone had done. A few board members told me that Bolze had done well. I heard that Bornstein, too, made a great impression because he seemed humble—not what some board members were expecting. Simonelli was brilliant—informed, decisive, strategic. Flannery, on the other hand, was not at his best, according to people in the room, but Brennan didn't think that it should eliminate him as a candidate.

VALUING THE COMPANY

During this period, I was dealing with something else that had been brewing since the days of Project Hubble: how to help the industrial analysts who followed GE stock figure out how to value the company in the wake of our GE Capital divestment.

Almost right away, in April 2015, I'd begun talking about an earnings-per-share target of two dollars by 2018. Jeff Bornstein and I had done a thorough bottom-up analysis, and both of us felt this was a more-than-reachable profit goal. Just a month after we'd announced the GE Capital divestiture, I'd unveiled the idea at the Electrical Products Group Conference, a group of analysts that met in Sarasota, Florida. Every year at this conference, I gave the final presentation. It was tradition. So in that May 2015 EPG speech I laid out the math. Exiting both our private-label credit business and GE Capital would be a drag on earnings, sure, but the stock buyback would help with that, I'd said. If we grew our industrial operating profit EPS just 4 percent a year, I'd asserted, that would get us to our promised number of two dollars a share.

Two years later, right before the 2017 EPG Conference in Sarasota, I was preparing to give the closing speech there, as usual. I knew some investors and analysts now wanted us to come off of the two-dollars-a-share guidance by as much as 10 percent. They felt we needed more flexibility given the headwinds in the global energy markets. But our team still had a plan to hit the two-dollar EPS target based on strong performance in Aviation and Healthcare and cuts we planned to make in GE Digital.

I felt about our two-dollars-a-share guidance much like I'd felt about my 2009 promise not to cut the dividend. That is: we'd made a public commitment and I wanted to honor it. I didn't want to give GE people permission to fail, and I felt coming off our guidance would do that. Most important, I was confident we could hit the two-dollar EPS target—so confident that I'd bought $8 million worth of GE stock in the open market in 2016 and 2017.

In mid-May 2017, I'd assembled a team to help me develop my EPG presentation. But as I did so, two factors weighed heavily on me. First: we had the succession race in its final heat. Second: there was the complexity around the two-dollars-a-share number itself. The situation was truly daunting.

On Wednesday, May 24, when I touched down in Florida just hours before delivering my remarks, I remember feeling nervous. We'd prepared a detailed and specific strategy that added up to two dollars a share but acknowledged there were challenges. When I took the stage, I was uncharacteristically jittery. I had a sense that the end was near for me, and I was coming to terms with that.

Close confidantes would later tell me that the person who stepped onto the EPG stage that day was not the CEO they'd known for sixteen years. Instead of owning the message, like I usually did, I was distinctly uncomfortable and weirdly vague. The closer I got to the part of my presentation that dealt with two dollars a share, the more rushed my delivery became. In the end, I left many people wondering what, exactly, I'd said.

In the Q&A afterward, it wasn't long before an analyst asked for clarification. "Just to confirm," he said, "you're reiterating that two dollars is a makeable number?" I didn't hesitate, but what I said next only muddied things further: "It's going to be in the range."

The blowback was swift. "Did GE's Immelt Just Waver on His $2 EPS Target for 2017?" read one headline. Cowen and Company analyst Gautam Khanna wrote that my comments amounted to a "subtle walk back." After the presentation, as Bornstein, Matt Cribbins, and I shared a car to the airport, I put on a brave face. "Mattie, how do you think that went?" I asked my investor relations guy, who shook his head.

"That did not go well," he said.

"No," I said, "it didn't." We sat in silence until we got to the air-port, where a plane waited to take me to Texas.

The next day I had to be in Houston to review the Baker Hughes/GE merger and integration plan. I also was the guest of honor at a luncheon held by the World Affairs Council of Greater Houston, which had chosen me as its 2017 International Citizen of the Year. This was a big deal within the oil-and-gas industry, and I was proud to receive it. The afterglow of that honor wouldn't last long, however. As I headed back to the airport that afternoon, I received a call from Peters, who told me our board chair wanted me to call him immedi-ately to discuss a timetable for my stepping down.

When I got Jack Brennan on the phone, he said the board wanted to choose my successor as soon as possible, at their next meeting, just two weeks away.

I was the only passenger on my flight home from Houston to Boston, alone but for the crew. Usually I would have embraced such solitude as a chance to get more work done, but on this night, I felt listless, angry, and hurt. Some have asked me whether I was simply burned-out. There's no question that I was, but at the same time, I just wasn't done being CEO. It wasn't that I felt I was owed more time. I hated the idea of being the guy who hung on too long. But I hadn't gotten the company where I wanted it to be.

I spent the following three-day weekend in a sort of fugue state. As luck would have it, it was Memorial Day, and my wife and I were hosting the parents of my daughter's fiancé at our home in South Carolina. It should have been a happy weekend for all of us—we loved Sarah's soon-to-be husband, Chris, and everyone was excited at the prospect of a September wedding. But it was difficult for me to act cheerful when I felt so dejected. I didn't want to ruin the week-end for Andy or Sarah, so I kept my mournful feelings to myself.

On Monday, when I told Andy what was going on, she was mad—both for me and at me. She didn't think I deserved to be pushed out the door so hastily. At the same time, she worried that the drama surrounding my sudden departure would steal the spotlight from Sarah. My family had made many sacrifices while I was CEO; Andy had always accommodated my 24/7 work ethic and GE's preeminence in our lives. But enough was enough. I promised I would do everything I could to keep GE from encroaching on our daughter's big day.

A jumble of feelings battled inside me now. First and foremost, I felt like I had let the team down. Since childhood, I'd been all in for GE. There was no overstating its importance to my life. Even before becoming CEO, I'd invested almost every waking hour in the company, as well as all of my earnings and nearly every ounce of my energy. People had a right to be frustrated with me, but it made me very sad. The company wasn't where anyone wanted it to be, and it was my fault. I was still simmering about Bolze—I wished the board had approved his ouster, and I was mad at myself for not pushing back when they repeatedly said no. My relationship with Brennan was getting worse—he was talking to me mostly through intermediaries. And yet it was not in my interest to step down midyear. Better to exit at year's end, when I could own my wins and losses (and not be blamed for every mistake—even those made after my departure). But that was not to be.

After sixteen years as CEO, I wanted to believe that my hard work would count for something. That night at the FDIC in 2009, when I refused to leave Sheila Bair's office until she heard me out? Those thousands of hours I'd spent traveling millions of miles to help our people close deals? Those ninety weekends sitting face-to-face with GE leaders? All the effort I'd put into remaking GE's portfolio and shoring up its culture to prepare it to thrive in the future? All the times I'd sat there with a grin on my face, gamely answering the one question I was asked more than any other: "What is it like to follow Jack Welch?"? I guess I'd hoped all that would come back to me someday, in some moment of grace. Now, especially, it felt like it never would. I'd spent thirty-five years busting my ass for GE, and in the end, none of that seemed to matter.

Now it was go time for the board. Who would be my replacement? They hadn't decided yet, except they agreed it wouldn't be

Bolze. There was, seemingly, only one person within GE who didn't know that: Bolze himself. In the days leading up to the meeting where the board would make its choice, Bolze approached more than one member of GE's leadership team to say that he really looked forward to working with them when he was named CEO.

The June 9 board meeting was on a Friday. Directors gathered in a big conference room at the Boston Harbor Hotel, across the river from GE's new temporary headquarters, which lacked a board room. I got there early, as I always do, and was in the room for the entire meeting. There wasn't much discussion; Brennan had reached out to the directors beforehand to seek consensus, and in the end, the board was unanimous in its choice of Flannery, whose extensive international experience, humility, and willingness to make significant change worked in his favor. The vote was over, and so was I. There was a beat of silence, and then board member Susan Hockfield, the former president of the Massachusetts Institute of Technology, spoke.

"Jeff, we just want to thank you for everything you've done for GE," she said as her fellow board members knocked quietly on the table to signal their agreement. Board member Andrea Jung walked over at that point to hug me, and as I rose from my chair, tears came into my eyes. I was overcome, and it surprised me. I tried to say something, but the words wouldn't leave my mouth. I had known what was going to happen. But the finality of it stung.

I walked out of the room, and Alex Dimitrief stayed at my side. We headed through the hotel lobby and out to the valet area, where my longtime security guy Eddie Galanek was waiting with a car. When he went to open the door for me, I told him not to bother—Dimitrief and I would return to GE headquarters on foot. I'll never forget how Galanek then turned to Dimitrief. "Take care of him," he said.

It was eighty degrees outside, but it felt like twice that as we plodded the mile back to the GE offices on Farnsworth Street. Dimitrief and I are both big guys, and we were wearing suits, so it wasn't long before we were both pouring sweat. As we crossed the Seaport Boulevard bridge, I could see the Boston Tea Party ships to the south of us, on display in the middle of the Fort Point Channel. What had I always said about military history? That everything goes wrong? That's how I felt now. Like a fallen general, defeated by fatigue.

Once we got back to GE headquarters, I called Beth Comstock, John Rice, and David Joyce to my office to tell them the news. I tried not to be emotional, but I cared about these people, so I didn't completely succeed. We kept it short. Next I called Flannery, who was in Chicago, and congratulated him. Get on the next plane to Boston, I said. We had an announcement to make.

Over the rest of that day, I met with the other finalists one by one, in person, to tell them the board had chosen Flannery. I could tell Simonelli was let down, but that was balanced by the fact that he had a very important job he was doing at Baker Hughes. He'd have many opportunities ahead.

When Bornstein arrived in my office, he already knew about Flannery. Brennan had told him. All along, Bornstein had been clear with the board that his first allegiance was to the company, not to being CEO. He had never been convinced that he was the right person for the job, so in addition to disappointment, he felt some relief. And he was aware of how much GE was about to change.

Finally, I met with Bolze. When I told him the board's decision, he looked surprised. But he quickly pivoted, saying he would now do what he'd threatened to do so many times before: leave GE. Then Bolze said something so uncharacteristically self-aware that I still marvel at it. "I am sorry I made it so hard for you," he told me. That would be the last time he ever spoke to me. Five days later, he announced via LinkedIn that he was retiring from the company, and six weeks later, he landed at Blackstone.

The next night was Saturday, June 10, and Andy and I had Flannery and his wife, Tracy, over to our home in the Back Bay for dinner. It was a pleasant evening. I'd supported the board's choice of Flannery, and I wished him the best. I knew he had a very difficult job ahead, and I told him I'd do anything I could to help. I only hoped that, aided by the experienced team that was in place, he could succeed.

On Sunday, the day before we announced Flannery's appointment, my communication team and I prepped for about an hour. I
then did a teleconference with the top thirty or so leaders of GE, letting them know that Flannery would become CEO on August 1 and
that I would remain as chairman until December 31, when Flannery
would take on that role as well. The tone of the call was somber, and
no one asked a single question.

Then I made five more phone calls—some out of courtesy, others out of love. I felt I owed Bill Conaty, my retired HR guy who I'd
nicknamed Mr. Wolf, a heads-up. "Aw, shit," he said when I told him.
"I'm sorry." I also called Sandy Warner, the former board member
who we'd asked not to stand for reelection in 2015. Some will be surprised that I called Warner, but despite our differences, I knew that
he loved GE. He was cordial to me. I think he appreciated the call.

I called my parents, of course. My dad said, "Why would you
leave now? You're doing a great job." I loved him for saying that, even
as my heart sank. When I reached my brother, Steve, who was then
the CEO of the international law firm Hogan Lovells, he was protec-
tive. He worried that Trian would push for me to exit before year's
end and that they'd continue to use the media to accomplish their
goals. "I fear you're not going to get to own the narrative on this," he
said. As usual, my brother was right.

Finally, I called Jack Welch. I wanted him to hear it from me.
He was supportive. "Hey," he said, "we both know you never caught
a break." Then, out of the blue, he added, "Thank God the board
didn't pick Bolze."

The next day we announced my retirement, and GE stock went up
4 percent, to $28.94. Apparently, investors felt my impending departure
was good for the company. The press coverage was brutal. I'd always
admired that Teddy Roosevelt quote: "It's not the critic who counts; not
the man who points out how the strong man stumbles . . . The credit
belongs to the man who is actually in the arena." Now I wasn't so sure.
I would always root for the man in the arena, but it seemed the critic
did count, because the critic could do a lot of damage.

GE's communication team did the best it could, but there was no way to make this transition look normal. At first I blamed my communications leader Deirdre Latour. But I was being a baby, and when I caught myself, I apologized. Had I merely locked myself in a room and read the headlines, I would have felt very much alone. But my friends wouldn't allow that. I sent personal notes to the 185 top officers of the company and to members of the GE board, thanking them for their partnership, but I was still surprised to hear from so many people—literally thousands—inside and outside GE. For a while there, the mail flooded my office. Customers sent handwritten letters and emails, as did scientists, investors, and CEOs at other companies who I knew well. "I'm not sure the press is willing to or can give you the credit you deserve," warned one. "Ignore the noise from those with less aptitude," said another.

Most of the letters, though, were from my GE colleagues. Many said what a privilege it had been to work with me and what an impact the company had had not just on their careers but on their ways of looking at the world. Several said that I'd taught them to put the company first. "I knew you would fire me in a minute if you thought it was in the best interests of the company," wrote one colleague who worked in the Global Growth Organization, "and this is exactly the way it should work." Others repeated things I'd said that had stuck with them. A GE Healthcare employee said the first time we met, I told him: "Focus on solving customer needs, cultivate world-class relationships with your peers, and always be bolder than you think is needed." An executive who worked on the Alstom integration quoted me like this: "When encountering a challenge, always look for a way to improve it and do better!" GE's chief information officer said I'd taught him to "take big swings and have the tenacity to stick with them." A top GE executive in China said, "Whatever I do in the future, I will always keep your words in mind: 'Lead in the moment and give fully of yourself.'"

Many reminded me of interactions I'd lost to the passage of time. "You trusted me at a crucial strategic moment, and I had a chance to grow," wrote one. Said another, "I was willing to take the high road less traveled because I knew you always had my back." Said a third: "I would follow you into any battle." Three separate people told me the end of my tenure made them think of a quote from Maya Angelou: "I've learned that people will forget what you said, people will forget what you did, but people will never forget how you made them feel."

The letters made clear GE employees and their families felt I knew them as people. One thanked me for my support during his difficult divorce, another recalled me intervening to help get the best treatment for her sick child. If you made me pick a favorite letter, though, it would be the one from the CEO of GE Onshore Wind, who ended with this postscript: "P.S. My 16-year-old daughter's reaction to your retirement was, 'How could Jeff do this to me?'" He recalled, as did I, one weekend when he'd come to work, toiling on some pressing project, and his daughter Meredith had tagged along. "You asked her if she wanted a job at GE," he recalled before passing along Meredith's career advice: "She is counting on you to stay active; she thinks Snap needs you most but would settle for Uber."

EVERY JOB LOOKS EASY
(UNTIL YOU'RE THE ONE DOING IT)

Anyone who reads the business pages knows the leadership transition didn't go as planned. There were challenges inside the company, for sure. But we compounded them through our own actions. It became clear right away that my main role would be Person to Blame. Trian dominated the narrative; I suspected they were behind a series of anonymously sourced stories. They'd wanted my scalp, and they'd gotten it.

My relationship with Flannery went south quickly. "We need to re-underwrite the place," he kept saying. "No number is too low. I want this to be a holding company, no headquarters, no corporate. I want to spin businesses out, and I want to lower the numbers. Everything's up for grabs." Early on, I tried when I could to counsel him to just run the place for a while. I told him that talking constantly about breaking up the company would be confusing in a conglomerate. In my view, it's not enough to stand at a podium and list the company's problems. You must motivate people to fix them. But Flannery had decided to perpetuate the "success theater" idea that would soon appear in the *Wall Street Journal*: that I had encouraged people to act like all was well, even when it wasn't. I was his scapegoat. Some people confided that he was trashing me in front of investors and others. He didn't want or need my input.

In September, the board had approved a board seat for Trian, effective in November. It was time to make myself scarce. On October 2, 2017, I stepped aside as GE chairman—three months ahead of schedule. From then on, I watched GE from the outside. Flannery had a lot to deal with during this period, some of which I'd helped create. I'd hoped we would be done with the GE Capital pivot and that the Alstom acquisition would be proving itself. But that wasn't yet the case, and the volatility that Trian created around the GE board didn't help.

ACTIVIST INVESTORS WEREN'T THE ANSWER FOR GE

I know I'm an imperfect messenger, but activist investors aren't always the answer. They have only four arrows in their quiver: fire the CEO, sell off parts of the business, cut costs, or spread blame. In some businesses, one or all of those are necessary. At a company whose problems are too complex to be solved by those four solutions, activist investors wreak only havoc.

Don't get me wrong, their focus on financial performance is justified. In fact, after I left GE I became the chair of Athenahealth at a time that another activist investor, Elliott Management, owned fifteen percent of the company's stock. While I was cautious, I believe they brought value to the company. But that isn't always the case.

While they usually show up in bad economic cycles, activist investors are particularly destructive in a crisis. They pull leaders' focus to the internal: right at the moment that you should be rallying to win in the marketplace, you must divert your energy to respond to their charges. When a company is in a tough cycle, leaders need to motivate their people. Activists stifle such efforts by building a culture of blame. They dominate the media and excel at vilification. Their voice drowns out those of other stakeholders.

Activists hire the best publicists—spin doctors who excel at getting their message out there. I'll never forget the moment that drove this point home. It was the day before we announced Trian's investment in GE, when we agreed to give the *Wall Street Journal* the scoop. That meant meeting with two reporters in my office in Connecticut—David Benoit, who covered Trian, and Ted Mann, who covered GE. When we all sat down, I couldn't help but notice that while the GE folks had a tense relationship with Mann, the Trian folks were buddy-buddy with Benoit.

Imagine this puzzle: it can take more than ten years to develop many lifesaving drugs. A gas turbine, once installed, lasts for thirty years. A stock is held for less than six months in a mutual fund. The average CEO tenure is now about five years. There is a mismatch in the time horizon. Add to all this the increasing prominence of activist investors, who push for even shorter-term results, and you get a big mess. Activists tax the system.

Trian studied GE for more than six months. But they invested right before major markets began cycling down. In response, they went after me personally and often unfairly. Later, they'd pit board members and GE's top managers against each other. Internally, GE leaders holed up in conference rooms; instead of making decisions, some leaked to the press. Externally, the narrative was increasingly toxic.

Peltz once said to me, "Winners make their numbers no matter what." But GE enjoys superiority in commercial aviation engines today precisely because we doubled R&D between 2008 and 2010, right in the midst of the financial crisis. The numbers were less important than the long-term goals. I could tell you hundreds of stories just like that, when we had to make big, expensive, future-looking decisions at the most difficult times. But that kind of big-picture thinking is impossible in the presence of activist investors.

A SHORT TENURE

In the end, Flannery wouldn't last long. I empathize with him. I know running GE is a bear of a job. But how did the company fall so far, so fast? Clearly some of our decisions didn't work out the way we planned. I own that. But the answer is more complicated than what's been reported.

First and foremost, the global energy markets were tougher than we expected. That gave Flannery no margin for error and made him even more dependent on his team to help him navigate these challenging conditions.

The tail from GE Capital proved more toxic than any GE leaders had ever imagined. The long-term care book metastasized so quickly it was shocking. Remember, it had been reviewed continuously, by multiple experts, including some at the Fed. The chair of our board's audit committee was a former SEC commissioner. Had we known what was coming, we would have put the proceeds of Project Hubble in reserve, and not done a stock buyback. In all, from the 1990s to today, GE's exposure in insurance has cost the company dearly. I'd tried to get us out, but we'd held on to a few of the worst pieces. The losses from policies written in the past proved worse than our carefully considered projections, and that became clear by the end of 2017, on Flannery's watch.

In my opinion, however, Flannery allowed GE's biggest business—Power—to be run poorly. Flannery was naive; it's always tempting for new leaders to lower the bar, protecting themselves by reporting that they've inherited big problems from their predecessor. However, Flannery flogged the "success theater" claim for too long. What he didn't realize was that he was creating his own failure narrative. The GE Power franchise had generated a lot of value for investors over time. Trashing the past didn't solve anything. Flannery should have been motivating the Power team to succeed, but he didn't. Most of the senior leaders in Power left or were pushed out.

Instead of moving quickly (as GE's Oil & Gas team had in a similarly down market), the people in charge at GE Power stopped moving altogether. Customers learned about quality issues on social media, not from GE salespeople. (In September 2018, when GE Power's new CEO, Russell Stokes, admitted a production issue with GE's next-generation HA turbines, he did it in a post on LinkedIn!) It was embarrassing. GE's gas-turbine share was 70 percent in the first quarter of 2017; a year later, it was 18 percent. In 2018, GE sold zero units of distributed power— usually a $2 billion annual business. GE lost deals in global markets like Mexico and Iraq—places where the company had enjoyed high share for decades. GE shut down its financing of power plants, which had been an essential way of creating demand. Mitsubishi Heavy Industries was the market leader for the first time in history. When you lose massive share, your factories become inefficient and clogged with inventory. Factory workers feel the burden of market loss. A business that generated more than $40 billion of cash over the previous fifteen years was now losing money. This failure to execute made debt levels look high and put pressure on the balance sheet.

It seemed to me that Flannery couldn't make decisions. This had always been my concern about his leadership. I think he was getting bad advice, both from inside the company and from bankers, that boiled down to, "Just do *something!*" I didn't expect him to follow my lead. But he kept tossing out ideas without taking action. Flannery put GE's Oil & Gas business up for sale in November 2017. Three years later, when I was finishing this book, GE still owned a large chunk of that business. He approved a "spin out" of GE Healthcare, because he said it didn't fit into GE's portfolio. Then, he changed his mind: GE Healthcare was a keeper. Later, the company sold GE's life sciences business, one of the few GE holdings that would have gotten a boost during the coronavirus pandemic. GE Digital was portrayed as a waste of money, then it was great, then it was on the auction block.

Worst of all, it seemed to me that Flannery lost the people who could have helped him and nobody seemed to care. By early 2018, GE had lost not just CFO Jeff Bornstein but also John Rice, Beth Comstock, Susan Peters, Alex Dimitrief, and most of the senior leaders at GE Power. Change is fine as long as replacements are working as a team. Earlier, I spoke about the importance of leaders absorbing pressure. Instead of solving problems, Flannery's team pointed fingers; some were even leaking to the media or going around him to the board. As I've said, your peers promote you, but an erosion in your relationship with your team gets you fired. This was Flannery's downfall.

With everyone fighting for themselves, no one was fighting for the brand. The narrative around the company went dark. Even when your results don't meet expectations, someone needs to publicly show that they know which direction to take, and then to lead people in that direction. This is the point at which the board needed to step in and take control. I have to believe that they were all impacted by Trian, which had initiated a process to shrink the GE board by a third. This downsizing was probably a good move, but it alienated everyone. The GE board was fractured at exactly the wrong time. As a result, the company wasted 18 months, freezing up precisely when it should have been taking action.

I'm sad that it didn't work out for Flannery, and this was bad for GE. Did he get dealt a tough hand? Sure. But GE needed clear, timely decision making, strong teamwork, accountable operations, and someone willing to fight publicly for the brand's reputation. In the absence of all those things, it seemed that GE's people quit following Flannery.

On October 1, 2018, a year after my departure, GE's board announced Flannery was out. Former Danaher CEO Larry Culp, who Flannery had added to the board earlier that year, was now GE's CEO.

One of the first moves Culp made, in November 2018, was to bring back John Rice, who Flannery had forced out, to help restructure the Power division. It seemed the narrative was starting to shift. In 2018, the Alstom steam business had a great year, earning almost $800 million. The market for natural gas in power generation is growing substantially. The current headwind is product quality in the GE gas-turbine business. My hunch is that GE Power will be a very profitable business again someday.

Now, Culp and his team are dealing with the COVID-19 crisis, which has severely impacted GE's aviation business. This is just another piece of bad luck. It seems that Culp is taking the action required. Perhaps Culp's biggest challenge is to restore the sense of pride that comes from working for a company that has purpose. In Jack Welch's day, and in mine, our people always had one another's backs, through good days and bad. Inside the company, we were open with criticisms that could make the company better, but outside, we were always united. I hope that cohesion can be rebuilt, and I am cheering Culp on from the sidelines as he seeks to do so.

I've always said that Truth = Facts + Context. The fact is that GE's stock performance trailed the market while I was CEO. There's no sugarcoating the numbers: the stock dropped significantly during my tenure. But here is the context: during my sixteen years in the job, GE had cumulative earnings of $240 billion, cumulative cash flow of $280 billion, and cumulative dividends of $145 billion. That's more than GE's previous 110 years combined. Put another way: in the first seven years of my tenure, GE generated more earnings and paid more dividends than during twenty years with Jack Welch at the helm.

During my tenure, GE was number one in almost every industry in which it competed. GE Aviation gained twenty-five points of share from 2001 to 2016, the year before I left GE. In Healthcare, we built a $20 billion innovation leader with the most respected brand in the industry. In Renewables, we built a $12 billion global business from scratch. We built a $75 billion company outside the United States, leading in markets such as China and India. We were on all the top-ten lists for patent applications, leadership development, brand value, and "Most Admired" companies.

It is hard to see today, but GE had a strong culture. People liked and respected one another; they were proud of their company. Other companies wanted to partner with us. GE had a strong foundation of integrity. We played by the rules and enforced high standards around the world. The team rode out the ups and downs of the most brutal cycles together and supported one another for the greater good.

I said in chapter 3 that we wanted to build a GE that was more technical, more global, more diverse and closer to our customers. We made progress on all of these fronts. We weren't perfect, for sure, but I believe that by making these improvements, GE set an example that had an impact on the world.

Yes, our PE ratio eventually went from 50X to 15X, while the burden of GE Capital added a layer of uncertainty that still looms today. When I took over, GE's stock was overvalued, and the company was about to encounter significant challenges. When I left, my team had made great progress transforming GE, but we weren't finished. And our stock price continued to lag.

In May 2019, I went to Australia for a conference and found myself at an impromptu mini GE reunion. Of twelve people around a table, five were CEOs, two were board members of public Australian companies, and the rest were division CEOs. They'd all worked for GE once, but not anymore. Give me the chance, and I could easily list more than thirty people who worked for me at GE who are now CEOs of S&P 500 companies. For a while there, in the wake of my departure, it seemed the only company that didn't value GE leaders was GE. I am hopeful that has begun to change.

CHAPTER 12

Leaders Are Optimists

In 2018, teaching my first class at the Stanford Graduate School of Business helped me see not only that I could write this book but also that I should. Two years later, teaching that class again in the midst of a pandemic clarified why I hope this book will resonate, now more than ever.

It was mid-March 2020 when COVID-19 caused Stanford to close its doors. Like so many others, my coteacher and I had to master the group-video-chat service Zoom, which we used to host our seventy-six students for two hours every Tuesday and Thursday afternoon. I also used Zoom to meet with each student one-on-one for an hour. But the adjustments we made weren't just technological. We also refocused our curriculum, zeroing in on a single theme: leadership in a crisis.

Like in past years, we built each class around a guest CEO—people we'd booked months earlier, who nonetheless could speak to our newly chosen topic because they were living it. One by one, these leaders, many of them GE alumni, opened up about how they were grappling with the unforeseen problems caused by the virus. A few of them, such as Michael Dowling, the CEO of New York State's largest healthcare provider, Northwell Health, faced a surge in sick people. But most were dealing with the ripples of a near-total economic shutdown.

Tom Gentile, a GE Capital veteran who was now CEO of Spirit AeroSystems, told us how even before the emergence of the novel coronavirus, his fuselage manufacturing business had been hurt by the grounding of Boeing's troubled 737 MAX. Now, with airline travel decimated, he said, "Our stock has lost about seventy-five percent of its value. We got downgraded to junk status. We had to raise liquidity to avoid violating our bank loan covenants." But, he added, "I'm actually quite optimistic. Air travel is going to come back. It will take some time. We may do things differently. But it's going to come back."

Anne Wojcicki, the CEO of the personal genomics company 23andMe, talked about the intersection of technology and healthcare, and how that linkage could change in a post-COVID world. "Put yourself in the shoes of an employer with 1,000 workers," she said. "How do you bring them back to work unless you know more about them and can guarantee they'll be safe?" She talked passionately about how more pooling of individuals' health data could help control spiraling healthcare costs, which account for nearly twenty percent of the US GDP. "If you want to disrupt healthcare, you have to be more creative than simply having a good idea," she said. "But to have an impact, we have to have critical mass."

Ryan Lance, the CEO of the oil-and-gas company Conoco-Phillips, said that nothing gets done without the products his company sells, so he felt good about the future. Still, it was unclear whether demand for energy would continue to grow 1 percent a year, as it had pre-COVID. Usually, he said, he followed a simple leadership model—"SAM," or "Set Direction. Align. Motivate." But now, with ten thousand employees working from home, he acknowledged he was spending most of his time on the latter two, calming his colleagues' anxieties—telling them their company would be okay.

Whether they worked for CNN or Ford Motor Company, for a large state university or for a fast-growth healthcare start-up, every guest CEO talked about the importance of staying flexible as they navigated the unknown. One had completely revamped her strategy in eight days. Another had restructured and automated his factory to allow for social distancing. Many spoke of resetting their clocks to deal with the crisis in real time.

| | | |

At the beginning of this book, I described how American leaders who came up in the 1980s, as I did, were the first to encounter multiple tail-risk events—those that are unlikely to happen but then *do* happen. But increasingly, as the guest speakers to our 2020 virtual classroom made clear, that kind of volatility isn't unlikely; it's the norm. My students' generation of leaders will have no choice but to be crisis managers. As my coteacher, Rob Siegel, told our class at one point, while no leader can stop all bad things from happening, "Your job, when you are running a company, will be to avoid the avoidable."

Between 2001 and 2017, if I'd had to choose one quality that defined my tenure it would have been uncertainty. My predecessor used to say, "Don't do anything we can't control." By the end of my time as CEO, I felt like there was little that any company could control. Increasingly, as the coronavirus has proven yet again, the best leaders must stay ready, must adapt, and must absorb their colleagues' and constituents' fears.

There is a popular idea that pessimism is a realistic way of looking at the world, while optimism is a naive illusion. I chose to lead GE with optimism and hope, not cynicism and blame. I would do that again today.

I was an optimist after 9/11. What was the alternative? I was an optimist on the day Lehman Brothers went bankrupt. Had I not been one, I wouldn't have been able to function. I was an optimist when we asked Warren Buffett for help and when we divested of most of GE Capital's holdings. Optimism doesn't mean ignoring reality.

I learned a lot about myself as CEO. Mainly, I learned that I could take a lot of abuse and keep leading. I never lost my curiosity or my determination to try new things. By the end of my tenure, though, I worried that I was losing my empathy—my ability to see the world through others' eyes. I just had too much scar tissue.

When I stepped down from GE, I packed a few knickknacks in a cardboard box, walked out of GE's Boston headquarters, and stepped into an Uber. Even then, though I was sad and I had no idea what was next, I remained optimistic. My tenure had ended the way it had begun: in volatility. Maybe, I thought, that experience would prove useful going forward.

OWNING SOME MISTAKES

The average tenure of a CEO keeps getting shorter. As many experts deride corporate short-termism, boards and investors keep demanding immediate performance (and forcing their CEOs out more quickly if they don't get it). Meanwhile, the public role of CEOs is getting more difficult as employees expect more policy activism, while at the same time governance and compliance get more complex. If you were the leader of a financial-services company in 2009, as I was, you had two jobs. First, keep your company alive. Second, prepare to get thrashed for a decade straight as the world changed forever. I did both while remaining GE's biggest cheerleader.

I also made some mistakes as CEO that had an impact on GE and sent us in a wrong direction. Had I not made these mistakes, I could have improved the long-term performance of the company. I want to own them here.

- I could have reset the company in the early 2000s, after 9/11 and the failure of the Honeywell deal. The power bubble and pension earnings had created a distortion in our results that would soon go away. I could have rightly argued that the world as we knew it had changed and that GE needed a different approach, one with dramatically lower growth. I didn't choose that path. I felt that the GE team needed stability after 9/11. And I was loyal to Jack Welsh and felt that a major shift in 2001 would tarnish his legacy. My failure to push reset, however, led to the growth of GE Capital, whose cash we needed to fix the industrial portfolio. That growth worked for a while. By 2007, it wouldn't look so smart.

- I did not develop a deep enough bench of rising leaders, especially given all the initiatives we had underway. I've thought about this the most since I retired. Lorenzo Simonelli was a superstar, but we should have had ten just like him at his age group, and we didn't. I should have created more opportunities for promising young leaders to learn and experiment, giving them jobs with profit-and-loss responsibility. By the 2000s, private equity—and even venture capital—was creating these opportunities and luring our people away. And then there's this: particularly as we added two new businesses—Baker Hughes, a GE Company, and Alstom—I should have paid more detailed attention to how those acquisitions overtaxed our front-line operating leaders (plant managers, sourcing leaders, and the like). We had siphoned off too many of these leaders to support our growth in renewables and oil and gas, leaving not enough skilled people in Power. This challenged our ability to execute. Had I realized this then, it could have made a huge difference.

- I wish I'd found a way to generate more shareholder value from GE Capital. This was a great team and a strong business. At one point, GE Capital had a market valuation of more than $200 billion. Ultimately, we captured just a fraction of that number for investors. We'd been guilty of arrogance. Had GE Capital stayed focused on the platforms it occupied in 1995, and merely grown them, we would have been better off. Most of GE Capital's expansion after that period was in areas where we lacked expertise and competitive advantage.

For sure, we had some bad luck. But at some point, before or after the financial crisis, we should have brought in an outside partner like Blackstone or Apollo or TPG.

- I wish I had said "I don't know" more frequently. Sometimes I sought to accomplish positive change by asserting how I believed things ought to be. I believed it was my job to set the course by telling people where we were going. But there were times when I may have tried to accomplish our aims through force of will. In those instances, instead of clarifying our mission, I muddied it.

- I took on too much, particularly at the end of my tenure. This was unfair to GE's board. In the midst of CEO succession planning, they had to deal with two difficult business transactions, a huge digital initiative, and volatile markets. Maybe I should have left at the end of 2015, after the GE Capital unwind. There is no question that, had I done so, my legacy would have been more positive. But I felt it was my responsibility to solidify the company before I handed it over. We had a five-year succession plan and I was trying to get the right people in place. At the end, I was still working hard and pushing the company forward, but maybe GE would have been better off if someone with a fresh perspective had taken over sooner.

As for the deals we did on my watch, smart people can debate their timing and valuation. Was selling NBCU to Comcast in 2010 perfectly timed? Probably not. We needed cash, though, and it was the best idea we had at the time. We had no plans to execute a bold strategy as Bob Iger was doing at Disney, so I thought it best to move on. Would I have created Baker Hughes, a GE Company in 2017 had I known that GE would announce a spin-off one month after I retired? Probably not. But it is a great franchise that will become even more valuable over time. Frankly, there are some criticisms of my tenure that I can only categorize as Monday-morning quarterbacking.

I know that you don't want to hear this, but luck really matters in business. It is easy to talk about controlling your destiny when you have the benefit of a tailwind. Think about the current COVID crisis. Because of the need to stay home, digital communication has benefited (many stocks have tripled) and global travel has gone dormant (airline stocks have been cut in half). I know both of these businesses; there are as many good leaders in aviation as there are in tech. Sometimes the difference is just luck.

As leaders, we must remember that the world turns. Be humble and empathetic when times are good. And learn to recognize the difference between tailwind and good management. If someone impresses you when they are benefiting from good markets, you still don't know much. When they thrive in a shit show, you have a gem.

THE CASE FOR LISTENING (MOST OF THE TIME)

The criticism I reject more than any other is: "GE would have been perfect, if only Jeff had listened to me."

During my tenure, we sustained the culture of GE with lively debate. Every year, we invited hundreds of outside leaders, teachers, and consultants into the company to help us hone our thinking and embrace the best ideas. I have been criticized, unfairly, I think, for being someone who stifled dissent. On the contrary, I sought out new voices and tried to empower those whose voices had been drowned out. Leaders must be willing to make decisions in a crowded room, out in the open, for everyone to see. But I'll admit: I didn't always listen to everyone.

Sometimes people are simplistic about the merits of listening, as if every comment anyone utters is valuable. I believe one of the most important elements of leadership is picking to whom you listen. If I had listened to every critic within GE, we wouldn't have launched our Ecomagination initiative, we wouldn't have bought Enron Wind, and we wouldn't have made the strides GE still benefits from in China. For years, members of the media and just about every sell-side analyst trashed me for paying $9.8 billion for Amersham in 2004. By 2015, it was indispensable to the company, and by 2019 it was generating

$2 billion of cash every year. (GE would ultimately sell a piece of the business, bioprocess manufacturing, which had been valued at $3 billion when we bought it, for more than $21 billion.) If I'd listened to the analysts, we would have missed that opportunity. In all four cases, my single-mindedness served GE. Here's a time that it didn't: Many smart people opposed the acquisition of the subprime mortgage lender WMC. We bought it anyway, at my direction. That was a mistake.

When you are driving change—especially inside a big company—there are a thousand voices. A few of them really matter, because they are saying, "Here's what you're not seeing; here's how we can make this work better." But those can be drowned out by the cacophony of voices saying, "Change is uncomfortable, so I don't want to change no matter what." To those attempting to transform their companies, I say this: make sure you're surrounded by enough differences of opinion to find the voices that matter.

In my experience, there are four types of people. One type is always switched on and focused in meetings, equally good at making relevant points and listening to others. The second type talks too much, drowning the room in detail and leaving little space for opposing views. The third type prefers to hang back but has lots of valuable insights—they need to be encouraged to contribute. The fourth group I call simply silent and smoldering. They believe they are smarter than others, but they don't want to dirty their hands by debating. They become the "unnamed source." If you worry about them, you will never get anything done.

You need intelligent people to serve as your guardrails, but in the end, it is your job to act. There is no simple rule for when to listen and when to act. But I do know this: in companies large and small, you must get rid of people you don't trust, even those who are unusually talented.

LIFE AFTER GE

In the three years since I left GE, I have chosen not to speak publicly about the company. I didn't want to have my words sliced into sound bites. I wanted to tell the whole story or not say anything at all. And I wanted to give the current leaders of GE the time and space to get their feet underneath them without my voice adding to the cacophony.

I needed to take some time to think. I've gone through periods of despair, embarrassment, and anger. I will always cheer for GE, even if it is different from the company I remember. But I've also learned I have to keep going, keep trying, keep learning. People often say to me, "You must have thick skin." But no one's skin is thick enough to fend off all pain. The haters hurt.

Now, as a venture partner at New Enterprise Associates, a Silicon Valley venture-capital firm, I spend a lot of time with founders of new kinds of companies, as well as legacy brands that are struggling to survive. That I have seen good and bad days gives me empathy, and people seem to value that. I've said that military history has much to teach entrepreneurs. Well, in California, I'm viewed to some extent as a combat veteran, back from battle, beaten up but still standing. People here want to learn from my successes and my mistakes.

You should know something I didn't in 2017: that it is possible to be happy, even when things don't work out the way you planned. For that reason alone, you can't give up. At GE, I learned lessons that have proved valuable to others. My mission now is to share those lessons. In doing that, I have felt satisfaction and happiness that I never would have expected when I first left GE.

Joining NEA has been a gift for me—a way to give back and to be of use. Sometimes the CEOs I advise, and on whose boards I sit, put me to work—giving pep talks before a sales kickoff, say, or closing deals or helping recruit talented executives. But a few have told me my most meaningful contribution has been empathy. Because I've sat in the CEO's seat, I know that what they need from outside advisers aren't marching orders—"Do it this way!"—but informed perspectives. And I understand how it feels to have the weight of all your employees' futures on your shoulders. I know how lonely that can be, so I make a point of being accessible and staying in touch.

Teaching, too, has given me another, valuable vantage point. At the end of each semester at Stanford, we ask our students where they hope to get jobs. I'm happy to say that these mostly twenty- and thirty-somethings are still willing to work at so-called classic companies such as GE. But they worry about how dedicated such companies are to remaining relevant. I have asked students, "Who will improve healthcare more in the future: GE or Apple?" I watch as they consider GE's history, record, and capability. But they still say Apple. This is not merely young people defaulting to a technology leader. It is young people backing a company perceived to have the will to be great.

This is GE's challenge today: to recapture and articulate the promise of the future. When I joined GE in 1982, probably 90 percent of college grads would have considered a career there. Now that number might be 50 percent.

CHANGE FOR THE BETTER

There are certain business icons who have created something out of nothing. I'm thinking of geniuses such as Jeff Bezos. Other leaders benefit from good luck or good timing. If you were the CEO of a bank from 2000 to 2007, you were seen as a hero. If you got the same job between 2008 and 2015, you were seen as a villain. Same person, same job, different circumstances.

Most leaders will not be perfect or lucky as they make hard decisions without a map to guide them. But especially in crisis, if they insist on waiting until the skies clear, they will never do anything at all. Inaction is bad leadership, but it can feel safer than action because to act is to open yourself up to criticism. There was never a time in sixteen years as CEO that I was sheltered from the critics—the media, our investors, my predecessor. But I always had my team and our customers on my side.

We live in a world without enough nuance. Too often, complicated situations or people are distilled down to simplistic judgments. When Jack Welch died in March 2020 at the age of eighty-four, the business press, which had glorified him in life, was critical of him and his legacy. But if you look at the totality of his contributions to

GE and the broader business world, there's no question that Jack was a great leader. I attended his service at St. Patrick's Cathedral in New York City, where no less than Babe Ruth and Bobby Kennedy had been memorialized before him. Ken Langone, the billionaire businessman, and the journalist Mike Barnicle gave eulogies, but I stayed quiet in a pew at the back of the church. I'd known him, loved him, and argued with him for most of my life. His absence is surreal.

I know there are some within GE who believe that I failed them. In October 2019, when GE moved to freeze the pensions of twenty thousand workers in the United States, it felt like a betrayal of trust. Many lay the blame for that setback, among others, at my feet. When I announced my retirement, the stock was at $28.94; as I complete this book, it's trading at less than $7. That makes my heart ache, and it always will. But I also know what my team accomplished, working together. We weren't perfect—I've made that clear. But GE is an incredible and purposeful company.

Every spring I tell my students that in this confusing world, leaders must be able to do contrary things well—to master conflicting principles at the same time. They must make their companies be at once big and fast, global and local, digital and industrial. They must manage in a way that is both competitive and empathetic. They must think short-term and long-term. They must deal with ambiguity.

In the spring of 2020, the situation we were all in—locked in our houses, uncertain about the future, staring at each other through our computer screens—brought that reality home. In our final class, I looked into the camera and told our far-flung students that I empathized with them. "Look," I said, "this really stinks, having to finish your business school career on Zoom. You have every right to be frustrated and anxious as you face this pandemic world. But believe it or not, you're going to be better for the experience."

I could see on their pixelated faces that they weren't convinced, but I pressed on. "Your career is going to have bad days and good days, but believe it or not, you need the bad days," I said. "They make you a better leader."

ACKNOWLEDGMENTS

Hot Seat was a very hard book to write because I wanted it to not just explore what happened during my time at GE, but also to examine my own strengths and weaknesses. It took an exceptional and empathetic team to bring it across the finish line, and I want to acknowledge them here. My agent, Elyse Cheney, was there from the beginning. She helped me find my cowriter, helped shepherd the proposal, and ultimately placed the project with an immensely talented editor: Ben Loehnen. For all that, I'm grateful.

My cowriter, Amy Wallace, is a tough-minded and talented storyteller. In addition to interviewing me relentlessly, she talked to seventy other people with knowledge of the GE story—many of them more than once. I want to thank them all for their help. These sources gave up many hours of their time, all in the service of getting the story right. Their input was invaluable, and it kept me honest. But accuracy wasn't our only goal. We wanted readers to understand what being in the hot seat in times of crisis actually feels like. I hope we accomplished that. (When it comes to dialogue, meanwhile, the intention was to recreate the essence of conversations rather than verbatim quotes.)

I also have to thank my communication advisor, Gary Sheffer. While my colleague at GE, Gary became a friend and he has remained so since. It was Gary who first counseled me about the pros and cons of writing this book and, when I decided to try it, he was frank about what would make the project worth the effort: it had to be a clear-eyed interrogation of my tenure. That directive made the experience brutal at times, but I felt it was something I had to do. In my lowest days, Gary was always there with solid advice. I couldn't have written the book without him.

As I write this "Acknowledgments" section, it occurs to me that throughout this book, I've tried where possible to acknowledge GE's wonderful people. By the time I retired, I probably knew several thousand of them by name. I admired the way they worked hard, often against great odds, always putting the company first. There were so many people who I worked with for decades: John Rice, Susan Peters, David Joyce, Beth Comstock, Lloyd Trotter, Nani Beccalli, and others. I truly loved them. It's easy to say your colleagues are family, but I really felt that way. Keith Sherin and I worked together in Milwaukee when his daughter was born; she just started medical school. I'd like to give a special shout out to Peter Foss and Steve Parks, two GE colleagues who were also my best friends. There were several GE leaders who I considered mentors. I put Glen Hiner and John Opie in that category. I learned so much from them and from so many others. Working at GE was a personal joy.

I also owe a huge debt to the colleagues who kept me organized and on time: Kathy Lorenz, Sheila Neville, Ed Pettway, and Ed Galanek. When you land at 3 a.m. from Bangalore, as I so often did, it is nice to see a friendly face—and for years I was fortunate to have the two Eds at my side. Back at headquarters, meanwhile, I was lucky to have Kathy and Sheila, who supported me with grace and patience.

There were many board members who gave so much to GE. As

I've said, I loved working with Ralph Larsen. But he wasn't the only one who made a large contribution. When you weather crises like 9/11 and the Great Financial Crisis, you see everybody's true colors. I was lucky that our directors, as a group, put GE first.

There were many outside of GE who helped the company win around the world and helped me understand what was at stake. I can't name them all, but I would like to call out a few. Bob Santamoor, the leader of our union, the IUE, stood up for our workforce. I listened to him and trusted him. Andrew Robertson and his advertising firm, BBDO, always understood where we were going and delivered great work that helped us get there. John Weinberg at Goldman Sachs and Blair Effron at Centerview Partners were fantastic advisors who, when delivering bad news, never failed to have a plan to make things better.

I learned so much from my peers, CEO's of other companies who became friends. There are too many to name. When you are on top, it is easy to be long on friends. When you hit bottom, there are a select few who reach out. For me, those standouts included American Express's Ken Chenault, Delta Airlines's Richard Anderson, and especially Cisco's John Chambers. Everybody should be lucky enough to have Chambers as a friend. He is brilliant and empathetic, an unbeatable combination.

I'd like to thank my partners at NEA and the company founders I now work with. They have helped me to reinvent myself in a new world. Their passion is contagious. I get up every morning determined to earn their trust in me.

Last and most important, my family has made everything possible. My mother and father gave me the tools to succeed. My brother set an example to strive for. My wife and my daughter (and, more recently, my son-in-law) have sacrificed, at times, to give me the room to devote myself to satisfying work. They have seen me in real pain, but they've never let me feel sorry for myself. My life with them gives me a reason to be an optimist.

INDEX

Abate, Vic, 70, 100
Abbott Diagnostics, 272
Accenture, 109
accountability, 10, 39, 64, 159, 164, 165, 168, 218, 231
action
   avoiding fear of, 87–91
   taking during a crisis, 318
activist investors, 254–56, 301–2
Acuson, 4
additive manufacturing, 67, 222–23
AFL-CIO, 180
Africa, 188
African American employees, 167–68, 169, 172
African American Forum, 86
AIG. *See* American International Group
Aigrain, Jacques, 89
Air Transportation Safety and System Stabilization Act, 22–23
AirAsia, 24
Airbus, 23, 71, 221
aircraft engines, 10, 13, 17, 21, 65, 71–75, 198, 199–200, 202
AiRXOS, 224
Alexanderson, Ernst, 63
Align Technology, 2

All Nippon Airways (ANA), 75
AlliedSignal, 288
Alphabet, 209, 222
Alstom, 4, 259, 262–83, 288, 299, 301, 305, 313
   carve out, 271
   closing the deal, 276
   criticism of deal, 263
   due diligence for transaction, 266–67
   final negotiations, 272
   initial negotiations, 265–68
   integrating into GE Power, 269–71
   perceived benefits of deal, 263–65
   transparency of transaction, 263, 271–76
Amazon, 209–10, 222
Amazon Web Services, 222
ambiguity, 162, 319
America West, 23–24
American Airlines, 24
American Clean Energy and Security Act, 105
American Express, 96, 153
American International Group (AIG), 127, 128, 238

Amersham, 77–81, 90, 111, 215, 262,
    315–16
Andreessen, Marc, 118
Angbazo, Lazarus, 194
Angelou, Maya, 300
anthrax attacks, 25, 57
AOL, 152
Apollo, 257, 314
Apple, 112, 117, 318
Apprentice, The (television program),
    85–86
Arab Spring, 181, 186
ARJ21 aircraft, 199–200
Arnold, Craig, 167
Arthur Andersen, 28
artificial intelligence (AI), 2, 65, 109, 203
artificial lift, 214
Asia, 188
Asian American employees, 168
Athans, Colleen, 155
Athenahealth, 301
A330x aircraft, 221
Atta, Mohamed, 17
Australia, 174–75, 184–85, 246
Autorité des marchés financiers (AMF), 246
Aviage Systems, 200
Aviation Industry Corporation of China
    (AVIC), 200
Avio, 219
Avitas, 223–24

Bair, Sheila, 139–40, 141, 295
Baise, Patrick Dane "P.D.," 38–39
Baker Hughes, 208, 214–16, 281, 288,
    294, 297, 313, 314
Baldwin, Alec, 150
Ballmer, Steve, 34–35
Bangladesh, 188–89
Bank of America, 127
Bank of Montreal, 257
Barnicle, Mike, 319
BASF, 37, 120
Bayer, 37, 120

Bayer AG, 288
BBDO, 97, 102, 112
BCG. *See* Boston Consulting Group
Bear Stearns, 124
Beattie, Geoff, 237, 257
Benioff, Marc, 153
Benoit, David, 302
Berardino, Joseph, 28
Berkshire Hathaway, 137, 209
Berlusconi, Silvio, 191
Bernanke, Ben, 130, 142
Bethlehem Steel, 20–21
Betty Crocker, 34–35
BetzDearborn, 76
Bewlay, Bernard, 63–64
Bezos, Jeff, 318
Biden, Joe, 180
Black Belts, 9
BlackRock, 248
Blackstone Group, 88, 217, 245–46,
    248–50, 257, 297, 314
Blueprint Reviews, 229–30, 231, 279
Boeing, 14, 54, 71, 72–75, 94, 203,
    219–20, 221, 222
Boeing Business Jet (BBJ), 79
Boeing 787, 219–20
Boeing 787 Dreamliner, 72–75, 107
Boeing 767, 15
Boeing 737 MAX, 222, 310
Bolsinger, Lorraine, 103–5, 111
Bolze, Steve, 206, 298
    Alstom deal and, 265–69, 272–83
    resignation of, 297
    in succession race, 267, 269, 274–76,
        281, 283, 289, 291, 295, 296
Bonderman, David, 217
Bornstein, Jeff, 124–25, 126, 139, 146,
    280, 282, 283, 293, 304
    Alstom deal and, 266, 276
    GE Capital divestment and, 239, 241,
        243, 244, 250, 253–54
    in succession race, 274, 281, 289,
        291–92, 297

Boston Consulting Group (BCG),
    35–36, 226, 227
BP, 212, 215
BP oil spill, 146
Brazil, 66, 67, 181–82, 201, 212
Brennan, Jack, 275, 276, 277–78, 288,
    291, 292, 294, 295, 296, 297
Bresenham, Terri, 188
Briggs, Mike, 33–34
Brokaw, Tom, 25, 57
Brussels, 246
Buffett, Warren, 136–37, 209, 311
Burger, Alec, 249–50
Burke, Steve, 35
Burlington Northern, 107, 208
Bush, George W., 22, 106, 138, 233
Business Council, 180, 217
Business Roundtable, 180

Calabar Free Trade Zone, 195
Calhoun, Dave, 51, 73, 218–19
Calpeter, Lynn, 273, 279, 280
Canada Pension Plan (CPP), 257
Capital One Financial Corporation, 257
Cash, Jim, 277
Cassidy, Kathy, 57–59, 131, 133–34
Castell, Sir William, 78–81
Caterpillar, 187, 208
Cathcart, James, 53
Cathcart, Silas, 53
CBS, 86
ceramic matrix composites, 65
Charles, Prince of Wales, 207–8
"chase planes," 192
Chenault, Ken, 96, 153
Cheney, Dick, 106
Chevron, 185, 212
Chih Chen, 198
China, 48, 52, 66, 67, 95, 123, 171, 172,
    175, 177, 209, 285–86, 306, 315
    Central Organization Department, 199
    criticisms of, 202–3
    GE CEO program, 198–99, 286

importance of, 196–204
investments of compared with US, 176
National Development and Reform
    Commission, 106, 201–2
SARS in, 61
technology "borrowed" by GE partners
    in, 200–201
China National Petroleum Corporation,
    203–4
China Railway, 201
Christensen, Clayton, 113
Chrysler, 127
Cisco, 110
Citigroup, 246
Clayton, Dubilier & Rice (CD&R), 217,
    219
Cleveland Clinic, 208
climate change, 43, 69, 101–2, 105,
    203, 207–8, 212, 265
Clinton, Hillary, 46, 193
CNBC, 11, 21, 125–26, 131, 138, 144,
    145, 146
C919 aircraft, 200
CNN, 28
CNN Worldwide, 152
coal, 70, 101, 106, 174, 281
Cohen, H. Rodgin, 132–33
Colao, Daniel, 240
collateralized mortgage obligations
    (CMOs), 122
Colvin, Geoff, 2
Comac, 199, 285–86
Comcast, 82, 86, 151, 152, 259, 314
commercial paper (CP), 58, 128, 131–
    33, 134, 135, 138, 140
commercial real estate business, 123,
    139
complaints, avoiding, 30
complexity, 162. *See also* conglomerates
Comstock, Beth, 21–22, 96–97, 98,
    100–102, 112, 204, 243, 290, 291,
    297, 304
Conaty, Bill, 60–61, 298

conglomerates
    advantages of, 208–9
    creating incremental value in, 209–11
    developing trustworthy leaders, 220–22
    disadvantage of, 209
    holding companies, 218
    innovation in, 222–24
    operating companies, 218
    peer learning and pressure in, 230–32
    private equity as, 216–20
    simplifying, 224–29
    transparency and, 229–30
ConocoPhillips, 310
Coolidge, William D., 63
Cordiner, Ralph, 63
Corporate Executive Council (CEC),
    172, 182–84
Council on Jobs and Competitiveness,
    179–82
country-to-country agreements (C2C),
    195–96
COVID-19 pandemic, 25, 95, 118, 147,
    176, 202, 209, 304, 305–6, 309,
    310, 311, 315
Cowen and Company, 293
Craighead, Martin, 214
Cramer, Jim, 21, 277
Crawford, Stephen, 87
Creative Artists Agency, 83
credit default swaps, 135, 146
credit rating of GE, 58–59, 121, 132,
    133, 143, 145
Cribbins, Matt, 243, 259–60, 280, 281,
    282–83, 293–94
crises. *See also* COVID-19 pandemic;
    financial crisis of 2008–2009;
    September 11 attacks
    globalization and, 182–85
    Immelt's course on leadership during,
    309–11
Crotonville, 101, 160, 199
    described, 10–11
    reimagining, 161–165

Crouthamel, Jake, 34
CT scanners, 21, 48–50, 52, 54, 108,
    198, 223
C3.ai, 116, 216
Culp, Larry, 305–6
culture of blame, 10, 147, 302
Curtiss-Wright, 30
customer relationship management
    (CRM), 225
customers
    assisting after September 11 attacks,
    22–25
    cementing relationships with global,
    190–94
    seeing through the eyes of, 36–41
CVC, 219

Daily Mercury, 174
Daley, Pam, 79
Daley, Sharon, 270
Dammerman, Dennis Dean "Triple D,"
    17, 19, 20, 75, 89, 90, 144
"Dancing Elephant" (ad), 102
Dangote Group, 195
Dartmouth College, 33, 36
Davis Polk, 248
Deere & Company, 277
Dekkers, Marijn, 288, 290
Delta Airlines, 118
Deng Xiaoping, 196
Denniston, Brackett, 139, 243, 246,
    247, 250, 271, 272
Deutsche Bank, 137
DG COMP, 270–71
Diasonics Vingmed Ultrasound, 47–48
DiCaprio, Leonardo, 130
digital technology, 107–18
    competing for talent, 112–13
    dismantling of project, 116–18
    resistance to, 113–16
"digital twins," 65, 111
Dignan, Aaron, 228
Diller, Barry, 81

Dimitrief, Alex, 243, 246, 280, 291, 296, 304

Dimon, Jamie, 35, 244

DiPietro, Maria, 258

Directorate-General for Competition, 268

Discovery, Inc., 152

Disney, 314

diversity, 62, 86, 166–72

Dodd, Chris, 234

Dodd-Frank Wall Street Reform and Consumer Protection Act, 151–52, 234–35

Donnelly, Scott, 290

Dow, 81, 120

Dow Jones Industrial Average, 18, 127, 136, 272

Dowling, Michael, 310

Dreamliner. *See* Boeing 787 Dreamliner

drones, 224

Duan, Rachel, 171–72

Dudley, Bill, 141–42

Dudley, Bob, 215–16

Duncan Hines, 34–35

DuPont, 81, 119–20, 125

dynamic complexity, 162

Eaton, 167

Ecomagination, 69, 96, 99–107, 111–12, 130, 150, 315
  impact on GE's business, 106
  initial resistance to, 101–2
  motivations for, 100–101

Edison, Thomas, 9, 62

Effron, Blair, 256

Egypt, 181, 193

Eisenhower, Dwight D., 234

Elam, Deborah, 86, 168, 169

Electrical Products Group Conference (EPG), 292–94

Electro-Motive Diesel (EMD), 210

Element Financial Corp., 241–42, 256

Elliott Management, 301

Emanuel, Rahm, 153

EMC, 215

empathy, 312, 317

employees
  connecting with, 154–59
  diversity in, 62, 86, 166–72
  retaining senior leaders, 164–66
  training leaders, 160–63

Enron, 28–29, 58, 59, 61, 68, 70, 96

Enron Wind, 68, 71, 315

enterprise risk, 237

environmental concerns, 99–100. *See also* climate change; Ecomagination; Hudson River pollution

Environmental Protection Agency (EPA), 27, 99, 102, 228

Erdoğan, Recep Tayyip, 191

Eurazeo, 219

European Commission, 54–55

European Union (EU), 55, 99, 268, 270, 271, 272

Executive Development Course (EDC), 163

exponential technology, 64–65

Export-Import Bank (EXIM), 176, 286

Exxon, 212, 225

Faber, David, 145

Facebook, 111

failure, fear of, 164

Falco, Randy, 152

Al-Falih, Khalid, 185

Fannie Mae (Federal National Mortgage Association), 127, 194

"fast-follower" strategy, 12

FDIC, 138–41, 295

fear
  absorbing, 19–22
  of acting (avoiding), 87–91
  of failure, 164

Federal Reserve, US, 127, 142, 235–37, 238, 241, 244, 246, 247, 248, 303

Federal Reserve Bank of New York, 131, 141–42, 247

Fernandes, Tony, 24
Fey, Tina, 149, 150
Fiat, 219
Fidelity, 137
Fields, Mark, 274
financial crisis of 2008–2009, 3, 88,
    120–47, 175, 180, 234, 302
  bailouts, 127, 128
  early indications of, 126–30
  GE investors' anxiety during, 134
  GE raises money during, 135–38
  lessons from, 147
  media coverage of, 145–46
Financial Guaranty Insurance Company
    (FGIC), 88
Financial Stability Oversight Council,
    234–35
Fink, Larry, 248
Finnigan, Pete, 64
First Boston Corporation, 254
Fitzgerald, Bill, 157
Fitzsimons, Shane, 105
Flannery, John, 179
  Alstom deal and, 266–67, 274
  appointed CEO, 296, 297–98
  in succession race, 267, 274, 281,
    289, 292
  tenure as CEO, 303–5
  transition to CEO position,
    300–301
Flannery, Tracy, 297
Fogg, Joe, 36
Ford Motor Company, 127, 274
Fortune magazine, 2, 3, 50, 54, 56, 89,
    255, 287
Fourtou, Jean-René, 81–82
Fowler, Jim, 111, 117
Fox Business, 146
Foxconn, 197
fracking, 67
France. *See* Alstom
Frank, Barney, 234
Frawley, Caroline, 237

Freddie Mac (Federal Home Loan
    Mortgage Corporation), 127
"French country risk," 266
Friedman, Thomas, 106
Friends (television program), 85, 150
Fukushima Daiichi nuclear reactor
    meltdown, 3, 146, 183–85
Future of Energy summit, 69

Galanek, Ed, 189, 296
Gambhir, Sam, 108
Gantt chart, 238
Garavel, Sharon, 258
Garcia, Jose Ignacio, 270
Garden, Ed, 282
Gartner, 116
gas turbines, 10, 61, 68, 185, 188, 189,
    191, 192, 193, 195, 202, 205, 264,
    265, 266, 267, 304, 305
GATT, 176
Gay, Lesbian, Bisexual, Transgender &
    Ally Alliance, 169
Gaymard, Clara, 267
GE Additive, 222
GE Aircraft Engines, 31
GE Antares, 256–57
GE Appliances, 11, 29–30, 41–44, 61,
    166, 259
GE Aviation, 11, 50, 51, 61, 70, 73–75, 94,
    103, 105, 111, 123, 155, 157, 159, 170,
    204, 205, 210, 220–22, 224, 290, 292
  China and, 200, 286
  COVID-19 pandemic and, 305–6
  September 11 attacks and, 15, 209
GE Capital, 4, 28–29, 54, 55, 62, 64,
    70–71, 85, 87, 90, 94, 111, 120–
    25, 132–33, 134, 142, 143, 153,
    175, 194, 210, 211, 217, 235–39,
    264, 289, 301, 303, 307
  bank business model compared with,
    120–21
  "The Blob Theory" of, 14, 88, 232
  breakup into separate businesses, 61

divestment of, 151–52, 239–60, 288, 292–94, 311, 314

excessive short-term debt, 132

growth of, 12–14, 57–61, 313–14

hedge funds spread rumors about, 146

steel industry bankruptcy restructuring, 20–21

TLGP and, 138–41

GE Capital Asia Pacific, 158, 174

GE Capital Commercial Finance, 168

GE Capital Real Estate, 158, 249

GE Commercial Finance, 61

GE Consumer Finance, 61

GE Current, 264

GE Digital, 96, 109–18, 157, 214, 292, 304. *See also* digital technology

GE Energy, 204, 206

GE Energy Management, 206

GE Equipment Services, 61

GE Healthcare, 142, 155, 157, 168, 171, 172, 175, 197–98, 210–11, 227, 286, 288, 289, 290, 292, 299, 304

accomplishments during Immelt's tenure, 306

day-care center in, 166–67

Immelt as manager of (GEMS), 4, 11, 18, 30, 40, 46–48, 49–50, 109, 166–67

naming of, 80

GE Healthcare Technologies, 80

GE India, 179, 182

GE Insurance, 61. *See also* insurance business

GE Insurance Solutions, 89

GE Latin America, 158, 270

GE Lighting, 61, 158

GE Medical Systems (GEMS), 46–48, 49–50, 61, 77, 96, 109. See *also* GE Healthcare

GE Middle East, North Africa & Turkey, 185

GE Oil & Gas, 113–14, 142, 158, 159, 184, 206, 211–16, 223, 230, 274, 279, 281, 282, 303, 304. *See also* oil and gas business

GE Onshore Wind, 300

GE Plastics, 61, 81, 119–20, 171, 196–97, 211

attempt to partner with Chinese firm, 203–4

Immelt as manager of, 11, 29, 36–39, 44–46, 82

sale of, 120

GE Power, 4, 50, 51, 64, 68, 103, 159, 209, 259, 262–63, 264, 265, 270–71, 272, 273, 276, 277, 286, 313

Alstom acquisition (*see* Alstom)

bubble, 10, 61

headquarters moved to Switzerland, 271

performance decline, 123, 278–83, 303–4

restructuring of, 305

GE Power & Water, 206

GE Renewable Energy, 142, 230, 306

GE Research Laboratory, 62–63

GE Service Council, 107

GE Silicones, 171

GE Store, 210–11, 213

GE Supply, 219

GE Transportation, 61, 70, 158, 214, 228–29, 289

GE Ventures, 223

GE Water, 157, 259

GE Water & Process Technologies, 76–77

GE Wind Energy, 69–71

Geithner, Tim, 130, 131, 140, 151–52, 180

GEMS. *See* GE Medical Systems

General Electric (GE). *See also* individual divisions of

anchor investor in equity raise, 136–37

bureaucracy of, 153, 221, 224–29

Corporate Executive Council, 102

credit rating, 58–59, 121, 132, 133, 143, 145

dividend cutting, 143–45

General Electric (GE) (*cont.*)
  founding of, 9
  mottoes, 97, 98, 235
  need for bold investments in, 61–62
  price-to-earnings ratio, 8–9, 13, 123, 307
  public offering/equity raise, 135–38
  repatriation of cash, 127, 181, 240
  stock performance, 1, 9, 10, 16, 18, 59, 60, 75, 80, 137, 143, 151, 153, 239, 240, 241, 243, 258–59, 276, 293, 298, 306, 307, 319
  Superfund site, 99
  taxes, 127, 240, 250–51, 271
  training for leaders, 160–65
  Treasury department, 57–59
  valuing in wake of GE Capital divestment, 292–94
General Motors (GM), 45–46, 127, 210
Genpact, 95
Gentile, Tom, 238, 310
Genworth Financial Inc., 87–88, 90
GEnx engine, 72–75, 107, 221
Germany, 66, 67, 101, 191–92, 246
Gettysburg (Sears), 234
Gexpro, 219
GGO. *See* Global Growth Organization
Ghana, 173–74
Ghana 1000, 174
Giuliani, Rudy, 16
Gladden, Brian, 119
Global Growth Organization (GGO), 182–84, 185, 188, 189, 264, 277, 299
  benefits of, 178–79, 210–11
  resistance to, 204–6
Global Research Center (GRC), 63–67, 68, 74, 107, 108, 161, 199, 210
globalization, 3, 47–48, 173–206
  cementing relationships, 190–94
  centralized US-decision making impeding, 175–76
  crises and, 182–85
  criticism of, 176–77, 187
  hiring local teams, 194–96
  investing in local capability, 185–87
  outsourcing, 176, 177
  pitfalls of, 55
  research presence in, 66–67
  "ROW segment," 176
  sales importance, 177–79
  volatility and, 187–90
  wage arbitrage, 177
Gogel, Don, 217
Goldman Sachs, 78, 87, 89, 121, 135, 136, 137, 138, 257
Goodwin, Doris Kearns, 162
Google, 109, 111, 112, 130–31, 222
Gore, Al, 43, 130
Gosk, Mike, 240
Gou, Terry, 197
Gould, Andrew, 208
Grasso, Dick, 89
Gray, Jonathan D., 245–46, 249
GRC. *See* Global Research Center
Green, Robert, 243
Greenspan, Alan, 23
Gross, Bill, 59, 60, 62
growth
  of GE Capital, 12–14, 57–61, 313–14
  pivoting for, 77–81
  stoking GE's engine of, 12–14
  technological, 62–67
  valuing, 46–48
guanxi, 199

H System gas turbines, 65, 106–7, 264
HA turbines, 304
Habayeb, Nabil, 142, 185, 186
Halliburton, 208, 214
Hammer, Bonnie, 84
Harbin Electric, 201, 286
Harrison, Bill, 89
Harvard Business School, 34, 35, 36
Hedegaard, Connie, 207, 208
hedge funds, 143, 146
Heidrick & Struggles, 52
Heintzelman, Dan, 159, 206
Herera, Sue, 11

Hinshaw, John, 253
Hispanic employees, 168
H.J. Heinz Company, 255
Hockfield, Susan, 296
Hogan, Joe, 51, 52, 77–78, 80
Hogan Lovells, 298
holding companies, 218
Hollande, François, 267–68
Holliday, Chad, 125
Home Depot, 54, 88–89
Honeywell International, 52, 54–55, 200, 225, 312
horizontal technology, 64–65
horizontal thinking, 94, 100
Hubschman, Henry, 23
Hudson River pollution, 27, 99, 102
Hudson, Steven, 241–42, 256
Hutchinson, Mark, 270, 272
Hyundai, 257

Ibarra, Herminia, 160
IBM, 63, 96, 108, 109
ideas (avoiding falling in love with), 76–77
Idelchik, Mike, 50
IDX Systems, 109
Iger, Bob, 314
Imagination Breakthroughs (IBs), 98
Immelt, Andy (wife), 15, 18, 37, 39, 41, 53, 93, 154, 158, 233, 261, 262, 294–95, 297
Immelt, Donna (mother), 11, 30, 53
Immelt, Jeff
    appointed CEO, 53–54
    blame placed on, 300–301, 302, 319
    connecting to senior leaders, 154–59
    declines bonus during financial crisis, 145
    first day as CEO, 6, 9–14
    GE accomplishments during tenure of, 306–7
    GE stock purchased by, 293
    hires on to GE, 36

International Citizen of the Year designation, 294
    as jobs czar, 179–82
    life after GE, 316–18
    mistakes owned by, 312–15
    personal history, 11–12, 30–36
    retirement announcement, 298–300
    Stanford course taught by, 1–4, 309–11, 317–18
    steps down as CEO, 1, 301
    succession process for replacement of, 267, 269, 274–76, 278, 281, 283, 286–92, 294–98, 314
    in succession runoff, 30, 50–54, 287
    tattoo of GE logo, 5, 261–62
    Welch and (*see under* Welch, Jack)
Immelt, Joe (father), 5, 11–12, 30, 31–32, 53, 298
Immelt, Sarah (daughter), 15, 18, 39, 41, 261, 262, 294–95
Immelt, Stephen (brother), 30, 31, 298
Imus, Don, 86–87
Imus in the Morning (television program), 86–87
India, 48, 66, 94, 109, 179, 182–84, 187–88, 190, 211, 246, 306
Indonesia, 201, 264
Infosys, 183
innovation, 9, 12, 222–24. *See also* technology
Innovator's Dilemma, 113–14
insurance business, 4, 10, 21, 62, 87–91, 303
    long-term care insurance, 14, 89–90
    mortgage insurance, 88
    primary care insurance, 14
    reinsurance, 14, 15, 17, 87, 89
    terrorism exception in, 19–20, 75
Intel, 180, 197
International Brotherhood of Electrical Workers, 180
Internet of Things (IoT), 108, 110, 116, 216
Iraq, 304

Ireland, Jay, 178
Ishrak, Omar, 47–48, 290
Italy, 191, 246

Jack: Straight from the Gut (Welch), 56
Janki, Dan, 206, 243
Japan, 48, 75, 183–85, 192, 246
Jarrett, Valerie, 180, 181, 246
JCPenny, 133
"Jeff Immelt—Unplugged" (forum), 2–4
Jian Zemin, 198
John Deere, 2
John F. Welch Leadership Development
    Center. *See* Crotonville
John Wood Group PLC, 190
Johnson & Johnson, 96, 144
Johnson, Kate, 117, 157
joint ventures, 48, 177, 200, 286
Jonathan, Goodluck, 195–96
Joyce, David, 204, 205, 220–22, 290,
    291, 297
J.P. Morgan & Co., 29, 276
JPMorgan Chase, 35, 118, 133, 134,
    146, 194, 244, 248
Jung, Andra, 296
Justice Department, US, 54, 122, 214, 271

Kazakhstan, 192
Kekedjian, Aris, 240, 241–42, 244,
    249–50, 256
Kemeny, John G., 33
Kent, Judy, 35
Kenya, 211
Kerry, John, 193
Khanna, Gautam, 293
Khashoggi, Jamal Ahmad, 186
Khurana, Rakesh, 160
Kidder Peabody, 126
"Killer Chart, The," 139
King Kong (film), 83–84
KKR & Co., 217
Kleiman-Lee, Kimberly, 166
Korea, 246

KPMG, 154, 272, 278
Kravis, Henry, 217
Krenicki, John, 204, 265–66, 269
Kron, Patrick, 265–66, 267
KTZ, 190
Kutner, Harold, 45–46

Lack, Andy, 15, 16, 84
Lance, Ryan, 310
Lane, Robert, 277
Langley, Donna, 152
Langmuir, Irving, 63
Langone, Ken, 88–89, 319
Larsen, Ralph, 144
Lash, Jonathan, 102–3
Late Night with Conan O'Brien
    (television program), 84
Latin America, 188
Latour, Deirdre, 299
Lawson, Jeff, 118
Lazarus, Shelly, 29
Leadership Explorations, 164–66
LEAP engine, 65, 157, 222, 230
Lee, Jimmy, 134, 244, 257
Lee, Robert E., 234
Legendary Entertainment, 2
Lehman Brothers, 126–27, 130, 133,
    147, 151, 311
leverage lending, 122
Lew, Jacob "Jack," 238, 246–47
Lexan, 46
LGBT employees, 168, 169
life sciences, 77–81, 304
LightSpeed QX/i, 48–50
listening, 95, 201–2, 315–16
Little, Mark, 67–68, 70, 108
Lockheed Martin, 63
locomotives, 10, 13, 107–8, 187, 190, 191,
    192, 195, 198, 200–201, 210, 228–29
Lone Pine Capital, 35
Longstreet, James, 234
Lucier, Greg, 288, 290
luck, 314–15, 318

Lumet, Sidney, 149
Lynch, John, 156
Lyons, Jim, 68

Mabe, 177
Macron, Emmanuel, 267
Mad Money (television program), 21
Maglathlin, Laurie, 35
Maglathlin, Pete, 35
Mahajan, Puneet, 243, 280
Mahindra & Mahindra, 183
Malaysia, 51
Malkin, Scott, 35
Malone, John, 85
Management Development and
    Compensation Committee, 275
Mandel, Steve, 35
Mann, Ted, 302
maquiladoras, 39
Markhoff, Heiner, 157
Marriott, 118
Marshall, Ernest, 167–68
Massachusetts Institute of Technology
    (MIT), 296
Massachusetts Institute of Technology
    (MIT) Sloan School of
    Management, 162
maternity and paternity leaves, 168–69
MBI, 35
McChrystal, Stanley, 153
McCullough, David, 233–34
McKinsey & Company, 123
McNerney, Jim, 50–51, 53, 54, 87,
    219–20, 287
Medtronic, 290
Meet the Press (television program), 84
Merkel, Angela, 5, 191–92
Merrill Lynch, 127
Merrill Lynch Global Private Equity, 219
Messier, Jean-Marie, 81
MetLife, 238
Mexico, 39, 177, 212, 304
Meyer, Ron, 83–84

Michaels, Lorne, 84, 149–50
Michelson, G. G., 16–17, 216–17
Microsoft, 34, 111, 117
Middle East, 142, 192
Miller, Jamie, 157
Minds + Machines conferences, 110,
    116, 118
Mineta, Norman, 23
Mitsubishi Heavy Industries (MHI),
    264, 266, 267, 304
money vs. purpose, 34–36
Monsanto, 81, 120
Montebourg, Arnaud, 268
Moody's Investors Service, 58, 60,
    87
Moonves, Les, 86–87
Moore's law, 65
Morgan Stanley, 36, 87, 135
Morgenson, Gretchen, 60
Morieux, Yves, 226–27
mortgage lending, 121–22
Mosci, Marcelo, 175
Motorola, 9
MR scanners, 65, 108, 211
MRI machines, 48, 198
MSNBC, 86
Mubadala, 137, 192
Mulally, Alan, 72
Mulcahy, Ann, 20
Murdoch, Rupert, 84
Murphy, Kieran, 157
Musk, Elon, 64
"My Mom" (ad), 169

NAFTA (North American Free Trade
    Agreement), 177
Nardelli, Bob, 50–51, 53, 54, 87,
    88–89, 287
Nason, David, 139, 235–36
National Governors Association
    conference, 99
Nationwide, 117
natural gas. *See* oil and gas business

Nayden, Denis, 12–13, 14, 20, 60–61
NBC, 15–16, 57, 61, 81–82, 85–86, 96, 149–50
NBC News, 142
NBCUniversal, 35, 90, 151, 314
    GE's acquisition of, 82–87
    sale of, 152–53
Neal, Mike, 121, 126, 146, 204, 239
Network (film), 149
Neville, Sheila, 185
New Enterprise Associates (NEA), 317
New York Daily News, 27
New York Fire Department, 22
New York Stock Exchange, 22, 60, 89
New York Times, 18, 60, 84, 106, 166, 253
News Corp, 152
Nielsen, 218–19
Nigeria, 194–96
Nightly News (television program), 25
Nobel Prize, 63
Nooyi, Indra, 96
North Africa, 142
North American Free Trade Agreement
    (NAFTA), 177
Northwell Health, 208, 310
Noryl, 36
nuclear power, 70, 105–6, 264. *See also*
    Fukushima Daiichi nuclear reactor
    meltdown
Nuovo Pignone, 212

Obama, Barack, 5, 142, 151, 179–81,
    234, 246
Ochsner, 208
O'Conner, Erin, 25
oil and gas business, 101, 173–74, 185,
    190, 192, 195, 196, 208, 212, 214,
    215–16, 264, 281, 294, 305, 313
Oil & Gas Technology Center, 66–67
One Belt One Road (OBOR) financing
    initiative, 286
O'Neill, Paul, 23
operating companies, 218
opportunity, seizing, 81–87

optimism, 310, 311–12
Oracle, 109, 117, 157
Osmonics, 76
Otellini, Paul, 180

Paine Webber, 126
Pakistan, 191
Palmisano, Sam, 96
Paris Agreement, 208
Parker, Doug, 23–24
patents, 9, 64, 222, 306
Patolawala, Monish, 154–55
Paulson, Hank, 89, 127–30, 131, 139, 140, 141
peers
    learning and pressure from, 230–32
    promotion by, 54–56
Peltz, Nelson, 255–56, 258, 272, 281–82,
    285, 302
Pemex, 212
pension earnings, 10, 312, 319
Penske, Roger, 135, 272
PepsiCo, 96
Perella, Joe, 254–56
Perella Weinberg, 254
Peters, Susan, 160, 161–62, 164, 171,
    269, 274, 275, 277, 283, 287, 290,
    291, 294, 304
Petrobas, 212
Pew Center on Global Climate Change, 106
phoniness, avoiding, 30–31
PIMCO, 59
Pioneer, 120
Play, 161
Porat, Ruth, 87
Pratt & Whitney, 12, 73
precision medicine, 77–78
Predix, 96, 111–18, 157, 214, 264
price-to-earnings ratio (PE) in GE, 8–9,
    13, 123, 307
Prius, 101
private equity, 216–20, 313
Procter & Gamble (P&G), 34–35
Project Beacon, 239

Project Hubble, 241–42, 244, 245, 247, 248, 252, 256, 258, 292, 303
Project Kingdom, 186
protectionism, 177, 268
Prudential Financial, 238
Prudential Regulation Authority (PRA), 246
purpose vs. money, 34–36
Putin, Vladimir, 190–91

Qantas Airways, 175

Radiological Society of North America, 53–54
"range effect," 55
Ratcliffe, David, 70
Ravin, Carl, 49
RCA, 81
Ready, The, 228
real estate holdings, 123, 139, 245–46, 249
Redstone, Sumner, 84
refrigerator compressor crisis, 41–44
Reinemund, Steve, 96
Reliance Group, 183
renewable energy, 101, 265
research, 12, 62–63, 66–67
Reserve Primary Fund, 130
revenue-recognition accounting rules, 278–79
Rexel, 219
R.H. Macy, 16
RhônePoulenc, 82
Rice, John, 51, 178–79, 183, 185–86, 192–93, 204, 277, 281, 290, 291, 297, 304, 305
Ringfencing of risk, 223
risk
    enterprise, 237
    "French country," 266
    ringfencing of, 223
    tail, 24–25, 146, 311
risk management, 234–37
Robb, Walt, 42

Roche, Gerry, 52
Rockwell Collins, 200
Rolls-Royce, 73, 75
Roosevelt, Franklin D., 217
Roosevelt, Teddy, 298
Rose, Charlie, 146
Rose, Matt, 208
Rosneft, 191, 212
Ross, Wilbur, 20–21
Rove, Karl, 233
Ruh, Bill, 110, 111, 112, 114, 115–16
rule of 40, 218
Russia, 190–91, 212
Ryan, Jack, 245, 248, 252–53

Salesforce.com, 153, 225
Santana, Rafael, 157–58
Santiago, Claudi, 212
Sarbanes-Oxley Act, 29
Sargent, Steve, 158, 174–75
SARS (severe acute respiratory syndrome), 61
Saturday Night Live (television program), 84, 149, 189, 259
Saudi Arabia, 66, 185–87, 211
Saudi Aramco, 185–86, 212
Saudi Basic Industries, 120
Saudi Electric, 185
Saunders, Barry, 161
Schlessinger, Mike, 240
Schlumberger Limited, 208, 213, 214, 215
Schneider, Steve, 198
Schwarzman, Steve, 217
Schwimmer, David, 150
Scotland, 190
Sears, Stephen W., 234
Securities and Exchange Commission, US (SEC), 59, 128, 279, 303
Senge, Peter, 162
September 11 attacks, 3, 14–25, 27–28, 29, 61, 75, 78, 96, 144, 145–46, 163, 189, 198, 219, 311, 312–13

September 11 attacks, (*cont.*)
  airlines in wake of, 17, 18, 19–20, 21, 22–24, 71, 73
  assisting customers following, 22–25
  dealing with fear caused by, 19–22
  dealing with impact of, 17–19
  GE accused of exploiting, 27
  GE connections to tragedy, 15–16
  GE donations to first responders, 16
  GE earnings following, 28
  GE employees killed in, 16, 17
  Immelt's visit to Ground Zero, 21–22
severe acute respiratory syndrome (SARS), 61
Shanghai Electric, 201
Sheffer, Gary, 130–31, 137, 142, 145
Shell Oil, 174, 212
Sherin, Keith, 15, 17, 47, 73, 90, 127, 131, 134, 135, 137, 146, 204
  GE Capital divestment and, 239, 240, 241, 242, 243–44, 245–46, 247, 248, 250, 252
  retirement of, 291
Shipchandler, Khozema, 111–12, 114, 115, 117
Siebel, Tom, 116, 117, 216
Siegel, Rob, 2, 311
Siegel, Sue, 223
Siemens, 4, 201, 264, 266, 267, 268
SIFIs. *See* systemically important financial institutions
Silk Road, 286
Simonelli, Lorenzo, 205, 213–16, 220, 281, 313
  background of, 213–14
  in succession race, 274, 289–90, 292, 297
simplification, 224–29
Simpson, Sir George, 8, 126
al-Sisi, Abdel Fattah, 193
Six Sigma, 9, 49, 117, 150, 164, 170
Six Simple Rules (Morieux and Tollman), 227
60 Minutes (television program), 181–82
Skilling, Jeffrey, 28

Slim, Carlos, 130
Sloan, Timothy, 249
Smith, Bill, 9
Smiths Aerospace, 75
Solomon, David, 87, 138
Sorkin, Aaron, 149
South Africa, 201
South America, 66
South Korea, 48, 246
Southern Company Energy Solutions, 70
Spirit AeroSystems, 310
Spitzer, Eliot, 89, 99
Splunk, 115
Squawk on the Street (television program), 145
St. Vincent's Hospital, 21
Stahl, Lesley, 181–82
Standard & Poor's, 58, 145
Stanford Graduate School of Business, 1–4, 309–11, 317–18
State Department, US, 193
Stefanovich, Andy, 161
STEM, 169
Steris Corporation, 223
stock performance of GE. *See under* General Electric
Stokes, Russell, 304
TheStreet, 277
Studio 60 on the Sunset Strip (television program), 149–50
"success theater" culture, 3, 279, 301, 303
Suez, 77
Sunday Night Football (television program), 86
Swieringa, Bob, 29
Swiss Re Group, 89
Synchrony Financial, 133
systemically important financial institutions (SIFIs), 235–37, 238–39, 240, 246, 247, 253, 254, 259
  defined, 235
  GE first to shed label, 260
systems thinking, 93–96

tail risk, 24–25, 146, 311
TARP (Troubled Asset Relief Program), 136, 138
Tarullo, Daniel, 247
Tata Consultancy Service, 186
Tea Party movement, 180
teamwork, 31–32, 147
technology. *See also* digital technology; innovation
  "borrowing" of by Chinese firms, 200–201
  exponential, 64–65
  GE's commitment to, 62–67
  GE's deemphasis of, 9
  GE's early inventions, 63
  horizontal and vertical, 64–65
Temporary Liquidity Guarantee Program (TLGP), 138–41
terrorism exception to insurance, 19–20, 75
Textron, 290
30 Rock (television program), 149–51, 235
3D printing, 67, 222–23
3M, 54, 155
Tier 4 regulations, 228–29
Tiger Management, 35
Time Warner, 152
TLGP (Temporary Liquidity Guarantee Program), 138–41
Tokyo Electric Power Company, 184
Tollman, Peter, 227
Toshiba Corporation, 192
Toyota, 101
TPG Capital, 217, 314
Transmec, 190
transparency, 19, 29, 96
  of Alstom transaction, 263, 271–76
  in conglomerates, 229–30
Treasury Department, US, 127, 151
Treasury Financial Institutions, 139
Trian Fund Management, 255, 256, 258–59, 272, 276, 282, 285, 286, 288, 298, 300, 301, 302, 305
Trott, Byron, 136–37

Troubled Asset Relief Program (TARP), 136, 138
Trumka, Rich, 180
Trump, Donald, 5, 21, 85–86, 147, 177, 268, 282
trust, 2, 24–25, 28, 67, 165
Tucci, Joe, 215
Turbomachinery and Process Solutions, 158
Turkey, 142, 191, 211
23andMe, 310
Twilio, 117, 118
TXU, 106
Tyson, Mike, 5

Ultrapure Water Corporation, 76
uncertainty, 93, 162, 311
United Arab Emirates (UAE), 137, 186, 192
United Nations Climate Change Conference, 207
United Technologies Corporation, 75
Universal Parks & Resorts, 83
Universal Studios, 81–83
Univision, 152
US Airways, 24

Value Retail, 35
ValueAct Capital, 255
Vanity Fair, 106
Vaughan, Matthew, 241
vertical technology, 64–65
vertical thinking, 94
Vestager, Margrethe, 270–71, 272
vice presidents of GE, retaining, 164–66
Vietnam, 264
Visa, 135
Vivendi, 81–82
Vivid, 48
VMware, 215
Voice, The (television program), 86
volatility, 162, 187–90
Von Essen, Thomas, 22

VUCA (volatility, uncertainty, complexity, ambiguity), 162

Wabtec, 158
Wachovia Bank, 135
Waldo, Jennifer, 111, 112, 117
Wall Street Journal, 3, 18, 118, 146, 190, 248–49, 258, 279, 301, 302
Walmart, 105, 133
Warner Bros., 85
Warner, Douglas "Sandy," 29, 90, 275–76, 298
Warner, Mark, 238
WarnerMedia News & Sports, 152
Washington Mutual, 134–35
Wasserstein Perella & Co., 254
water-treatment business, 76–77
Watson, John, 212–13
Weil, Gotshal & Manges, 87, 248
Weinberg, John, 87, 137, 138
Weiner, Edie, 162
Welch, Jack, 4, 5, 6, 7–9, 12, 14, 19, 30, 37–38, 39–42, 43, 44–45, 49–54, 58, 62, 63, 79, 81, 84, 88, 90, 96, 117, 166–67, 199, 203–4, 206, 217, 295, 306, 313
    death and funeral of, 318–19
    Immelt compared with, 7–8
    Immelt publicly criticized by, 125–26, 144
    Immelt seeks guidance from, 144–45
    on Immelt's departure from GE, 298
    Immelt's final advice from, 56
    Immelt's first meeting with, 36
    Immelt's most important lesson from, 40
    Jack: Straight from the Gut, 56
    jobs eliminated by, 39–40
    "Neutron Jack" moniker, 40
    retirement of, 55–56
    retirement package of, 59
    rise in value of GE under, 9
    succession process, 50–54, 287

Weldon, Bill, 96
Wells Fargo & Company, 249, 258
Wen Jiabao, 67
Westinghouse Electric Company, 272
"What if?" thinking, 65, 162
Wilder, John, 106
Williams, Reggie, 33–34
Williams, Tom, 83
Wilson, Harry, 34
Wilson, Russell, 34
wind business, 67–71, 77, 100
wind turbines, 230, 264
Wipro Limited, 183
Wiseman, Mark, 257
WMC, 121–22, 316
Wojcicki, Anne, 310
women (GE employees), 166–67, 168, 169–72, 186
Wood, Sir Ian, 190
Woodburn, Bill, 76
World Affairs Council of Greater Houston, 294
World Resources Institute, 102
World Trade Organization (WTO), 176, 177
WorldCom, 58, 59, 61
Wright, Bob, 15–16, 17, 25, 81–82, 84–85
Wright, Orville and Wilbur, 97–98

Xerox, 13, 14, 20
Xi Jinping, 5, 147

Yakunin, Vladimir, 190
Yellen, Janet, 247

Zadek, Sue, 35
Zanin, Ryan, 243
Zaslav, David, 152
Zeitgeist conference, 130
Zenon, 76
Zucker, Jeff, 84–87, 152
Zuckerman, Mort, 27

ABOUT THE AUTHOR

JEFF IMMELT is the former ninth chairman of General Electric and served as CEO for sixteen years. He has been named one of the "World's Best CEOs" three times by *Barron's*. During Immelt's tenure as CEO, GE was named "America's Most Admired Company" by *Fortune* magazine and one of the "World's Most Respected Companies" in polls by *Barron's* and the *Financial Times*. Immelt has received fifteen honorary degrees and numerous awards for business leadership and chaired the President's Council on Jobs and Competitiveness under the Obama administration. He is a member of the American Academy of Arts and Sciences and a lecturer at Stanford University. Immelt earned a BA in applied mathematics from Dartmouth College and an MBA from Harvard University. He and his wife have one daughter.